Outlook 97™
One Step at a Time

Outlook 97™
One Step at a Time

Trudi Reisner

IDG Books Worldwide, Inc.

An International Data Group Company

FOSTER CITY, CA · CHICAGO, IL · INDIANAPOLIS, IN · SOUTHLAKE, TX

Outlook™ 97 One Step at a Time

Published by
IDG Books Worldwide, Inc.
An International Data Group Company
919 E. Hillsdale Blvd., Suite 400
Foster City, CA 94404
www.idgbooks.com (IDG Books Worldwide Web site)

Library of Congress Catalog Card No.: 97-76682

ISBN: 0-7645-3128-X

Printed in the United States of America

10 9 8 7 6 5 4 3 2

1E/QV/QS/ZX/IN

Distributed in the United States by IDG Books Worldwide, Inc.

Distributed by Macmillan Canada for Canada; by Transworld Publishers Limited in the United Kingdom; by IDG Norge Books for Norway; by IDG Sweden Books for Sweden; by Woodslane Pty. Ltd. for Australia; by Woodslane Enterprises Ltd. for New Zealand; by Longman Singapore Publishers Ltd. for Singapore, Malaysia, Thailand, and Indonesia; by Simron Pty. Ltd. for South Africa; by Toppan Company Ltd. for Japan; by Distribuidora Cuspide for Argentina; by Livraria Cultura for Brazil; by Ediciencia S.A. for Ecuador; by Addison-Wesley Publishing Company for Korea; by Ediciones ZETA S.C.R. Ltda. for Peru; by WS Computer Publishing Corporation, Inc., for the Philippines; by Unalis Corporation for Taiwan; by Contemporanea de Ediciones for Venezuela; by Computer Book & Magazine Store for Puerto Rico; by Express Computer Distributors for the Caribbean and West Indies. Authorized Sales Agent: Anthony Rudkin Associates for the Middle East and North Africa.

For general information on IDG Books Worldwide's books in the U.S., please call our Consumer Customer Service department at 800-762-2974. For reseller information, including discounts and premium sales, please call our Reseller Customer Service department at 800-434-3422.

For information on where to purchase IDG Books Worldwide's books outside the U.S., please contact our International Sales department at 415-655-3200 or fax 415-655-3295.

For information on foreign language translations, please contact our Foreign & Subsidiary Rights department at 415-655-3021 or fax 415-655-3281.

For sales inquiries and special prices for bulk quantities, please contact our Sales department at 415-655-3200 or write to the address above.

For information on using IDG Books Worldwide's books in the classroom or for ordering examination copies, please contact our Educational Sales department at 800-434-2086 or fax 817-251-8174.

For press review copies, author interviews, or other publicity information, please contact our Public Relations department at 415-655-3000 or fax 415-655-3299.

For authorization to photocopy items for corporate, personal, or educational use, please contact Copyright Clearance Center, 222 Rosewood Drive, Danvers, MA 01923, or fax 978-750-4470.

is a trademark under exclusive license to IDG Books Worldwide, Inc., from International Data Group, Inc.

ABOUT IDG BOOKS WORLDWIDE

Welcome to the world of IDG Books Worldwide.

IDG Books Worldwide, Inc., is a subsidiary of International Data Group, the world's largest publisher of computer-related information and the leading global provider of information services on information technology. IDG was founded more than 25 years ago and now employs more than 8,500 people worldwide. IDG publishes more than 275 computer publications in over 75 countries (see listing below). More than 60 million people read one or more IDG publications each month.

Launched in 1990, IDG Books Worldwide is today the #1 publisher of best-selling computer books in the United States. We are proud to have received eight awards from the Computer Press Association in recognition of editorial excellence and three from *Computer Currents'* First Annual Readers' Choice Awards. Our best-selling *...For Dummies®* series has more than 30 million copies in print with translations in 30 languages. IDG Books Worldwide, through a joint venture with IDG's Hi-Tech Beijing, became the first U.S. publisher to publish a computer book in the People's Republic of China. In record time, IDG Books Worldwide has become the first choice for millions of readers around the world who want to learn how to better manage their businesses.

Our mission is simple: Every one of our books is designed to bring extra value and skill-building instructions to the reader. Our books are written by experts who understand and care about our readers. The knowledge base of our editorial staff comes from years of experience in publishing, education, and journalism — experience we use to produce books for the '90s. In short, we care about books, so we attract the best people. We devote special attention to details such as audience, interior design, use of icons, and illustrations. And because we use an efficient process of authoring, editing, and desktop publishing our books electronically, we can spend more time ensuring superior content and spend less time on the technicalities of making books.

You can count on our commitment to deliver high-quality books at competitive prices on topics you want to read about. At IDG Books Worldwide, we continue in the IDG tradition of delivering quality for more than 25 years. You'll find no better book on a subject than one from IDG Books Worldwide.

John Kilcullen
CEO
IDG Books Worldwide, Inc.

Steven Berkowitz
President and Publisher
IDG Books Worldwide, Inc.

Eighth Annual
Computer Press
Awards ≥1992

Ninth Annual
Computer Press
Awards ≥1993

Tenth Annual
Computer Press
Awards ≥1994

Eleventh Annual
Computer Press
Awards ≥1995

IDG Books Worldwide, Inc., is a subsidiary of International Data Group, the world's largest publisher of computer-related information and the leading global provider of information services on information technology. International Data Group publishes over 275 computer publications in over 75 countries. Sixty million people read one or more International Data Group publications each month. International Data Group's publications include: **ARGENTINA:** Buyer's Guide, Computerworld Argentina, PC World Argentina; **AUSTRALIA:** Australian Macworld, Australian PC World, Australian Reseller News, Computerworld, IT Casebook, Network World, Publish, Webmaster; **AUSTRIA:** Computerwelt Osterreich, Networks Austria, PC Tip Austria; **BANGLADESH:** PC World Bangladesh; **BELARUS:** PC World Belarus; **BELGIUM:** Data News; **BRAZIL:** Annuário de Informática, Computerworld, Connections, Macworld, PC Player, PC World, Publish, Reseller News, Supergamepower; **BULGARIA:** Computerworld Bulgaria, Network World Bulgaria, PC & MacWorld Bulgaria; **CANADA:** CIO Canada, Client/Server World, ComputerWorld Canada, InfoWorld Canada, NetworkWorld Canada, WebWorld; **CHILE:** Computerworld Chile, PC World Chile; **COLOMBIA:** Computerworld Colombia, PC World Colombia; **COSTA RICA:** PC World Centro America; **THE CZECH AND SLOVAK REPUBLICS:** Computerworld Czechoslovakia, Macworld Czech Republic, PC World Czechoslovakia; **DENMARK:** Communications World Danmark, Computerworld Danmark, Macworld Danmark, PC World Danmark, Techworld Denmark; **DOMINICAN REPUBLIC:** PC World Republica Dominicana; **ECUADOR:** PC World Ecuador; **EGYPT:** Computerworld Middle East, PC World Middle East; **EL SALVADOR:** PC World Centro America; **FINLAND:** MikroPC, Tietoverkko, Tietoviikko; **FRANCE:** Distributique, Hebdo, Info PC, Le Monde Informatique, Macworld, Reseaux & Telecoms, WebMaster France; **GERMANY:** Computer Partner, Computerwoche, Computerwoche Extra, Computerwoche FOCUS, Global Online, Macwelt, PC Welt; **GREECE:** Amiga Computing, GamePro Greece, Multimedia World; **GUATEMALA:** PC World Centro America; **HONDURAS:** PC World Centro America; **HONG KONG:** Computerworld Hong Kong, PC World Hong Kong, Publish in Asia; **HUNGARY:** ABCD CD-ROM, Computerworld Szamitastechnika, Internetto online Magazine, PC World Hungary, PC-X Magazin Hungary; **ICELAND:** Tolvuheimur PC World Island; **INDIA:** Information Communications World, Information Systems Computerworld, PC World India, Publish in Asia; **INDONESIA:** InfoKomputer PC World, Komputek Computerworld, Publish in Asia; **IRELAND:** ComputerScope, PC Live!; **ISRAEL:** Macworld Israel, People & Computers/Computerworld; **ITALY:** Computerworld Italia, Macworld Italia, Networking Italia, PC World Italia; **JAPAN:** DTP World, Macworld Japan, Nikkei Personal Computing, OS/2 World Japan, SunWorld Japan, Windows NT World, Windows World Japan; **KENYA:** PC World East African; **KOREA:** Hi-Tech Information, Macworld Korea, PC World Korea; **MACEDONIA:** PC World Macedonia; **MALAYSIA:** Computerworld Malaysia, PC World Malaysia, Publish in Asia; **MALTA:** PC World Malta; **MEXICO:** Computerworld Mexico, PC World Mexico; **MYANMAR:** PC World Myanmar; **NETHERLANDS:** Computer! Totaal, LAN Internetworking Magazine, LAN World Buyers Guide, Macworld Netherlands, Net, WebWereld; **NEW ZEALAND:** Absolute Beginners Guide and Plain & Simple Series, Computer Buyer, Computer Industry Directory, Computerworld New Zealand, MTB, Network World, PC World New Zealand; **NICARAGUA:** PC World Centro America; **NORWAY:** Computerworld Norge, CW Rapport, Datamagasinet, Financial Rapport, Kursguide Norge, Macworld Norge, Multimediaworld Norge, PC World Ekspress Norge, PC World Nettverk, PC World Norge, PC World ProduktGuide Norge; **PAKISTAN:** Computerworld Pakistan; **PANAMA:** PC World Panama; **PEOPLE'S REPUBLIC OF CHINA:** China Computer Users, China Computerworld, China InfoWorld, China Telecom World Weekly, Computer & Communication, Electronic Design China, Electronics Today, Electronics Weekly, Game Software, PC World China, Popular Computer Week, Software Weekly, Software World, Telecom World; **PERU:** Computerworld Peru, PC World Profesional Peru, PC World SoHo Peru; **PHILIPPINES:** Click!, Computerworld Philippines, PC World Philippines, Publish in Asia; **POLAND:** Computerworld Poland, Computerworld Special Report Poland, Cyber, Macworld Poland, Networld Poland, PC World Komputer; **PORTUGAL:** Cerebro/PC World, Computerworld/Correio Informático, Dealer World Portugal, Mac*In/PC*In Portugal, Multimedia World; **PUERTO RICO:** PC World Puerto Rico; **ROMANIA:** Computerworld Romania, PC World Romania, Telecom Romania; **RUSSIA:** Computerworld Russia, Mir PK, Publish, Seti; **SINGAPORE:** Computerworld Singapore, PC World Singapore, Publish in Asia; **SLOVENIA:** Monitor; **SOUTH AFRICA:** Computing SA, Network World SA, Software World SA; **SPAIN:** Communicaciones World España, Computerworld España, Dealer World España, Macworld España, PC World España, PC World Turkiye, PC World Turkiye; **SWEDEN:** CAP&Design, Computer Sweden, Corporate Computing Sweden, Internetworld Sweden, it.branschen, Macworld Sweden, MaxiData Sweden, MikroDatorn, Nätverk & Kommunikation, PC World Sweden, PCaktiv, Windows World Sweden; **SWITZERLAND:** Computerworld Schweiz, Macworld Schweiz, PCtip; **TAIWAN:** Computerworld Taiwan, Macworld Taiwan, NEW ViSiON/Publish, PC World Taiwan, Windows World Taiwan; **THAILAND:** Publish in Asia, Thai Computerworld; **TURKEY:** Computerworld Turkiye, Macworld Turkiye, Network World Turkiye, PC World Turkiye; **UKRAINE:** Computerworld Kiev, Multimedia World Ukraine, PC World Ukraine; **UNITED KINGDOM:** Acorn User UK, Amiga Action UK, Amiga Computing UK, Apple Talk UK, Computing, Macworld, Parents and Computers UK, PC Advisor, PC Home, PSX Pro, The WEB; **UNITED STATES:** Cable in the Classroom, CIO Magazine, Computerworld, DOS World, Federal Computer Week, GamePro Magazine, InfoWorld, I-Way, Macworld, Network World, PC Games, PC World, Publish, Video Event, THE WEB Magazine, and WebMaster; online webzines: JavaWorld, NetscapeWorld, and SunWorld Online; **URUGUAY:** InfoWorld Uruguay; **VENEZUELA:** Computerworld Venezuela, PC World Venezuela; and **VIETNAM:** PC World Vietnam.   3/24/97

CREDITS

Acquisitions Editor
Juliana Aldous

Development Editor
Susannah D. Pfalzer

Technical Editors
Paul Summitt
Rima Regas

Copy Editor
Nate Holdread

Production Coordinator
Katy German

Book Designer
seventeenth street studios

Graphics and Production Specialists
Ritchie Durdin
Shannon Miller
Maureen Moore
Dina F Quan
Andreas F. Schueller
Deirdre Smith
Trevor Wilson
Elsie Yim

Proofreader
Melissa D. Buddendeck

Indexer
Caroline Parks

ABOUT THE AUTHOR

Trudi Reisner is a computer technical writer specializing in software technical writing and courseware development. Trudi has written numerous books, including *Word 97 One Step at a Time*, published by IDG Books Worldwide, Inc. Trudi has also written software documentation manuals on manufacturing, clinical, financial, and font-creation software, as well as courseware on Lotus 1-2-3 and Lotus Notes Web Navigator.

WELCOME TO ONE STEP AT A TIME!

The book you are holding is very special. It's just the tool you need for learning software quickly and easily. More than a book, it offers a *unique learning experience*. Along with our text, the dynamic *One Step at a Time On-Demand* software included on the bonus CD-ROM in this book coaches you through the tutorials at *your own pace*. You'll never feel lost!

See examples of how to accomplish specific tasks. Listen to clear explanations of how to solve your problems.

Use the *One Step at a Time On-Demand* software in three ways:

- **Demo mode** shows you how to perform a task in movie-style fashion — in sound and color! Just sit back and watch the *One Step* software demonstrate the correct sequence of steps on-screen. Seeing is understanding!

- **Teacher mode** simulates the software environment so you can practice completing a task without worrying about making a mistake. The *One Step* software guides you every step of the way. Trying is learning!

- **Concurrent mode** allows you to work in the actual software environment while still getting assistance from the friendly *One Step* helper. Doing is succeeding!

Our goal is for you to learn the features of a software application by guiding you painlessly through valuable and helpful tutorials. Our *One Step at a Time On-Demand* software — combined with the step-by-step tutorials in our One Step at a Time series — will make your learning experience fast-paced and fun.

See it. Try it. Do it.

To Preston Curtis, in gratitude for helping me not take life too seriously.

PREFACE

Welcome to *Outlook 97 One Step at a Time*. This book is part of a unique new series from IDG Books Worldwide, Inc. Our goal with this series is to give you hands-on exercises to help you with every step of learning the many features of a software program, such as Outlook 97.

Your *One Step at a Time* book has been designed to support your learning in the following ways:

- The lessons are paced to present small, manageable chunks of information so that you never feel in over your head. You always feel prepared for each step you're asked to take.

- You learn Outlook 97 by doing; every lesson is packed with hands-on examples and procedures.

- You are told at the start of each lesson what you'll need to complete the lesson, and how much time to set aside to complete it.

- A CD-ROM with exercise files accompanies this book, so you can begin working with typical business and personal information manager files right from the start. You can also use these exercise files to help you create your own polished personal information manager files.

WHO SHOULD READ THIS BOOK

If you have a basic knowledge of computers and haven't used Outlook 97 before, then this book is for you. You should already understand basic computer skills, such as turning on a computer, using a mouse and keyboard, and the like. However, detailed steps for each procedure are provided, so even if you feel uncertain to start with, you'll be comfortable working through these lessons.

If you are new to Windows 95 itself, Lesson 1 provides some Windows basics to help you. If you are already comfortable with Windows, you can skip over the Windows basics in that lesson and move on to the sections that teach you the various parts of Outlook 97.

If you have used Outlook before, you can read only those sections that relate to the portion of Outlook you want to learn. You can also start from Lesson 1 and proceed in a linear fashion through the entire book (recommended if you are a newcomer to Outlook).

SPECIAL ELEMENTS TO HELP YOU LEARN

The designers of this series thought long and hard about how people learn. They came up with some features that are structured to make you feel in control of your learning, yet challenged in a way that keeps you interested. Every lesson has a consistent structure so you can quickly become comfortable using all the following elements:

- **Suggested completion time.** Because the best way to learn is to complete each lesson without interruption, we've provided a stopwatch symbol at the beginning of each lesson. This stopwatch tells you approximately how much time to set aside to work through the lesson.

- **Goals.** The goals of each lesson are provided at the beginning, so you can anticipate what skills you'll learn and practice.

- **Get Ready.** This section explains what you need to complete the steps in the lessons. It shows you an illustration of a document you will be able to create after completing the exercises.

- **Visual Bonus.** This is a one- or two-page collection of illustrations with callouts that helps you understand a process, procedure, or element of a program more clearly.

- **Skills Challenge.** Every lesson ends with a long exercise that incorporates all the skills you've learned in the individual exercises. The Skills Challenge is a little less explicit about the steps to take, so you are challenged to remember some of the details you've learned. This section reinforces your learning and significantly improves your retention.

- **Bonus Questions.** Sprinkled throughout the Skills Challenge section are Bonus Questions. If you want to push yourself a little harder, you can answer these questions and check Appendix C to see if you got them right.

- **Troubleshooting.** This section appears near the end of each chapter and contains a table of troubleshooting questions and answers that addresses common mistakes or confusions that new users of Outlook often encounter.

- **Wrap Up.** This section provides you with an overview of the skills you learned, as well as a suggested practice project you might try to get more experience with these skills.

Appendix B contains suggestions of real-world projects for you to work on to get further practice with Outlook. Projects, such as creating a business and personal to-do list or personal address book, help you take that all-important step from learning to doing.

Finally, you'll see two icons sprinkled throughout the book, **Notes** and **Tips.**

Notes provide some background or detail that is helpful for you to know about the feature being discussed.

Tips offer reassurances or solutions to common problems.

HOW THIS BOOK IS ORGANIZED

Outlook 97 One Step at a Time has a simple structure. The **Jump Start** session flexes your Outlook muscles by having you run through some typical features and tools of the Outlook program and giving you your first glimpse of the Outlook product.

Part I: Outlook Basics introduces you to the Outlook environment. You'll learn basic Outlook and Windows skills and how to manage Outlook information.

Part II: Managing Contacts shows you how to build a Contacts list and how to do cool things with contacts, such as send a letter to a contact, use AutoDialer, go to a contact's Web page, and print your address book.

Part III: Handling Outlook E-Mail teaches you how to connect to your mail-delivery service, how to send and receive mail, and how to manage your e-mail by tracking messages, recalling messages, flagging messages for follow-up, creating templates, and voting with e-mail.

Part IV: Managing Your Schedule demonstrates how to use Calendar to schedule appointments, events, and meetings; how to change appointments; how to view your schedule; and how to customize Calendar.

Part V: Managing Tasks introduces you to the Task list and teaches you how to create tasks and view and track tasks in various ways.

Part VI: Working with Outlook Components gives you instruction on how to record journal entries and then view the entries; how to create notes, change notes, and view the notes; and how to manage Outlook components and items.

Finally, four appendixes cover installing Outlook 97, provide practice projects, provide the answers to the Bonus Questions, and cover what's on the CD-ROM. You'll also find a glossary of terms and feature names for Outlook, as well as a CD-ROM with sample files for Outlook.

CONVENTIONS USED IN THIS BOOK

Understanding a few simple conventions will help you use this book:

- Many illustrations in the book contain callouts listing step numbers that relate to each part of the figure. There is no need to search around for figure numbers; the visual reinforcement you need is always right where you need it.

- In numbered steps, actual text that you are to type is in **boldface.**

- You will be asked from time to time to import a file located on the CD-ROM that accompanies this book. Each lesson has its own folder, which can be found in the Exercise directory on the CD-ROM. Each lesson folder also contains saved versions of these same files after all the exercises have been completed; these files contain the word "Result" at the beginning of their name to indicate final versions.

That's it! Sit back, relax, and enjoy your lessons with *Outlook 97 One Step at a Time.*

ACKNOWLEDGMENTS

My sincere thanks to a superb professional team at IDG Books. A gracious thank you to Ellen Camm, Acquisitions Editor, who offered me the opportunity to write this book; Susannah Pfalzer, my development editor, who did a fine job developing the content, and whose wit and good humor helped me keep my sense of humor throughout the project; and Paul Summitt, my technical editor, who corrected the manuscript. Also, much appreciation for all the hard work done by the copy editor, Nate Holdread, and the production staff that proofread and produced the entire book. Finally, a special thank you to the sales team at IDG Books.

Special thanks to Tom McCaffrey, Marilyn Russell, and everyone at Real Help Communications, Inc. (http://www.realhelpcom.com) for creating the several thousand sound files required for the CD-ROM in this series, under very aggressive deadlines.

CONTENTS AT A GLANCE

TABLE OF CONTENTS

Jump Start

30 MINUTES

GOALS

In this lesson you learn the following skills:

- Opening Outlook 97
- Reading e-mail
- Adding appointments
- Adding contacts
- Adding tasks
- Recording journal entries
- Creating notes

Opening Microsoft Outlook

GET READY

You're about to tackle learning one of the most robust personal information-manager products on the market today—Microsoft Outlook 97. Your goal is to learn how the program works. To help you prepare to achieve this goal, I've included this Jump Start section. By working through this section, you'll get used to following the step-by-step structure of this book and get a glimpse of the key functions in Outlook 97.

   Don't be concerned about remembering all the procedures or features you're about to see. You'll revisit each of them in more detail within the lessons that follow. Just work your way through these steps to get comfortable with the Outlook environment and the look and feel of the program.

   For this Jump Start section, you need to turn on your computer and have the Windows desktop on your screen (this usually appears automatically when you first turn on your computer).

TRY OUT THE

INTERACTIVE TUTORIALS

ON YOUR CD!

OPENING MICROSOFT OUTLOOK

The first step in working with Outlook is to open the program (see Appendix A for installation instructions). You therefore begin by opening Outlook 97 for a first glimpse.

1 Click the Start button on the Windows taskbar.

2 Choose Programs from the Start menu.

3 Choose Microsoft Outlook from the Programs menu.

   You now have Microsoft Outlook open (see the accompanying figure).

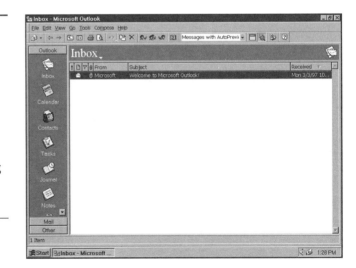

TIP *A quick way to start Outlook is to double-click the Microsoft Outlook shortcut icon on the Windows desktop.*

4 Click the Maximize button to maximize the Outlook window.

Your screen probably looks different from the one in the figure, depending on the mail you received in your Inbox.

READING E-MAIL

The first screen you see in Outlook is the Inbox. From here you can read and send your e-mail messages. Go ahead and read an e-mail message to see how it works.

❶ Click the Mail button at the bottom of the Outlook Bar (the Outlook bar is the toolbar that runs along the left side of the Outlook window).

The Outlook Bar changes to the Mail Bar that contains buttons for sending and receiving e-mail.

❷ Double-click the Welcome to Microsoft Outlook! message.

The accompanying figure shows the e-mail message in a window.

❸ After you read the message, click the Close button to close the e-mail window.

❹ Click the Outlook button at the top of the Mail Bar to return to Outlook Bar.

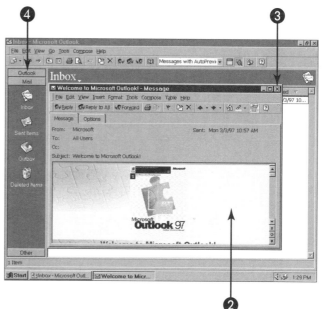

ADDING APPOINTMENTS

To keep track of appointments in your daily schedule, Outlook gives you a calendar. To add an appointment to the calendar, follow these steps:

❶ Click the New button on the Inbox toolbar.

❷ Choose Appointment.

You see the Appointment window.

Adding Appointments

TIP

You'll frequently see windows in Outlook that are similar to dialog boxes. You use these windows to enter data and make most choices and settings for your data. Typically, you'll see lists with scroll bars, lists that drop down when you click the arrow next to them (the Start time and End time choices in this window function that way), and check boxes such as the ones for All Day Event and Reminder. You can usually leave a window without entering your data and applying your choices simply by clicking the Close button and choosing No to cancel any entries.

❸ In the Subject text box, type **My first meeting.**

❹ In the Start time section, click the date drop-down arrow.

❺ Choose the next weekday date on the month calendar.

❻ In the Start time section, click the time drop-down arrow.

❼ Choose 9:00 AM.

❽ Click the Save and Close button on the Appointment toolbar.

❾ Click the Calendar button on the Outlook Bar.

❿ Click tomorrow's date in the current month calendar located on the upper-right side of the Calendar window.

Now you can see the appointment you added to the schedule— a meeting at 9:00 a.m. tomorrow, like the one in the accompanying figure.

ADDING CONTACTS

Outlook provides an address book in which you can store your business and personal names and addresses. To add a contact to the Contacts list, follow these steps:

❶ Click the New button on the Calendar toolbar.

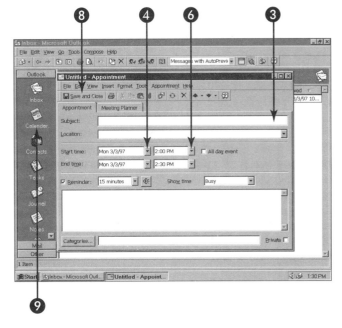

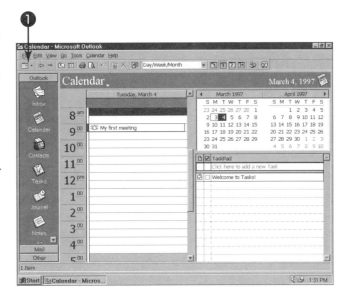

2 Choose Contact.

You see the Contact window.

3 Type the following contact information in the Contact window:

(When you type information in the text boxes in the Contact window, you can press the Tab key to move from one text box to another. Pressing the Tab key is one of several methods for moving between text boxes. To move backward between text boxes, you can press Shift+Tab.)

Claudia Brooks [Tab]

Sales Manager [Tab]

Bookworm Books [Tab]

4 Click in the Address box.

5 Type **100 Reader's Lane** and press Enter.

Next you type the address information. Be sure to press the comma key following the city, and press the spacebar twice after the state.

6 Type **Scarsdale, NY 10011.**

7 Click in the empty text box next to Business in the Phone section.

8 Type **914–555-1300.**

9 Click the Save and Close button on the Contacts toolbar.

10 Click the Contacts button on the Outlook Bar.

Your Contacts list should now look like the one in the accompanying figure, except that you won't have an entry for Reisner, Trudi. Your own name or the name of the person who set up your computer should appear in the Contacts list.

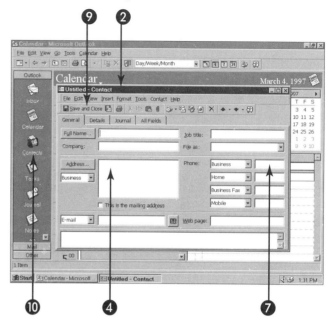

Adding Tasks

ADDING TASKS

You can track your tasks, projects, and people involved in these tasks and projects by using Outlook's Tasks list. Follow these steps to add a task to your Tasks list:

① Click the New button on the Contacts toolbar.

② Choose Task.

Outlook displays the Task window.

③ In the Subject box, type **create contacts list.**

④ In the Due date section, click the Due option button.

⑤ Click the Due drop-down arrow.

⑥ Choose this Friday's date on the month calendar.

⑦ In the Due date section, click the Start drop-down arrow.

⑧ Choose this Thursday's date on the month calendar.

⑨ Click the Save and Close button on the Tasks toolbar.

⑩ Click the Tasks button on the Outlook Bar.

Your Tasks list should resemble the one in the accompanying figure. This is the simple list view; however, there are many views you can switch to, and they're discussed later in Lesson 9.

RECORDING JOURNAL ENTRIES

You can record any activity you perform in Microsoft Office and use the Outlook journal to find it. For example, when you've worked on a document or task or made a phone call to a contact in the Contacts list, you may not remember where you stored the information. Use the Journal feature to manually track the phone call to a particular contact.

① Click the New button on the Tasks toolbar.

② Choose Journal Entry.

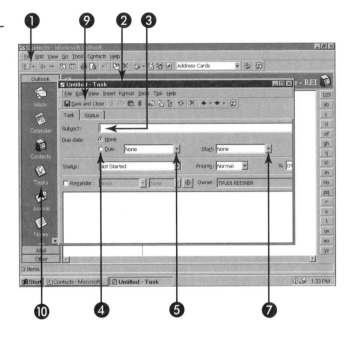

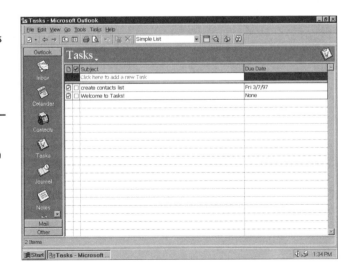

Outlook displays the Journal Entry window shown in the accompanying figure.

3 In the Subject box, type **book conference.**

4 Press Tab twice.

5 In the Contact box, type **Claudia Brooks.**

6 Click the Start Timer button to manually record the phone call activity.

7 In the large empty box, type **Discussed presentation that Claudia is giving at book conference. Will meet her at breakfast on first day of conference to review her speech.**

8 Click the Pause Timer button to stop recording the entry.

The time spent on the phone call appears in the Duration box. In this example the duration time is measured in minutes. However, Outlook also measures duration time in hours and days.

9 Click the Save and Close button on the Journal toolbar.

10 Click the Journal icon on the Outlook Bar.

The Phone Call journal entry is added to the end of the Journal list. Your Journal should look like the one in the accompanying figure.

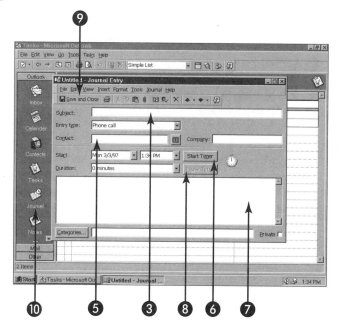

CREATING NOTES

You've probably used many sticky notes in your life to make a note about something or remind you of an important thing you need to do. Outlook lets you create and view sticky notes right on your screen, so you can keep the little reminders at your fingertips and view them any time.

1 Click the New button on the Journal toolbar.

2 Choose Note.

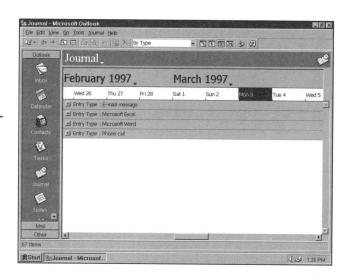

Creating Notes

Outlook displays a blank yellow note onscreen.

3 Type **Bring task list to staff meeting.**

4 Click the Notes button on the Outlook Bar.

The first note in the Notes window is yours.

5 Open the File menu.

6 Choose the Exit command to close Outlook.

7 Click the Close button in the upper-right corner of the note to close the note.

Now it's time to delete all the items you created in Jump Start so that you have a clean slate in each Outlook component for all the lessons in this book. Start by deleting items in Notes.

1 Click the first note to select it.

2 Hold down the Ctrl key and click the next note to select it.

This is how you select multiple items. As you can see, both items are selected, indicated by their text in dark blue.

3 Click the Delete (X) button on the Notes toolbar.

Both notes are gone. Outlook displays a message in the Information Viewer, letting you know that no items are in Notes.

4 Click Journal in the Outlook Bar.

5 Repeat Steps 1–3 to delete all the items in Journal.

6 Repeat Steps 4–5 to delete all the items for each of the remaining Outlook components.

WRAP UP

You've now learned several key operations used in Outlook. You learned how to

■ Open Outlook 97

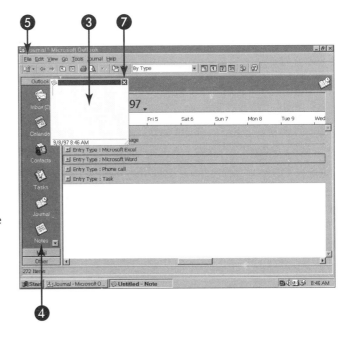

- Read your e-mail
- Insert appointments
- Add some contacts
- Create tasks
- Record journal entries
- Create notes

Examining some of the tools and menus in Outlook gave you a sneak preview of the program. Now you know that accomplishing tasks in Outlook is simply a matter of learning to use the tools, menus, and dialog boxes that the program presents. The lessons in this book give you a working knowledge of these features and much more so that you can master the Outlook 97 basic skills.

PART I

Outlook Basics

This part shows you the Outlook environment. You learn about the different parts of Outlook and how to manage Outlook information.

This part contains the following lessons:

- Lesson 1: Meet Microsoft Outlook
- Lesson 2: Managing Outlook Information

Meet Microsoft Outlook

GOALS

In this lesson you learn these basic skills:

25 MINUTES

- Creating folders
- Opening Microsoft Outlook 97
- Starting Outlook Online or Offline
- Working with the Menu Bar
- Exploring shortcut menus
- Touring the Outlook Bar
- Learning to use the toolbars
- Getting Help
- Exiting Microsoft Outlook 97

What Is Outlook 97?

GET READY

To complete this lesson's exercises, you need to have Outlook 97 installed (see Appendix A). You also need the accompanying Outlook 97 One Step at a Time CD-ROM.

When you're finished with these exercises, you will be familiar with the elements of the Outlook window. For example, the accompanying figure shows the Outlook window, the Office Assistant window, and a Help dialog box.

WHAT IS MICROSOFT OUTLOOK 97?

Microsoft Outlook 97 is a personal information manager that comes with the Microsoft Office 97 suite of programs. Microsoft Outlook 97 includes the former Microsoft Exchange (the Windows message system), the former Microsoft Schedule+, and more—all rolled into one information-management program. Outlook 97 functions like a three-ring binder you might tote around during your business day.

You can jot down appointments and events on a calendar, write names and addresses in an address book, keep a to-do list, record your daily activities in a journal book, and write on sticky notes, but Outlook 97 makes entering data, managing information, and printing the results much easier. You can use Outlook 97 to computerize your daily appointments and events, contacts, tasks, projects, journal entries, sticky notes, and much more. You can create almost anything in Outlook 97 that involves managing information.

In addition to managing your personal information, Outlook 97 can help you keep track of e-mail and faxes. Its capability to send and receive e-mail and faxes (including a cover sheet) enables you to communicate with others from one place—Outlook 97—instead of using e-mail in a different program and a fax machine in your office.

Here's what you find in Outlook 97:

- **Inbox** lets you send and receive e-mail and faxes, preview messages before you open them, and mark messages with message flags to follow up on any action necessary. With Inbox you can share Outlook's management information with others, either over a company computer network or in a printout.

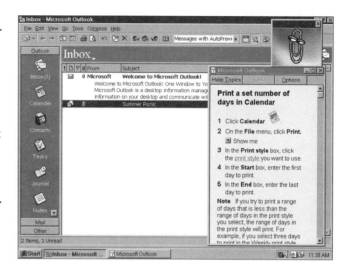

What Is Outlook 97?

- **Calendar** enables you to schedule and keep track of appointments, events, holidays, and meetings, and even set up meetings. You can also set up a reminder—an alarm that rings to remind you of an appointment. The Date Navigator helps you find and view information in your schedule. Calendar helps you better manage the way you control your own time.

- **Contacts** assists you with building a contacts list that contains names, addresses, phone numbers, fax numbers, and e-mail addresses. You can sort and store the contacts in various ways. For example, you can store several addresses, phone numbers, and e-mail addresses for each contact. You can also go to a contact's Web page on the World Wide Web.

- **Tasks** gives you a way to organize your daily or weekly projects and tasks in one place, as well as prioritize tasks and assign tasks. The TaskPad lets you see the day's tasks and schedule time to work on them. This feature is useful for project management.

- **Journal** enables you to record interactions with important contacts; Outlook items such as e-mail messages; files (Microsoft Word, Excel, and PowerPoint documents) important to you; and appointments, tasks, or notes. The Journal can record past entries of e-mail messages you sent to others, files you created, past appointments, and completed tasks. Journal is another handy tool for project management.

- **Notes** are the electronic versions of paper sticky notes. You can use notes to jot down ideas, reminders, questions, instructions, and anything else you may write as a note on paper. You can leave notes open onscreen as you work.

TRY OUT THE

INTERACTIVE TUTORIALS

ON YOUR CD!

Whether you are working on an individual computer or computers linked together in workgroups, you can use Outlook 97 to manage your time. If you are working on a computer linked to a workgroup, you can access, view, and share files from within Outlook 97.

You can buy Outlook 97 as a stand-alone product or as part of a suite of programs called Microsoft Office 97. Office 97 contains Outlook 97 and several other programs that complement one another, such as a word processor (Word 97), spreadsheet (Excel 97), and presentation (PowerPoint 97).

Creating Folders

▶ Creating Folders

Before you get further into the nitty-gritty of Outlook, you need to set up a folder for the exercise files on your hard drive.

Generally, your computer works more efficiently with files located on the hard drive rather than a floppy disk or CD-ROM. To make your work in this book easier, copy the exercise files from the CD-ROM into a folder on your hard drive. You can then import and work with the files from that folder when indicated in an exercise. In Lesson 2 you learn how to import files in Outlook 97.

1 Double-click the My Computer icon on your desktop.

2 In the My Computer window, double-click the hard drive (C:).

3 Open the File menu.

4 Choose the New command.

5 Choose Folder from the submenu. A new folder appears at the end of the list with the name New Folder.

6 Type **One Step** to name the folder.

7 Press Enter.

8 Place the accompanying CD-ROM in the CD-ROM drive.

9 In the My Computer window, double-click the CD-ROM icon, usually labeled D:, to open the drive in which you placed the CD-ROM.

10 In the CD-ROM (D:) window, click the folder named Exercise to select it.

11 Point to the Exercise folder, hold down the left mouse button, and drag the folder from the CD-ROM (D:) window to the One Step folder.

The One Step folder is highlighted while you hold the other folder over it, letting you know that if you release your mouse button, the item you're dragging will drop into that folder.

12 Release your mouse button.

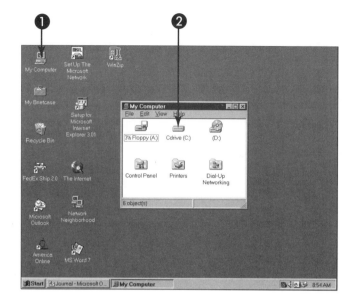

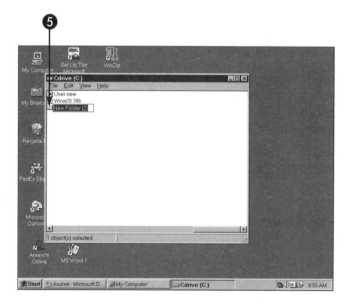

⑬ Double-click the One Step folder.

All the files for your exercises are now located within this folder, and you can work with them from here.

⑭ Close all the open windows on your desktop.

FIRST LOOK AT OUTLOOK 97

Before you can start Outlook 97, you must install it on your hard disk. If Outlook 97 is installed, it appears in your Windows Programs menu and as a shortcut icon on the Windows desktop. The exact installation procedure depends on whether you bought Outlook 97 as part of the Microsoft Office 97 suite or as a separate program. For installation instructions, refer to Appendix A, "Installing Microsoft Outlook 97."

Starting Outlook 97 is simple — it's as easy as starting the engine in your car! When you turn on your computer and monitor, Windows 95 appears on your screen. You can start Outlook 97 from the Windows desktop or by using the Start menu (covered in Exercise 2).

In this book I want you to imagine that you work for All Sports Promotions, Inc., a fictional company that manages, markets, and promotes professional athletes for professional sports. All Sports Promotions, Inc. has grown rapidly in recent years, and it is now a medium-size company with several departments, including marketing, promotions, advertising, human resources, sales, and accounting.

As a sports agent for All Sports Promotions, Inc., you have just had your computer upgraded to run Windows 95, with a copy of Outlook 97 installed. Your first assignment is to become familiar with the basic control and help features of the program.

The following exercises introduce you to Outlook 97, one of the best personal information manager programs.

Opening Microsoft Outlook 97

You can use either of two methods for starting the Outlook program:

- Microsoft Outlook shortcut icon on the Windows desktop

Opening Outlook 97

- Microsoft Outlook on the Windows Programs menu

A quick way to open Microsoft Outlook 97 is to double-click the Microsoft Outlook 97 shortcut icon (an icon with a clock, envelope, and piece of paper) on your Windows 95 desktop (see the accompanying figure). A shortcut icon always has an arrow that curls up and to the right located in the lower-left corner of the shortcut icon.

NOTE *When you install Outlook, the Setup program looks for a user profile. If you don't have a user profile, Setup creates one for you. A user profile contains a group of settings that specifies how you are set up to work with Outlook. For example, your user profile may let you send and receive messages with your Internet connection, or specify that you don't use e-mail at all and have a personal folder file.*

If you see the Choose Profile dialog box, open the Profile Name drop-down list and make a selection. Then click OK. If no Profile name exists, you need to create one. To do so, click the Start button on the Windows taskbar and select Settings ➢ Control Panel. In the Windows Control Panel, double-click the Mail icon, click the Services tab, and click Show Profiles. Then click the General tab and click Add, and the Inbox Setup Wizard walks you through creating a Profile name.

Follow these steps to open Outlook 97:

1. Click the Start button on the Windows taskbar.

2. Select Programs from the Start menu.

3. Select Microsoft Outlook from the Programs menu.

   After a brief introductory screen, the Outlook window appears. This window contains the Inbox view (by default) with a list of e-mail messages. The Inbox view is where you can read, send, and receive your e-mail messages. The Menu Bar is located directly below the title bar. The toolbar on the left side of the window is called the *Outlook Bar,* and the one at the top is the *Inbox toolbar.*

4. In the Office Assistant balloon, click the Show these choices at startup check box to remove the check mark.

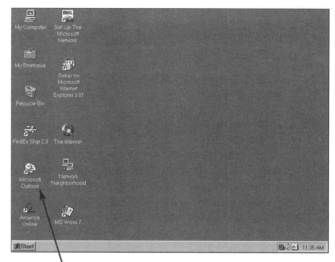

Outlook Shortcut Icon

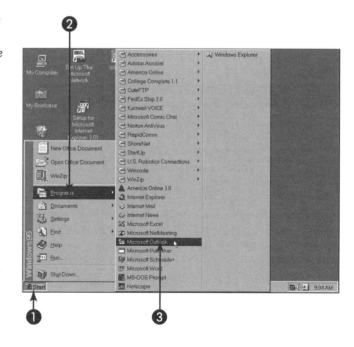

⑤ Click OK to remove the Office Assistant from your screen.

⑥ Click the Maximize button in the upper-right corner of the Outlook window.

The Outlook window enlarges to full-screen size as shown in the accompanying figure.

⑦ Click the Minimize button in the document window.

The Outlook window shrinks to a button at the bottom on the Windows taskbar.

⑧ Click the Inbox-Microsoft Outlook button on the Windows taskbar.

The Outlook window reopens and fills the screen.

The six main components of this compact little program are represented by icons in the Outlook Bar. At any time you just choose an icon in the Outlook Bar to work with any component you want.

Keep an eye on the Status bar at the bottom of the screen as you change the view. For example, the number of items in a view is explained at the left end of the Status bar.

Starting Outlook Online or Offline

Outlook lets you work online or offline, your choice, depending on what kind of work you're going to do in Outlook. For example, if you're going to work with mail, the Internet, or fax, you need to connect to a network and get online. Otherwise, you can work offline in Outlook.

To send, store, and receive messages and Outlook items and to designate where to store your Outlook information, you use a group of settings in Outlook referred to as an *information service.* Some examples of information services include the Microsoft Network online service, personal folders, Microsoft Exchange Server, EarthLink, and any ISP (Internet service provider) that can connect you to a network.

If you want to use e-mail in Outlook, you need to add the appropriate information service to your user profile. A *user profile* is a group of settings that specifies how you are set up to work with Outlook. If you don't plan to use e-mail, or if you have an existing

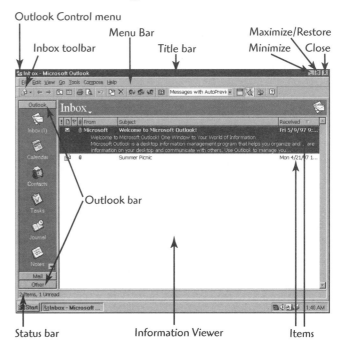

Outlook Control menu
Menu Bar
Maximize/Restore
Inbox toolbar
Title bar
Minimize Close

Outlook bar

Status bar
Information Viewer
Items

Starting Outlook

user profile with the information service and settings recommended by your network administrator, then you don't have to read any further in this section. You can open Microsoft Outlook without any further ado.

To set up Outlook to work online, you need to add an information service for either your e-mail service provider or for Internet mail. Some of the more common protocols used by an e-mail service provider or Internet mail include SMTP—Simple Mail Transfer Protocol—and POP—Post Office Protocol Version 3. Outlook supplies you with the software necessary for several popular e-mail service providers and for the Internet. If your e-mail service provider is not included, you must get the appropriate software from your Internet service provider.

To add an information service for e-mail, start Outlook and click Inbox on the Outlook Bar. Select Tools ➢ Services and click Add on the Services tab. In the Add Service to Profile dialog box, choose the information service you want to add. If the information service you want is not in the list, you need to install it. Choose any other options you want, such as filename and location, and then click OK.

To set up Outlook to work offline, follow these steps:

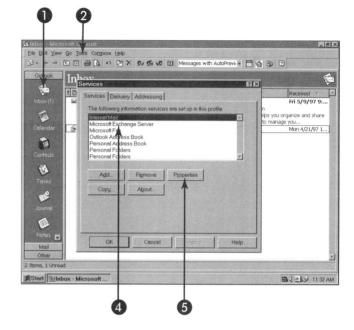

❶ Click Inbox on the Outlook Bar.

❷ Open the Tools menu.

❸ Choose the Services command. The Services dialog box appears.

❹ In the The following information services are set up in this profile box, choose Microsoft Exchange Server.

❺ Click the Properties button.

The Microsoft Exchange Server dialog box appears.

❻ Click the General tab.

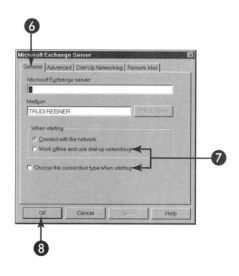

❼ Choose the Work offline and use dial-up networking option. If you want to choose whether to work offline or online each time you start Outlook, select the Choose the connection type when starting option.

❽ Click OK.

(9) Exit Outlook.

(10) Restart Outlook to enable these connection types.

USING MENUS AND TOOLS

The Menu Bar is a row of main menu commands. You select a menu command to perform operations such as saving a file, formatting text, or printing a document. The Menu Bar contains pull-down menus similar to window shades. You pull down a menu to get a list of commands. A pull-down menu shows a list of commands like a list of items on a restaurant menu. To select a command, simply point to the command and then click it.

When you select a command followed by an ellipsis (. . .), Outlook displays a dialog box. Some dialog boxes have more than one set of options, indicated by tabs at the top of the dialog box. You can display a different set of options by clicking a tab.

Many of the menu commands have shortcut keys for which you use a function key, such as F1. Or, sometimes you can use the Ctrl and/or Shift key in addition to a keyboard character. Using these substitutes is often faster than using the menu commands.

When you point to an item in Outlook and then click the right mouse button, you see a shortcut menu. This menu appears next to the item. Shortcut menus contain fewer commands than a menu in the Menu Bar. The commands on the shortcut menus vary depending on the item you select. You may find it quicker and easier to use a shortcut menu than to select commands from the Menu Bar and the pull-down menus.

A toolbar contains buttons for common commands and provides quick access to commands you use frequently. The Outlook toolbar appears on the left side of the main Outlook window. In the documentation, Microsoft calls the Outlook toolbar the Outlook Bar. No matter what you call it, it's quick and ready for you to use. This set of tools is a powerful aid when you enter and manage your information. You can customize the Outlook Bar to contain icons for the features you use most frequently, which is discussed in Lesson 2.

After you start Outlook 97, you see the Inbox toolbar at the top of the Inbox window beneath the Menu Bar. Outlook 97 displays many different toolbars that appear automatically when you switch

Working Out with the Menu Bar

folders and select various commands to enter data. Each folder has its own toolbar. For example, when you switch to Calendar, you see the Calendar toolbar at the top of the Calendar window. When you compose an e-mail message, the Mail toolbar appears at the top of the message window. You'll use many of these toolbars as you work in Outlook.

You need a mouse to use the toolbars. To perform a task, select a toolbar button instead of a menu command as a shortcut. As you become more comfortable with Outlook, you will find that using the tools on the toolbar is easier and faster than selecting commands in menus.

Working Out with the Menu Bar

Outlook's Menu Bar has some commands in common with the standard Windows menu bars. You've probably seen many of those commands before in other software you use. But many menu commands are unique to Outlook. The menu names appear in the Menu Bar at the top of the screen. You can select menu commands by using the mouse or the keyboard. In this exercise and throughout the exercises in this book, you select commands using the mouse. However, if you want to use the keyboard, press Alt and the underlined letter in the menu name to open the menu. Then press the underlined letter of the command you want to select in the menu.

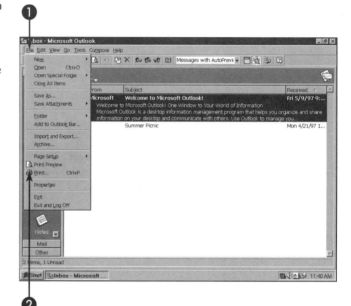

❶ Point to File in the Menu Bar and click the left mouse button.

The File menu opens and you see a list of File commands.

❷ Point to Print in the File menu and click the left mouse button.

You've selected the Print command; Outlook opens the Print dialog box.

❸ Click Cancel to close the dialog box.

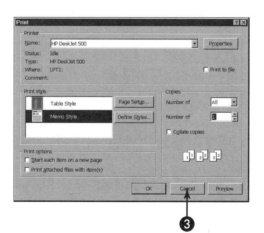

TIP

To close a menu without making a selection, press Esc or click anywhere outside the menu.

Exploring Shortcut Menus

You learn and use many different menu commands during subsequent exercises in this book.

Exploring Shortcut Menus

In this exercise you explore one of Outlook's shortcut menus.

1 Right-click the dark gray area of the Outlook Bar—don't click a button.

A shortcut menu opens and you see a list of Outlook Bar commands.

2 Select Small Icons.

The Outlook Bar now contains small icons with their names at the top half of the toolbar, making room for any buttons you may want to add in the future. See the accompanying figure.

3 Right-click the dark gray area of the Outlook Bar.

4 Select Large Icons.

You see large icons in the Outlook Bar again.

TIP

To close a shortcut menu without making a selection, press Esc or click anywhere outside of the menu.

Touring the Outlook Bar

You get three toolbars in one in the Outlook Bar:

- **Outlook** contains a collection of tools for choosing a particular Outlook folder. Outlook's most important folders include Inbox, Calendar, Contacts, Tasks, Journal, and Notes.

- **Mail** gives you a set of tools for sending and receiving e-mail messages.

- **Other** lets you open My Computer and the My Documents and Favorites folders.

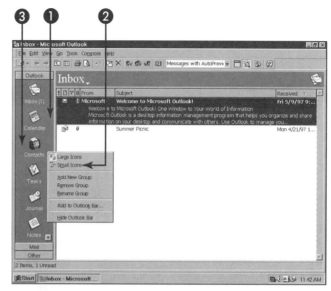

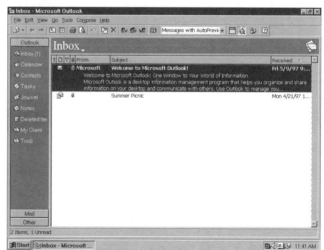

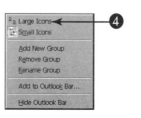

Touring the Outlook Bar

The tools on all the toolbars operate as point-and-click. When you point to a tool, you click it to perform an operation quickly. These are shortcuts to Outlook operations. In this exercise you use the Outlook Bar to switch from one Outlook component to another, as well as look at all three toolbars.

❶ Click the Calendar button on the Outlook Bar.

Outlook displays the Calendar folder.

❷ Click the Contacts button on the Outlook Bar.

You see the Contacts folder with the name and address you entered earlier in the Jump Start.

❸ Click the Tasks button on the Outlook Bar.

You see the Tasks folder with the task you entered earlier in the Jump Start.

❹ Click the Journal button on the Outlook Bar.

As you can see, the Journal folder appears with several journal entries.

❺ Click the Notes button on the Outlook Bar.

Notice that the Notes folder contains two sticky notes—one you created and one from Microsoft.

Next look at the More Icons (down arrow) button at the bottom of the Outlook Bar. When you click this button, Outlook shows you more buttons on the Outlook Bar.

❻ Click the More Icons button at the bottom of the Outlook Bar.

The Outlook buttons slide up and you see the Deleted Items button at the bottom of the Outlook Bar (see the accompanying figure).

❼ Click the Deleted Items button at the bottom of the Outlook Bar.

The Deleted Items folder appears, showing all the items deleted in earlier Outlook sessions.

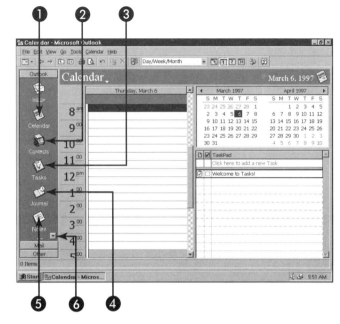

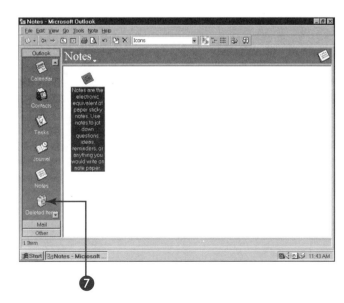

Notice the More Icons button at the top of the Outlook toolbar. Clicking this button shows you more buttons at the top of the Outlook Bar.

8 Click the More Icons button at the top of the Outlook Bar.

The Outlook buttons slide down and you see the Inbox button again at the top of the Outlook Bar. Notice that the More Icons button shows up again at the bottom of the toolbar.

9 Click the Inbox button at the top of the Outlook Bar to return to the Inbox view.

10 Click the Mail button at the bottom of the Outlook Bar.

The Outlook toolbar slides up and the Mail toolbar appears (see the accompanying figure). These buttons give you shortcuts for the most frequently used mail commands. You'll use these buttons later in Lesson 5.

11 Click the Other button at the bottom of the Mail toolbar.

The Mail toolbar slides up and the Other toolbar emerges, as shown in the accompanying figure. These tools provide shortcuts for the most common Windows operations and for storing your information in the most frequently used folders.

12 Click the Outlook button at the top of the Other toolbar.

This takes you back to the Outlook toolbar.

In some cases you may want to change the width of the Outlook Bar to accommodate the information that shows in the Information Viewer on the right. Notice the gray vertical bar that divides the Outlook Bar and the Information Viewer window. This is called the *split bar*. Point to the split bar until you see a vertical bar with a left and right arrow. Then drag the split bar to the left to make the Outlook Bar skinnier and widen the Information Viewer. Drag the split bar to the right to make the Outlook Bar wider and the Information Viewer skinnier.

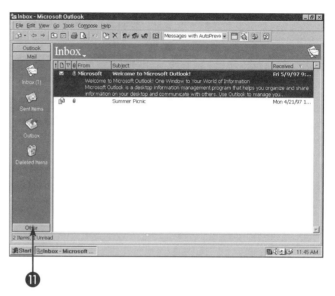

Outlook Toolbars

The Outlook Bar contains buttons for the most common Outlook commands. It is located on the left side of the screen. If this toolbar doesn't appear on your screen, then select View ➤ Outlook Bar.

The Outlook Bar.

The Mail toolbar contains tools for the most common Outlook mail commands. Click the Mail button at the bottom of the Outlook toolbar to display the Mail toolbar on the left side of the screen. To return to the Outlook toolbar, click the Outlook button at the top of the Mail toolbar.

The Mail toolbar.

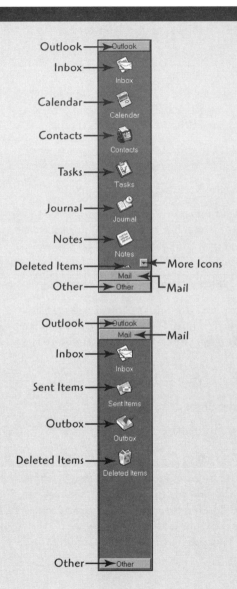

The Other toolbar contains tools for the most frequently used Windows operations and folders. Click the Other button on the Outlook toolbar to display the Other toolbar on the left side of the screen. To return to the Outlook toolbar, click the Outlook button at the top of the Other toolbar.

The Other toolbar.

You can hide the toolbars to make more room onscreen. To hide the Outlook Bar, select View ➤ Outlook Bar. To hide a toolbar, double-click any part of the toolbar—do not double-click a button to hide the toolbar.

To display the Outlook Bar, select View ➤ Outlook Bar again. To display a toolbar, right-click the Menu Bar or a toolbar to display the Toolbar shortcut menu. Select a toolbar from the shortcut menu.

Learning to Use the Toolbars

Outlook's component toolbars allow fast selection of commands. Each component you select in the Outlook Bar displays a toolbar with a set of tools specific to the component. For example, when you select Contacts, the Contacts toolbar appears beneath the Menu Bar. When you select Tasks, Outlook displays the Tasks toolbar beneath the Menu Bar, and so on. Other toolbars appear in other places in Outlook. When you create a new item such as a mail

Learning to Use the Toolbars

message, an appointment, contact, or task, Outlook displays a dialog box that has its own toolbar for creating and working with the item.

Microsoft's ScreenTip feature makes it easy to recognize the Outlook tools you work with on the toolbars. This feature displays the button names on a toolbar. In this exercise you view ScreenTips and use some of the buttons on the toolbars.

❶ Point to the New Mail Message button on the Inbox toolbar.

You see the button's name, New Mail Message, in a light yellow box near the button. This is the ScreenTip feature. If you're unsure what a toolbar button does, leave the mouse pointer on a toolbar button for a second or two. Outlook then displays the button name.

❷ Click the New Mail Message button on the Inbox toolbar.

Outlook opens the Message window. Notice the Message toolbar at the top of the Message window.

❸ Point to the Save button (the button with a floppy diskette) on the Message toolbar.

Notice the ScreenTip for the button name—Save.

❹ Click the Close button to close the Message window.

The more you use Outlook, you'll notice that the New button's name changes depending on what folder is currently displayed in the Outlook window. For example, when the Inbox folder is displayed, the New Mail Message button name displays, as you saw in Step 1. However, if you switch to the Calendar folder, the New Appointment button name is displayed. Check it out.

❺ Click the Calendar button on the Outlook Bar.

Outlook switches to the Calendar folder.

❻ Point to the New Appointment button on the Calendar toolbar.

You see the ScreenTip for the button's name—New Appointment.

You use many of the tools on the toolbars in subsequent lessons.

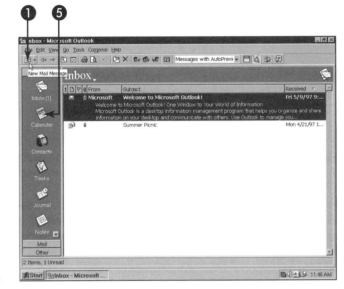

Help!

Sometimes you may want to have a clean screen, or you may want to make more white space visible in a window. You can hide the toolbars to make more room onscreen. Double-click any part of the toolbar (except on a button) to hide the toolbar.

To display a toolbar, right-click the Menu Bar or a toolbar to display the Toolbar shortcut menu. Select a toolbar from the shortcut menu.

HELP!

Help is always there when you need it, and Outlook makes sure of that by giving you as much help as you can handle. There are several ways to get help:

- **Help menu with Help Contents and Index.** At the right end of the Menu Bar is the Help menu. Through the Help Contents and Index command, you can access an extensive set of online documentation about various commands and procedures.

- **F1 key (context-sensitive help).** A more direct way to get help about a specific topic is through the F1 key, which opens the Help window in a context-sensitive way. Context-sensitive means that the help message applies to the current operation. Outlook displays relevant information about the most recently activated command, procedure, or window.

- **Shift+F1 (Help pointer).** Another way to get context-sensitive help is to press Shift+F1 (you'll see a question mark (?) next to the mouse pointer arrow) and then select a command. Instead of executing the command, the program displays the Help window with the appropriate information.

- **Office Assistant.** This provides a quick way to search for help on a particular topic and find shortcuts in Outlook.

1

Meet Microsoft Outlook

Getting Help

Getting Help

The four ways to get help in Outlook include the Help menu with Help Contents and Index; the F1 key; Shift+F1 and the Help pointer; and the Office Assistant. In this exercise you use the built-in Office Assistant to get help printing a calendar.

1 Click the Office Assistant button on the Calendar toolbar.

The Office Assistant balloon appears. The Office Assistant enables you to search for help, get tips, and change Office Assistant options.

2 Type **print calendar** in the text box, replacing the text that you see there.

3 Click the Search button or press Enter.

The Office Assistant displays a list of help topics for printing a calendar, as shown in the accompanying figure.

4 Click the topic called Print a set number of days in Calendar.

A dialog box appears that contains steps for you to follow to print a set number of days in Calendar.

5 Click the Close button in the dialog box's title bar to close the Help dialog box.

6 Click the yellow light bulb in the Office Assistant window.

The Office Assistant Tips balloon appears. You see one of Outlook's shortcuts—which could be called F.Y.I, Try This, or Tip of the Day—in a light yellow balloon.

TIP *If the Office Assistant balloon is displayed, you can click the Tips button to display F.Y.I and Tip of the Day information.*

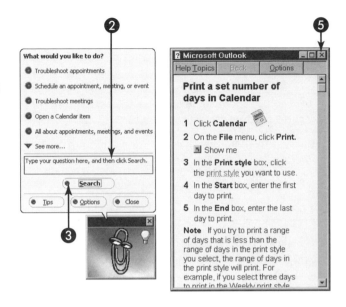

7 Click the Back or Next button to display the previous or next shortcut.

8 Click the Close button to close the Tips balloon.

9 Click the Close button to close the Office Assistant window.

Exiting Microsoft Outlook

To exit Outlook, follow these steps:

1 Open the File menu.

2 Choose the Exit command.

Outlook closes and you are back to the Windows desktop.

TIP

You can also double-click the Control menu icon or click the Close button in the upper-right corner of the Outlook window.

SKILLS CHALLENGE: EXPLORING THE OUTLOOK PROGRAM

In this exercise you open Microsoft Outlook, select menu commands, open a shortcut menu, use tools on the toolbars, get some help with the Office Assistant, and exit Microsoft Outlook. This exercise gives you the opportunity to apply the skills you've learned in this lesson. Answer the bonus questions to review the skills and help you determine your understanding of the topics covered. The answers to these bonus questions are located in Appendix C.

1 Open Microsoft Outlook.

1 *Can you identify the Window Control buttons on the Outlook window?*

2 Click OK to remove the Office Assistant from your screen.

Meet Microsoft Outlook

Skills Challenge

 2 *What does an ellipsis next to a menu command indicate?*

TRY OUT THE

INTERACTIVE TUTORIALS

ON YOUR CD!

3 Open the File menu.

4 Choose the Print command.

5 Close the Print dialog box.

6 Right-click the Outlook Bar.

7 Select the Hide Outlook Bar command to hide the toolbar.

8 Open the View menu.

9 Choose the Outlook Bar command.

10 Click the New Mail Message button on the Inbox toolbar.

11 Close the Message window.

 3 *If you're unsure what a toolbar button does, how do you find the button's name?*

12 Using the Office Assistant, search for help on the Status bar.

13 Click the Close button to close the Status bar Help dialog box.

14 Click the yellow light bulb in the Office Assistant to open the Tips balloon.

15 Click the Back and Next buttons in the Tips balloon to look at Outlook's shortcuts.

16 Click the Close button in the Tips balloon to close it.

17 Then, click the Close button to close the Office Assistant.

18 Exit Microsoft Outlook.

 4 *What are the two shortcuts for exiting Outlook?*

TROUBLESHOOTING

You've learned many of the basics of getting around Outlook. The following table may answer some questions that have come up during this lesson.

Problem	Solution
My Outlook window shrunk to a button at the bottom of the screen.	Click the Outlook button on the Windows taskbar to maximize the Outlook window.
When I clicked the mouse button to execute a command, nothing happened.	Be sure you point to the right thing and click the left mouse button. If nothing happens, or if a strange menu appears, check the location of the mouse pointer and try clicking again.
I accidentally opened a menu.	Press Esc or click anywhere outside the menu.
I accidentally opened a dialog box.	Click the Cancel button or the Close button in the dialog box to close the dialog box.
I tried to view a toolbar button's name, and the ScreenTip doesn't appear.	Try moving the mouse pointer again and pause a few seconds.

Although you may experience some of these issues as you learn Outlook, most are not catastrophic, and resolving them is part of the learning process.

WRAP UP

In this lesson you learned how to

- Create new folders
- Open Microsoft Outlook

Wrap up

- Start Outlook Online or Offline

- Use the Menu Bar

- Look at shortcut menus

- Discover what's on the Outlook Bar

- Use the toolbars

- Get help

- Exit Microsoft Outlook

For more practice, review the Outlook screen elements in this lesson and the Visual Bonus: Outlook Toolbars. Explore all the menus and view the ScreenTips for the buttons on all the toolbars.

In the next lesson you learn how to store and manage your Outlook information in folders.

Managing Outlook Information

35 MINUTES

GOALS

This lesson covers the following Outlook information management skills:

- Naming Outlook folders
- Changing the order of Outlook folders
- Moving items to different folders
- Exporting items to a file
- Importing items from a file
- Switching Outlook views
- Creating a filter on a view

Working with Outlook Folders

GET READY

To complete this lesson's exercises, you need the accompanying CD-ROM. When you're finished with these exercises, you will have created a new Personal folder in the Folder List called My Client, shown in the accompanying figure.

WORKING WITH OUTLOOK FOLDERS

Before you begin to add gobs of information to your Outlook folders, you should familiarize yourself with how the folders and information are organized. It's important to know where the information is located, where it will be stored, and how you can access it.

The most important folder you will be working with in Outlook is called the Personal folder. Each major Outlook component has a Personal folder identified by the component's name. A Personal folder is a file stored on your hard disk drive, not on a network server. For example, CALENDAR is the Personal folder for the Calendar component.

A Personal folder can hold other folders, files, messages, and forms, just like any other folder on your computer. You can even have incoming e-mail messages sent directly to your Personal folder, if that's your preference. Because Personal folders contain so much valuable information, it is recommended that you make backup copies of your Personal folder files on floppy diskettes from time to time.

Before I go any further, you need to know that the term *item* is frequently used in Outlook, and you need to know what it means. An item refers to a mail message, appointment, contact, journal entry, task, and note. Items are stored in the Personal folders.

If you want, you can save your Outlook items in different folders — maybe you want to organize your work by type and use separate folders for different project types. Outlook stores your information in various folders you designate on your hard disk drive.

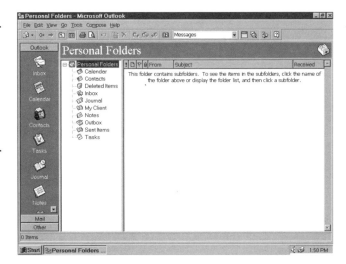

Naming Outlook Folders

After you have all the folders you need in Outlook, you can reorder them in the Folder List any way you want. That way you can find a folder quickly whenever you need to work with it. Also, you can add your own Personal folders to the Outlook Bar. They become shortcuts to viewing the contents of your Personal folders. Simply click a Personal folder's button on the Outlook Bar to see its contents.

Outlook gives you a couple ways to store your items. You can move items to any folder or, if you want to store multiple items in a file, you can export the items to a file. Then you can import that file to display the items in the Information Viewer and work with them.

In the next set of exercises, you name and reorder Outlook folders for your own personal use, move an item to a folder, and import and export items in files.

TRY OUT THE

INTERACTIVE TUTORIALS

ON YOUR CD!

Naming Outlook Folders

You learned in Lesson 1 that Outlook is comprised of folders representing the six major components of the program. When you choose a component from the Outlook Bar, that component is presented visually in the Information Viewer. This perspective may make it a little difficult to think of each component as a folder, but this exercise will help you see that each component truly is a folder.

Also, as a sports agent you need your own Personal folder to store your first and only client's information.

❶ Open the View menu.

❷ Choose the Folder List command.

The Folder List appears. Notice the split bar between the Folder List and the Information Viewer. Earlier in Lesson 1 you changed the width of the Outlook Bar using its split bar. Now you can do the same with the Folder List. Some of the folder names are long and partially hidden. Widen the Folder List to see all the complete folder names.

Naming Outlook Folders

TIP

There are two other ways to display the Folder List. You can click the component name's (in large letters) drop-down arrow located in the upper-left corner of the Information Viewer. For example, click the Inbox drop-down arrow. You can also click the Folder List button (the button with two windowpanes—a narrow pane on the left and a wider pane on the right) on the component's toolbar.

3 Point to the split bar on the Folder List until you see a vertical bar with a left and right arrow.

4 Drag the split bar to the right until the long folder names are visible.

Now your Folder List should look like the one in the accompanying figure.

5 Click the Calendar folder.

Notice the reduced size version of the Calendar's contents in the Information Viewer. You can work with a component this way, too. Now create a new Personal folder.

6 Click Personal Folders, which is the parent folder.

7 Select the File menu.

8 Choose the Folder command.

9 Next, choose the Create Subfolder command.

The Create New Folder dialog box appears.

10 Type **My Client** to name the folder.

11 Click OK.

There's your first Personal folder in the middle of the Folder List. Next, add this folder to the Outlook Bar.

12 Select the File menu.

13 Click the Add to Outlook Bar command.

14 Click OK.

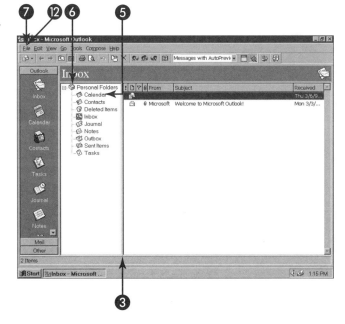

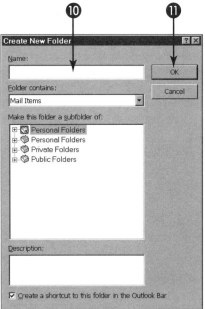

⑮ Click the My Client folder in the list.

⑯ Click OK.

Bingo! Your Personal folder is added to the bottom of the Outlook Bar automatically.

⑰ Click the More Icons button at the bottom of the Outlook Bar.

Now you can see the My Client folder button shown in the accompanying figure.

Suppose you no longer need a Personal folder that you created. Of course, you don't want to delete an Outlook folder such as Calendar, Contacts, and so on, but you can delete another personal folder you've created and remove its icon from the Outlook Bar. (You wouldn't want to, but you can remove Calendar, Contacts, and so on from the Outlook Bar.) To do so, click the folder you want to delete and press the Delete key. Outlook asks you to confirm the deletion. Choose Yes.

The deleted item ends up in the Deleted Items folder. If you want, you can see a list of the deleted items in the Information Viewer. Simply click the Deleted Items button on the Outlook Bar. If you want to delete a deleted item, click the one you want to get rid of and press the Delete key. Choose Yes to confirm the deletion.

What if you want to get rid of all the deleted items in the list? No problem. Just select Tools ➤ Empty "Deleted Items" Folder, and choose Yes to confirm the deletion.

You can also ask Outlook to delete all items in the Deleted Items folder automatically. I highly recommend this option so that you don't have to worry about emptying the Deleted Items folder manually. To set up this option, select Tools ➤ Options, click the General tab, and choose the Empty Deleted Items Upon Exiting option. Then click OK. From this point forward you are prompted to confirm the deletion of the deleted items in the Deleted Items folder when you exit Outlook. Choose Yes so that Outlook deletes all those deleted items, and then exit Outlook.

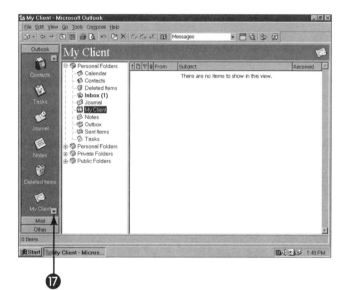

2

Managing Outlook Information

Changing the Order of Folders

Changing the Order of Outlook Folders

By default, the Outlook folders appear alphabetically in the Folder List. You can expand and collapse folders and subfolders the same way you do in the Windows Explorer. A plus sign (+) next to a folder indicates that it contains subfolders and can be expanded. A minus sign (−) next to a folder indicates that the folder can be collapsed.

What if you want to change the order of the folders? That's an easy task in Outlook. You can move folders around in the Folder List as you normally do in the Windows Explorer. An advantage to reordering folders is that you can put the folders you use most frequently at the top of the list and the ones you rarely use at the bottom.

To get comfortable with navigating the Folder List, practice expanding and collapsing folders and subfolder. Then move the My Client folder to the Tasks folder.

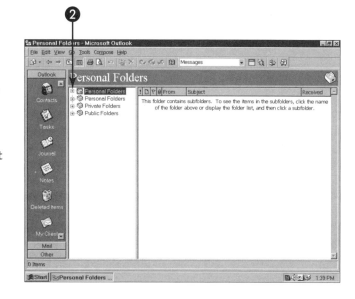

❶ Click the minus sign (−) next to the Personal Folders folder.

All the Personal folders in the list collapse.

❷ Click the plus sign (+) next to the Personal Folders folder.

All the Personal folders in the list expand.

❸ Click the My Client folder.

This folder is empty, as you can see from the message in the Information Viewer window.

❹ Drag the My Client folder to the Tasks folder.

The My Client Personal folder is now a subfolder of the Tasks folder. Notice the minus sign (−) next to the Tasks folder, which indicates the subfolders can be collapsed.

❺ Drag the My Client folder to the Personal Folders folder.

Your Personal folder is back in the middle of the Folder List.

❻ Click the Folder List button on the Calendar toolbar to close the Folder List.

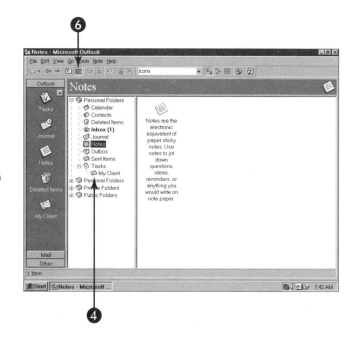

Moving Items

VISUAL BONUS

Outlook's Personal Folders

There are three ways to display Outlook's Personal folders:

- Select View ➢ Folder List.

- Click the component name's (in large letters) drop-down arrow located in the upper-left corner of the Information Viewer.

- Click the Folder List button on the component's toolbar.

The Outlook Personal Folders.

Personal Folders

Collapse ➤
Contacts ➤
Inbox ➤
Notes ➤
Sent Items ➤

- Personal Folders
  - Calendar ← Calendar
  - Contacts
  - Deleted Items ← Deleted Items
  - Inbox
  - Journal ← Journal
  - Notes
  - Outbox ← Outbox
  - Sent Items
  - Tasks ← Tasks

← Split bar

Moving Items to Different Folders

After you have your folders in the order you want them to appear in the Folder List, you can move items to any folder you want. Follow these steps to see how it works.

1 Click the first mail message in your Inbox.

This selects the item.

2 Click and drag the message into the My Client folder in the Folder List.

3 Click the My Client folder.

This folder now contains one item, the mail message.

Exporting Items to Files

Exporting Items to Files

Outlook is somewhat different from other programs when it comes to storing and retrieving your information. Traditionally, you save and open files, but in Outlook you export and import files. In other words, to "save" items, you export them to an Outlook file. These items have the file extension .PST. Then you import the .PST file when you want to work with the items again. Undelete the item you entered in Contacts during the Jump Start exercise, and then export the contact.

1 Click the Deleted Items icon on the Outlook Bar. Select the contact and drag it to the Contacts icon on the Outlook Bar.

2 Click the Folder List button on the Inbox toolbar to hide the Folder List.

3 Click Contacts on the Outlook Bar.

4 Open the File menu.

5 Choose the Import and Export command.

The Import and Export Wizard dialog box appears.

6 Choose Export to a personal folder file (.PST).

7 Click Next.

Now choose the folder to export from. In this case, Contacts is the folder you want.

8 Click Next.

Here's where you tell Outlook where you want to store the file on your hard disk or floppy disk. Save the file in the One Step folder and name it contact1.

9 In the Save as exported file box, type **c:\one step\contact1.pst.**

TIP

If you're not sure exactly in which folder you want to save the export file, then click the Browse button to see the existing folders on your disk. Double-click a folder to choose one.

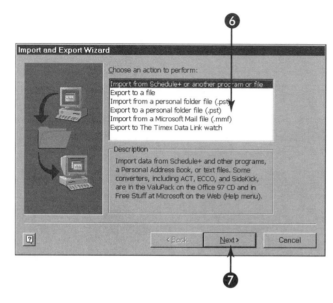

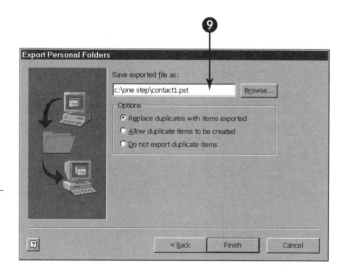

⑩ Choose the Allow duplicate items to be created option.

⑪ Click Finish.

Importing Items from Files

After you export items to a .PST file, you can import the file to use the information stored in the file. This concept is similar to opening a file. Now import the .PST file you just created. But first delete the contact that appears in Contacts.

❶ Click the contact to select it in the Information Viewer.

❷ Click the Delete button (with a big X) on the Contacts toolbar.

The Contacts folder is now empty.

❸ Open the File menu.

❹ Click the Import and Export command.

The Import and Export Wizard appears.

❺ Choose Import from a personal folder file (.pst).

❻ Click Next.

In this box, tell Outlook the file location and filename stored on your hard disk or floppy disk.

❼ In the File to import box, type **c:\one step\contact1.pst.**

TIP

If you can't remember in which folder you stored the export file, click the Browse button to see the folders on your disk. Double-click a folder to choose one.

❽ Choose the Allow duplicates to be created option.

❾ Click Next.

Now choose the folder to import from. In this case, Personal Folders is correct.

⑩ Click Finish.

Your contact is in the Information Viewer again.

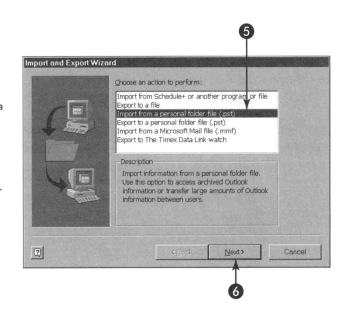

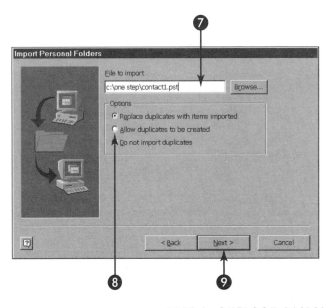

Managing Outlook Information

2

Working with Offline Folders

At any time you can refer to these steps when you are asked to import an exercise file in a lesson in this book. After you're finished with the lessons in this book, feel free to delete the items in Outlook and all the exercise files on your hard disk.

WORKING WITH OFFLINE FOLDERS

You have the option of using offline folders only if you are working with Microsoft Exchange. Offline folders let you take a folder from a server, work with the contents when you're not connected to the network, and then update the folder and its corresponding server folder so that both have identical contents. With offline folders you can add, delete, and change the contents the same way you do with a folder on a server. For example, you can move and change items in your offline Inbox, send messages placed in your offline Outbox, and read your offline public folders. When you work on the server, you can receive new messages in your Inbox, and other users can add, delete, and change items in public folders. However, these activities taking place on the server while you're offline will not be visible to you until you go online to see the activities that occurred.

Offline folders are stored in the offline folder file, OST, which is located on your hard disk. It is also available when the network is down. When you want to update the contents of the offline folder and its server folder so that they have the same contents, you need to synchronize the folders before you can continue to work offline. There are three ways to synchronize offline folders:

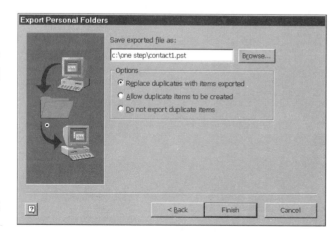

- **One offline folder.** Select the offline folder you want to synchronize, select Tools ➢ Synchronize, and choose This Folder.

- **All offline folders.** Select Tools ➢ Synchronize and choose All Folders.

- **Automatically synchronize all folders upon exiting Outlook.** Select Tools ➢ Options, click the General tab, and choose the option When online, synchronize all folders upon exiting (see the accompanying figure).

When you synchronize your offline folders, Outlook creates a log file that appears as a message in the Deleted Items folder. This log file includes the following information: the time you synchronized, the folder names you synchronized, and the number of items you added.

CHANGING OUTLOOK VIEWS

Compared to other information-management programs, Outlook has a unique feature. You can view the information in a folder in several views. Because each folder holds different information, some views are specific to a particular folder. By changing Outlook views in a folder, you can work more effectively and the way you want.

In this book I show you some of the views for a couple folders, but the list of available views is quite lengthy. For details on all Outlook views, see *Discover Microsoft Outlook 97* by Julia Kelly (Foster City, CA: IDG Books Worldwide, 1997).

You can also custom-tailor a view by creating a filter on a view. A filter lets you specify conditions that *filter out* only the items you want to view. For example, you can filter all items with the name Terry Asher in the From field to see only items from Terry Asher. All the other items are still in the folder. You just need to remove the filter to see all these items again.

Switching Outlook Views

Outlook offers a wide variety of views that enable you to look at items in each component in just about any way you want. Each component gives you several predefined views that you can choose from the Current View list box on the toolbar. Take a peek at some of the views in Calendar and Contacts.

1 Click the More Icons button (up arrow) at the top of the Outlook Bar to scroll up to the top of the toolbar.

2 Click the Calendar button on the Outlook Bar.

3 Click the Current View drop-down arrow on the Calendar toolbar.

Outlook displays a list of Calendar views.

Creating a Filter on a View

④ Choose Active Appointments.

You see the meeting you added earlier in the Jump Start. Active Appointments view shows all scheduled appointments and events and their details, beginning with the currently selected day and extending into the future.

⑤ Click the Current View drop-down arrow on the Calendar toolbar.

⑥ Choose Day/Week/Month.

You're returned to the default Day/Week/Month schedule.

⑦ Click the Contacts button on the Outlook Bar.

⑧ Click the Current View drop-down arrow on the Contact toolbar.

Outlook displays a list of Contacts views.

⑨ Choose By Company.

You see a company directory list organized by company, full name, job title, company name, and department. The rest of the list is not visible, so scroll over to see the other fields.

⑩ Click the right scroll arrow on the horizontal scroll bar to scroll to the right.

Now you can see home phone, mobile phone, and category.

⑪ Click the Current View drop-down arrow on the Contact toolbar.

⑫ Choose Address Cards.

You're back to the Address Book.

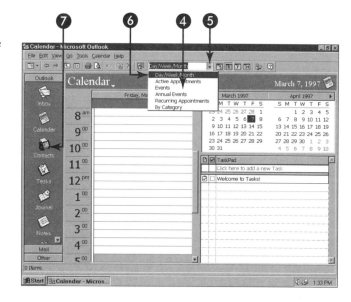

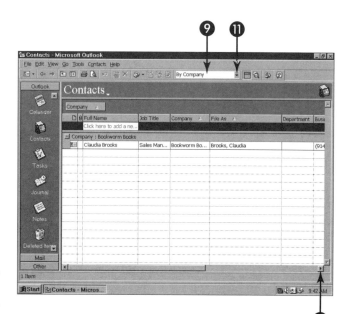

Creating a Filter on a View

Outlook lets you customize your own view by filtering out only the items you want to view. Microsoft calls this view a *dynamic data view*. For example, you can filter all the mail message items from one contact. You need to specify that you want to filter the contact field. Then you will see only the mail message items from that one contact, even though all the other mail message items are still in the folder. You remove the filter to see all the items again.

In this exercise you create a filter on the Inbox Messages view to see only the messages sent from one contact.

1 Click Inbox on the Outlook Bar.

2 Select the View menu.

3 Choose the Filter command.

The Filter dialog box opens with the Messages tab in front.

4 In the From box, type the name of a person from whom you received some mail.

5 Click OK.

As shown in the accompanying figure, you see the mail only from that one person you filtered in the Information Viewer. At the left end of the Status bar, notice the words *Filter Applied*, which indicate that you have applied a filter to a selected folder. Now clear the filter to see all the messages again.

6 Select the View menu.

7 Click Filter.

8 Click Clear All.

9 Click OK.

You see all the messages again.

SKILLS CHALLENGE: NAMING OUTLOOK FOLDERS

In this exercise you create a new Personal folder and switch to different Outlook views. This final exercise brings together all the skills you've learned in this lesson. Answer the bonus questions to review the skills and help you determine your understanding of the topics covered. The answers to these bonus questions are located in Appendix C.

1 Select the View menu.

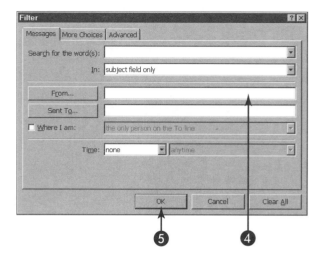

2

Managing Outlook Information

Skills Challenge

2 Choose Folder List to open the Folder List

 Name two ways to open the Journal folder.

3 Click the Personal Folders icon.

 Before you name a subfolder, what is the folder called that you select in the Folder List?

4 Select the File menu.

5 Choose the Folder command.

6 Choose Create Subfolder.

7 Type your own name to name the folder.

8 Click OK.

9 Click the minus sign (–) next to the Personal Folders icon to collapse the entire folder.

⭐**3** *What does a minus sign (–) next to a folder in the Folder List mean?*

10 Click the plus sign (+) next to the Personal Folders icon to expand the personal folders.

⭐**4** *What does a plus sign (+) next to a folder in the Folder List mean?*

11 Click the Folder List button on the Contacts toolbar to hide the list.

12 Open the File menu.

13 Click the Add to Outlook Bar command.

14 Choose the folder you created in Step 7 of this Skills Challenge.

15 Click OK.

16 Click the More Icons button (down arrow) to see your folder in the Outlook Bar.

TRY OUT THE

INTERACTIVE TUTORIALS

ON YOUR CD!

⑰ Click the More Icons button (up arrow) to scroll back to the top of the Outlook Bar.

⑱ Click the Calendar icon on the Outlook Bar.

⑲ Click the Current View drop-down arrow on the Calendar toolbar.

⑳ Choose Active Appointments.

㉑ Click the Current View drop-down arrow on the Calendar toolbar.

㉒ Choose Day/Week/Month.

TROUBLESHOOTING

You've learned quite a bit about Outlook folders and views. The following table may answer some questions that have come up during this lesson.

Problem	Solution
My Folder List is very long and I can't see the folders at the bottom of the list.	Use the vertical scroll bar in the Folder List to scroll down to the bottom of the list.
I moved my new Personal folder in the Folder List, and I don't see the folder anymore.	Your new folder may now be a subfolder of a folder. If there is a plus sign (+) next to a folder, click that plus sign to expand the folder. Your folder should be there. If it is and you want to move it somewhere else, just click it and drag it to the new location.
I have a Personal folder that I no longer need.	Select the Personal folder, press the Delete key, and choose Yes to delete the folder.
I'm in the wrong view in the Calendar folder.	Click the Current View drop-down arrow on the Calendar toolbar, and choose the view you want.

Wrap up

Although you may have any of these questions as you learn Outlook, most are not detrimental, and finding the answers to them is part of the learning process.

WRAP UP

Before you leave this lesson, let's go over some of the things you learned in this lesson. You learned how to

- Name Outlook folders
- Change Outlook folder order
- Move items to different folders
- Export items to a file
- Import items from a file
- Change Outlook views
- Create a filter on a view

For more practice, create a subfolder of the Contacts list for your personal names and addresses. Explore all the views for each Outlook component.

PART II

Managing Contacts

In this part you learn how to build a list of your contacts, and you learn about the different things you can do with Contacts.

This part contains the following lessons:

- Lesson 3: Building a Contacts List
- Lesson 4: Working with a Contacts List

Building a Contacts List

GOALS

In this lesson you learn about the following features for creating a contacts list:

- Adding new contacts
- Adding a contact from the same company
- Categorizing a contact
- Changing a contact's information
- Deleting a contact
- Locating a contact
- Navigating through the Address Book
- Showing contacts in different views

45 MINUTES

Building Your Contacts List

GET READY

To work through this lesson's exercises, you need the files EX03-1.PST and EX03-2.PST from the Outlook 97 One Step at a Time CD-ROM.

When you're finished with these exercises, you will have created a contacts list, as shown in the accompanying figure.

BUILDING YOUR CONTACTS LIST

When you're working on your computer and talking on the phone, Outlook can help you organize your business and personal contact information so that it's right at your fingertips. You can build a list of contacts and their addresses, phone numbers, and e-mail addresses. The list is an electronic version of an address book or Rolodex card file. Some users have been known to replace their traditional paper-based Rolodex by using Outlook's Contacts feature.

Contact information in Outlook is treated the same way as a database. Each contact is a separate record that contains fields such as name, address, business phone, and so on. You can add, delete, search for, sort, and print records for contacts you create in Outlook.

To better organize your contacts, you can assign contacts to one or more categories. A *category* is basically a word or phrase that helps you keep track of items in Outlook. For example, if you want to send holiday cards and gifts to some of your clients, assign those contacts to the Holiday Cards and Gifts categories. Then you can use the By Category view to look at only the contacts assigned to the cards and gifts categories. You can even print this view to use as your holiday shopping list. Another benefit to having categories is that they can help you hunt down items quickly—you can find, sort, filter, and group items.

Some of the many categories offered are Gifts, Holiday Cards, Hot Contacts, International, Time & Expenses, Business, Personal, and Phone Calls. These categories are provided in a list referred to as the *Master Category list.* If you can't find a category in the list that suits your needs, then you can make up your own categories and add them to the Master Category list.

By the way, you can assign contacts not only to categories but also to any items in Outlook, such as tasks, meetings, and messages.

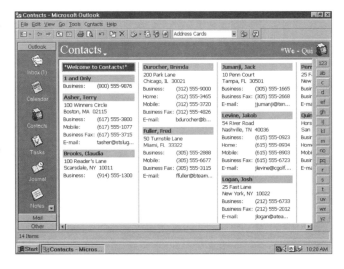

TRY OUT THE
INTERACTIVE TUTORIALS
ON YOUR CD!

Adding New Contacts

Assigning items to categories can make your life much easier, letting you track and monitor different types of items that are related but stored in different Outlook folders. For example, you can trace all contacts, meetings, and messages for a particular project when you assign these items to a category called Time & Expenses.

After you set up the names, addresses, phone numbers, fax numbers, and e-mail addresses, you can use the contacts to create mailing and holiday card lists, dial phone numbers, dial up other computers with a modem, and much more.

Adding New Contacts

For this exercise, import the file named EX03-1.PST from the One Step folder. You can select File ➢ Import and Export to import the file. For more help on importing a file, see Lesson 2. This file is a contacts list that contains ten of the contacts for All Sports Management. You'll use this contacts list to practice adding new contacts. As a sports agent, you have many business contacts. Now add one of those contacts to Outlook.

❶ Click the New Contact button on the Contacts toolbar.

The Contact window opens. The contact is a file in which you store your data. The filename UNTITLED appears in the title bar until you save the file and give it a name. Outlook copies the name from the Full Name text box for each contact file you create. The menu bar is located directly below the title bar. The Contacts toolbar is below the menu bar. The insertion point (blinking vertical bar) is in the Full Name text box. This is where you can start typing. See the Visual Bonus later in this lesson to examine all the elements of the Contact window.

❷ Type the following contact information to fill in the text boxes, pressing Tab to move between boxes. You can also click in a box to place the insertion point in the text box and begin typing.

In the Full Name box, type **Fred Fuller.**

❸ In the Job title box, type **Head Coach.**

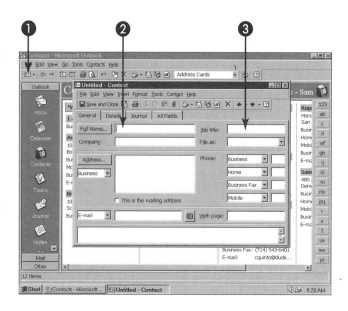

3

Building a Contacts List

Contacts from the Same Company

④ In the Company box, type **The B Team.**

⑤ In the Address box, type **50 Turnstile Lane** [Enter] **Miami, FL 33322.**

⑥ In the Business Phone box, type **305-555-2888.**

⑦ In the Business Fax box, type **305-555-3115.**

⑧ In the E-mail box, type **ffuller@bteam.com.**

Your Contact window should look like the accompanying figure when you're finished typing.

TIP *To move backward between text boxes, press Shift+Tab. If you make a mistake while typing, press the Backspace or Delete key. The Backspace key deletes characters to the left of the insertion point, and the Delete key deletes characters to the right of the insertion point.*

⑨ Click the Save and Close button on the Contacts toolbar.

This saves the contact and clears the boxes in the Contact window so that you can enter the next contact.

Adding a Contact from the Same Company

Outlook lets you add a contact from the same company by copying the previous contact's company information to the new card. You don't have to type the company information over and over again for each contact from the same company. Your task is to add another contact and then add a contact from the same company.

① Type the following contact information in a new contact window. Remember to press Tab to move between boxes.

In the Full Name box, type **Martin Sedgewick.**

② In the Job title box, type **Trainer.**

③ In the Company box, type **The Tennis Academy.**

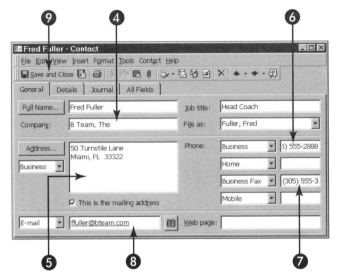

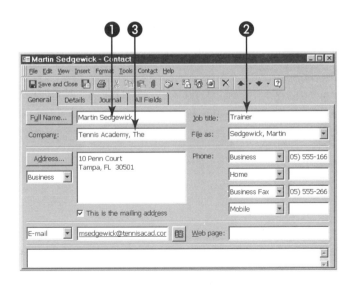

Contacts from the Same Company

④ In the Address box, type **10 Penn Court** [Enter] **Tampa, FL 30501.**

⑤ In the Business Phone box, type **305-555-1665.**

⑥ In the Business Fax Phone box, type **305-555-2668.**

⑦ In the E-mail box, type **msedgewick@tennisacad.com.**

⑧ Open the File menu.

⑨ Click the Save and New in Company command.

This saves the contact and displays the Contact window, leaving the company, address, and phone number from the previous contact. The name, job title, and file as information were cleared.

⑩ Type the following contact information in the appropriate text boxes:

In the Full Name box, type **Jack Jumanji.**

⑪ In the Job title box, type **Tennis Pro.**

⑫ In the E-mail address box, type **jjumanji@tennisacad.com.**

TIP *It's never too late to add a contact from the same company. Yes, you can use an existing contact's company information at any time. Just double-click a contact that contains the company information you want to use, select File ➢ Save and New in Company, and then enter the new contact information.*

⑬ Click the Save and Close button on the Contacts toolbar.

This saves the contact and closes the Contact window. You see the address cards for Fred Fuller and Jack Jumanji in the Information Viewer. The default view is Address Cards, which shows you an address book with tabs dividing it into alphabetical sections. You should have quite a few names and addresses now. Compare your address list to the one in the accompanying figure.

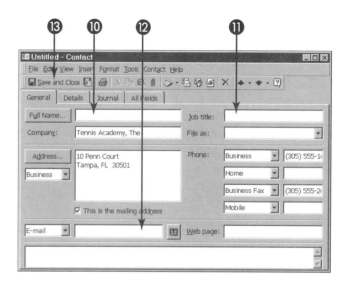

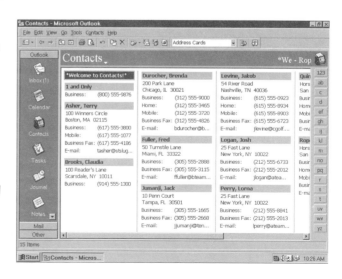

Changing a Contact's Information

⑭ Using the horizontal scroll bar, scroll right to see Martin Sedgewick.

⑮ Then scroll left to return to the beginning of the contact list.

Changing a Contact's Information

After you add contacts in Outlook, you can change a contact's information by using the editing functions such as *insert* to add information, *overtype* to type over existing text, and *delete* to remove information. You make the changes in the Information Viewer or open the contact's dialog box. One of your contacts, Fred Fuller, has purchased a mobile phone. Add the mobile phone number to that contact.

① Click anywhere on the Fred Fuller contact to select it.

② Open the File menu.

③ Choose the Open command.

This opens the Contact window.

 TIP *For faster editing, double-click anywhere on a contact to open its Contact window.*

④ In the Mobile text box, type **305-555-6677.**

⑤ Click the Save and Close button on the Contacts toolbar.

Notice that the mobile phone number has been added to the contact.

 TIP *You can also change existing information directly in Address Cards view. Click the information and then make the changes using Outlook's editing functions, such as overtype, insert, and delete. Overtype lets you type over existing text; insert lets you add text; and delete lets you*

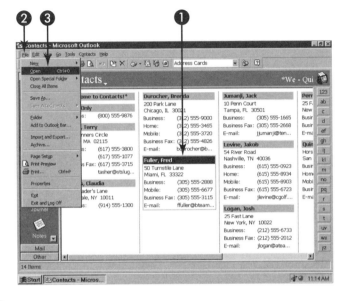

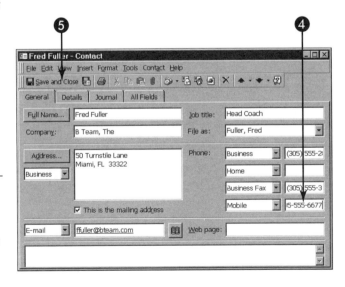

remove unwanted text. You probably know these functions already because they're used in any Microsoft Office program.

One of your contact's business fax number has changed. You need to edit his information.

6 In the Terry Asher contact, click anywhere on the Business Fax number.

You see a dotted line border surrounding the Business Fax number, indicating that the element is currently selected (see the accompanying figure).

There are a couple ways you can tackle this editing task:

- Type over text or numbers on a one-for-one basis—click and drag over the text or numbers you want to edit, and then type the new entry.

- Press Backspace or Delete to remove the text or numbers and type the new entry. Let's use the first method.

7 Click before *4* and drag over the numbers to highlight *4186*.

8 Type **3715.**

9 Click anywhere on the Terry Asher contact to deselect the fax number.

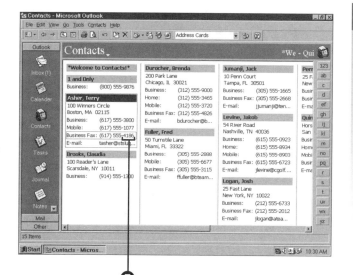

TIP

Because Outlook doesn't let you change a contact's name in the Address Cards view, there has to be another way to make this change. You can change a contact's name by opening the contact first and then making the name change.

Categorizing a Contact

When you start to build up a large number of contacts in Outlook, it would be nice to be able to organize your contacts in a certain way. You can do just that by categorizing them. Outlook provides many categories that include Holiday Cards, Hot Contacts, Business,

Deleting a Contact

Personal, International, and Phone Calls. You can assign a contact to one or more categories. All Sports Management will be sending a gift to a couple of your contacts, so you should assign those contacts to the Gifts category.

① Click Claudia Brooks to select her name.

② Hold down Ctrl and click Josh Logan.

Both contacts are now selected.

③ Select the Edit menu.

④ Click the Categories command.

The Categories dialog box appears. You see a long list of categories.

⑤ Choose Gifts.

A check mark appears next to Gifts, and the category is highlighted with a colored bar. Notice that Gifts has been added to the Item(s) belong to these categories box at the top of the dialog box.

NOTE *If you want to add a category of your own, click the Master Category List button in the Categories dialog box. Type the category name in the New text box. Click Add and then click OK.*

⑥ Click OK.

Outlook doesn't change anything on a contact's address card to indicate that the contact is assigned to a category. However, you will be able to view the contacts by category later in this lesson.

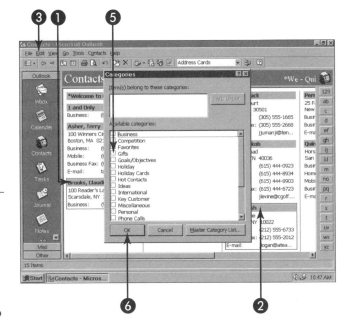

Deleting a Contact

If you have a contact in your list that you no longer deal with, you can delete that contact at any time. In this exercise you delete one contact.

Changing Contacts List Views

① Scroll to the far right.

② Select Marisa Samuels.

③ Click the Delete button on the Contacts toolbar.

The contact's address card disappears from the Address Book. All remaining cards shift accordingly.

④ Scroll back to the left.

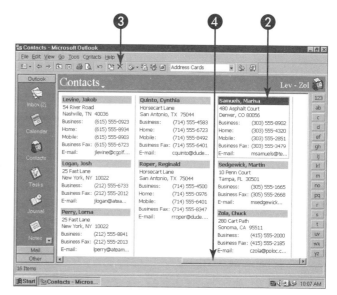

TIP *It's never too late to change your mind about deleting a contact. Just click the Undo button on the Contacts toolbar to restore the deleted contact.*

What if you want to delete more than one contact in one fell swoop? Select Edit ➤ Select All to select all contacts, and click the Delete button on the Contacts toolbar.

CHANGING CONTACTS LIST VIEWS

After you add contacts, you might want to find a particular contact that you want to change. Outlook lets you find contacts easily with its Find Items feature. You just give Outlook some search criteria with which to search, and Find Items will display the item(s) you're looking for. The search criteria can be any field entry you made for a contact. As with categories, Find Items can also be used to find any items in Outlook.

If you have a Rolodex card file in your office, you flip to the index tab and then thumb through the cards to find names and addresses. In your personal address book you keep at home, you thumb through the indexed pages to locate an address. Outlook makes it just as easy for you to move through the address cards in your electronic address book. Just flip through the index tabs to find what you want. You can also use the navigation keys as you normally would in other Microsoft Office programs. Table 3-1 lists these navigation keys.

3

Building a Contacts List

Contacts Toolbar

The Contacts toolbar gives you tools for creating and managing your contacts.

The Contacts toolbar.

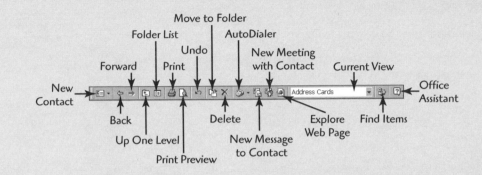

When you click the New Contact button on the Contacts toolbar or open a contact, Outlook opens the Contact window. From here you can insert contact information to add contacts to Outlook. The Contacts toolbar in the window provides tools for adding contacts.

The Contacts toolbar in the Contact window.

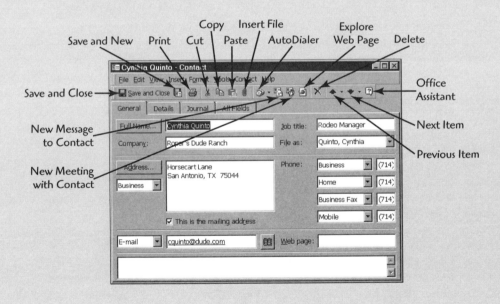

Changing Contacts List Views

TABLE 3-1 NAVIGATION KEYS

To Move	Press
To the next card	Ctrl+↓
To the previous card	Ctrl+↑
To the first card in the list	Ctrl+Home
To the last card in the list	Ctrl+End
To the first card on the previous page	Ctrl+PgUp
To the first card on the next page	Ctrl+PgDn
To the closest card in the previous column	Ctrl+←
To the closest card in the next column	Ctrl+→
To go to a specific card	Type one or the first few letters of the name the card is filed under.

Your contact information is organized into fields such as Full Name, Company, Address, and so on. Outlook has arranged these fields in some useful views in Contacts. You select a view from the Current View list on the Contacts toolbar to display in the Information Viewer. These Contact views include:

- **Address Cards.** Looks similar to a Rolodex card file with one mailing address plus business and home phone numbers.

- **Detailed Address Cards.** Shows you more complete information, including business and home addresses, additional phone numbers, and other details.

- **Phone List.** Displays Full Name, Company, File as, Business Phone, Business Fax, Home Phone, Mobile Phone, Journal, and Categories fields. This view is useful for a company phone directory.

- **By Category.** Shows fields sorted by categories. The contact for each category is in alphabetical order. This view is handy if you use categories. You can assign categories to your contacts, such as Gifts, Holiday Cards, Hot Contacts, International, Phone Calls, and a myriad of others.

3

Building a Contacts List

Locating a Contact

- **By Company.** Organizes list by company and displays the Job title, Company, Department, Business Phone, and Business Fax fields. This view is useful for a company directory list.

- **By Location.** Creates a geographical contact list ordered by country and shows the Company, State, Country, Business Phone, and Home Phone fields.

Keep in mind that you can also filter the items in any view that you pick. For example, you may want to view only the contacts that have Terry Asher in the Full Name field. Feel free to check back in Lesson 2 for details on how to create a filter on a view.

Locating a Contact

After you build your contacts list, you're going to need a quick way to locate a particular contact instead of wading through the list with the navigation keys. Outlook's Find Items feature lets you locate a contact in a snap. Find Martin Sedgewick using the Find Items feature.

1 Click the Find Items button on the Contacts toolbar.

Outlook displays the Find dialog box. The Look for box and In box already contain Contacts because you're currently in Contacts. But you can change to any Outlook component by choosing one from the Look for drop-down list. Also notice that the Contacts tab is currently selected.

2 Type **Sedgewick.**

3 Click Find Now.

Outlook displays the contact in a list at the bottom of the Find dialog box, as shown in the accompanying figure. From here you can open the contact.

TIP

*If Outlook doesn't find what you're searching for, the message **There are no items to show in this view** appears in the list at the bottom of the Find dialog box. Verify your search criteria, and then enter the correct search criteria to search again.*

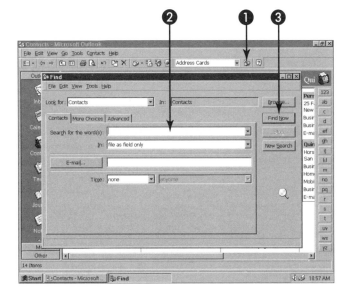

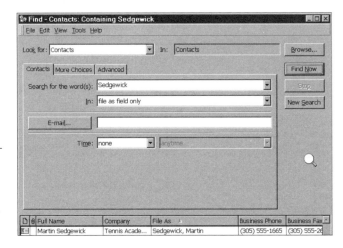

4 Double-click Martin Sedgewick in the list.

At this point you can make changes to the contact. But for the purpose of this exercise, close everything because you're finished finding items.

5 Click the Close button in the upper-right corner of the Contact window.

6 Click the Close button in the upper-right corner of the Find dialog box.

Navigating Through the Address Book

Outlook gives you many ways to navigate through the cards in the Address Book. You can use the alphabetical index tabs and the navigation keys to find the card you're looking for. Let's move around the Address Cards list using the tabs on the right side of the list and the navigation keys.

1 Click the *yz* tab.

Outlook finds and highlights the first contact whose name begins with the letter Z.

2 Press the Home key.

You move to the beginning of the list.

3 Press the End key.

You move to the end of the list.

4 Click the *ab* tab.

The first contact whose name begins with the letter A is highlighted.

Suppose a contact begins with a number, such as 456 Hike Mike. You probably want to know where this contact appears in the Address Book. It is at the beginning of the list before the contact that begins with the letter A. Outlook puts numbers before letters in the ascending alphabetical sort order. And how do you quickly navigate to a contact that begins with a number? You can simply click the 123 tab (first tab at the top) on the right side of the contact Address Cards list.

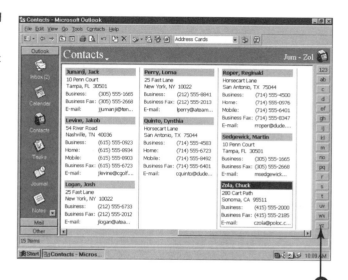

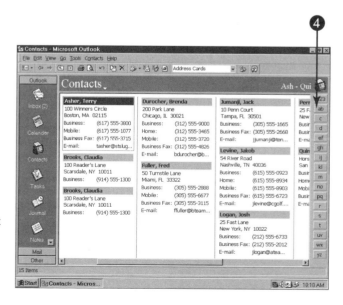

3

Building a Contacts List

Showing Contacts in Different Views

Showing Contacts in Different Views

By default, the Address Cards view displays in the Information Viewer. This is a good all-purpose view that gives you enough information to work with on a daily basis. But what if you want to see more detail on those address cards? Outlook's Detailed Address Cards view can show you all the details you want. Take a look at all the different views for Contacts.

1 Click the Current View drop-down arrow on the Contacts toolbar.

2 Choose Detailed Address Cards.

You see more complete information, including business and home addresses, additional phone numbers, and other details.

3 From the Current View list, choose Phone List.

The Phone List view shows you contact information in a grid, as shown in the accompanying figure. Notice that the address is omitted, which leaves you with the phone numbers and a few other details.

4 Use the horizontal scroll bar to see the rest of the fields on the right side of the grid.

5 From the Current View list, choose By Category.

By Category shows fields sorted by categories. Notice that Gifts has a plus sign (+) button next to it. The plus sign indicates that the category is expandable.

6 Click the plus sign (+) button.

The contacts for the Gifts category are in alphabetical order, as shown in the accompanying figure.

7 From the Current View list, choose By Company.

By Company displays a list organized by company and shows the Full Name, Job Title, Company, File As, Department, and other fields, as shown in the accompanying figure.

8 Scroll to the far right.

Now you can see the Business Phone, Business Fax, Home Phone, Mobile Phone, and Categories fields.

9 From the Current View list, choose By Location.

You see a geographical contact list ordered by country that shows the Full Name, Company, File As, State, Country, and other fields. See the accompanying figure.

10 Scroll to the far right to see the rest of the fields.

11 Now choose the Address Cards view, the default view.

To prepare for the Skills Challenge exercise coming up, you need to delete all the contacts.

12 To delete the contacts, open the Edit menu.

13 Choose the Select All command.

14 Click the Delete button on the Contacts toolbar.

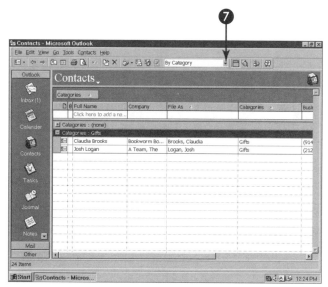

3

Building a Contacts List

Skills Challenge

SKILLS CHALLENGE: ADDING A CONTACT TO OUTLOOK

This final exercise reinforces the contacts skills you've learned in this lesson.

TRY OUT THE

INTERACTIVE TUTORIALS

ON YOUR CD!

1 Import the file named EX03-2.PST.

2 Add a new contact using the following information:

Name: **Olaf Linkovich**

Job title: **Marketing Manager**

Company: **Hoop it Up**

Address: **380 Baylor Avenue** [Enter] **Dallas, TX 77005**

Business Phone: **714-888-5000**

Business Fax Phone: **714-888-2244**

E-mail address: **olinkovich@hoop.com**

 How do you move backward from box to box in the Contact window?

3 Save and close the contact.

 If you want to add a few contacts consecutively, what button on the Contacts toolbar helps you do it?

4 Select Lucy Drake.

5 Select the File menu.

6 Click Open.

3 *What's the shortcut for opening a contact's file?*

7 In the Mobile Phone text box, type **617-888-5633.**

8 Save and close the contact.

9 Select Super Hooper.

 4 *Can you describe what a contact looks like when it's selected?*

10 Delete the contact.

11 Restore the contact with Undo.

12 Find the first contact that begins with the letter *W*.

13 Switch to the Phone List view.

14 Scroll to view all the contact information in the grid.

15 Now switch back to Address Cards view.

TROUBLESHOOTING

You've learned about adding contacts to Outlook and viewing them in different ways. The following table may answer some questions that have come up during this lesson.

Problem	Solution
I want to include a birthday reminder for my contacts.	Open a contact's window and click the Details tab. Next click the Birthday drop-down arrow. You see the current month calendar. At the top of the calendar, click the left or right arrow to choose a month, and then choose a day.
I need to add a middle initial to a contact's name, but when I clicked the name in Address Cards view, Outlook wouldn't let me make any changes to the name.	You won't be able to make changes to a contact's name in Address Cards view. The only way to make changes is to open the contact's window and change the name in there.

continued

3

Building a Contacts List

Wrap up

Problem	Solution
I want to delete a couple of contacts in one clip.	Select the first contact, hold down the Ctrl key, and click the second contact. Then click the Delete button on the Contacts toolbar.
In my contacts list I want to get to a contact that begins with a number.	Click the 123 tab on the right side of the Address Cards list.

Although you may run into some of these predicaments as you learn Outlook, most are not catastrophic, and finding the solutions to them is all of the learning process.

WRAP UP

Let's review the skills you learned in this lesson. You learned how to

- Add new contacts
- Create a contact from the same company
- Categorize a contact
- Change a contact's information
- Delete a contact
- Find a contact
- Navigate through the Address Book
- Display contacts in different views

For more practice, add personal contacts with their birthdays. Also, experiment with switching to all the different views to see which views suit your needs.

In the next lesson you put the contacts to good use by utilizing them with other Outlook features, Microsoft Office programs, and the Internet.

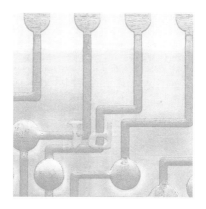

Working with a Contacts List

GOALS

This lesson helps you make good use of contacts by walking you through the following skills:

35 MINUTES

- Sending a letter to a contact

- Calling contacts using AutoDialer

- Going to a contact's World Wide Web page

- Creating a unique "File As"

- Printing your Address Book

Sending a Letter to a Contact

GET READY

To work through this lesson's exercises, you need the files EX04-1.PST and EX04-2.PST from the Outlook 97 One Step at a Time CD-ROM.

When you're finished working on these exercises, you will have used contacts in various ways. The accompanying figure shows what a contacts list looks like when printed.

WORKING WITH CONTACTS

You can do many useful things with contacts to help you get the most out of your contact information. Some of these things require only Outlook skills; others require some familiarity with Microsoft Word and the World Wide Web.

If you're interested in sending a letter to a particular contact in your contacts list, you can use Word's Letter Wizard to whip up a professional-looking letter. It takes only a few minutes to do—the wizard walks you through the procedure, and you don't have to type the contact's name or any of the contact information that you want to include in the letter. Outlook and Word do the job for you.

Outlook's AutoDialer can make your phone calls for you automatically. To do this, you need to have a modem. You also need to set up your computer and modem for automatic phone dialing. AutoDialer is not available with Microsoft Windows NT Server 3.51 or Windows NT Workstation 3.51.

Some of your contacts may have Web pages on the Internet that you might want to view. If you're connected to the Web with Internet Explorer, you can go directly to a contact's Web page when you're working in Outlook.

Sending a Letter to a Contact

In this exercise you use a file named EX04-1.PST stored in the One Step folder. This is a contacts list that contains several contacts for All Sports Management. You'll use this contacts list to practice working with contacts. This exercise assumes that you have Microsoft Word 97. You'll send a letter to one of these contacts using Word's Letter Wizard. This wizard steps you through the process of creating a letter

123
Welcome to Contacts!

a
Adesso, Andre
1000 Fifth Avenue
New York, NY 10021
Bus: (212) 789-9632
Bus Fax: (212) 789-6547
E-mail: aadesso@ata.com

b
Beckman, Boris
1000 Fifth Avenue
New York, NY 10021
Bus: (212) 789-9632
Bus Fax: (212) 789-6547
E-mail: bbeckman@ata.com

c
Carston, Jimmy
1000 Fifth Avenue
New York, NY 10021
Bus: (212) 789-9632
Bus Fax: (212) 789-6547
E-mail: jcarston@ata.com

e
Eichensevic, Goran
1000 Fifth Avenue
New York, NY 10021
Bus: (212) 789-9632
Bus Fax: (212) 789-6547
E-mail: geichensevic@ata.com

g
Gray, Stephanie
1000 Fifth Avenue
New York, NY 10021
Bus: (212) 789-9632
Bus Fax: (212) 789-6547
E-mail: sgray@ata.com

i
IDG Books, Foster City

k
Kaufmann, Yanni
1000 Fifth Avenue
New York, NY 10021
Bus: (212) 789-9632
Bus Fax: (212) 789-6547
E-mail: ykaufmann@ata.com

l
Lansbury, Ivan
1000 Fifth Avenue
New York, NY 10021
Bus: (212) 789-9632
Bus Fax: (212) 789-6547
E-mail: ilansbury@ata.com

m
MacDougal, John
1000 Fifth Avenue
New York, NY 10021
Bus: (212) 789-9632
Bus Fax: (212) 789-6547
E-mail: jmacdougal@ata.com

Marovovich, Martina
1000 Fifth Avenue
New York, NY 10021
Bus: (212) 789-9632
Bus Fax: (212) 789-6547
E-mail: mmarovovich@ata.com

Mueller, Thomas
1000 Fifth Avenue
New York, NY 10021
Bus: (212) 789-9632
Bus Fax: (212) 789-6547
E-mail: tmueller@ata.com

s
Santana, Pete
1000 Fifth Avenue
New York, NY 10021
Bus: (212) 789-9632
Bus Fax: (212) 789-6547
E-mail: psantana@ata.com

Sen, Michael
1000 Fifth Avenue
New York, NY 10021
Bus: (212) 789-9632
Bus Fax: (212) 789-6547
E-mail: msen@ata.com

to a contact. If you need some help creating a letter in Word, refer to IDG Books Worldwide Inc.'s *Word 97 One Step at a Time*.

1 Import the EX04-1.PST file.

2 Click Contacts in the Outlook Bar if you're not already there.

3 Click Jimmy Carston to select a contact.

4 Open the Contacts menu.

5 Choose the New Letter to Contact command.

Outlook opens Microsoft Word 97 and then displays the Letter Wizard Step 1 of 4 dialog box. This is the first of several Letter Wizard dialog boxes that you will see. After you follow the instructions in the Letter Wizard, you will switch to Word automatically. All you have to do is type a few entries and pick some options in the dialog boxes to complete the letter.

6 Click the Date line check box to insert today's date.

7 Click the Next button to continue.

You see the recipient's name and address as shown in the accompanying figure. You can leave the salutation as Informal.

8 Click the Next button to continue.

9 Because you won't be adding any other elements, click the Next button again.

10 Click the Complimentary closing drop-down arrow.

11 Choose Best regards.

Outlook displays the letter closing you selected in the Preview box on the right.

12 Click the Finish button.

The Office Assistant pops up and asks if you want to do more with the letter. In this exercise you're only creating a letter.

13 Click Cancel to remove the Office Assistant from the screen.

14 Click the Maximize button in the upper-right corner of the Word window so you can work on a full screen.

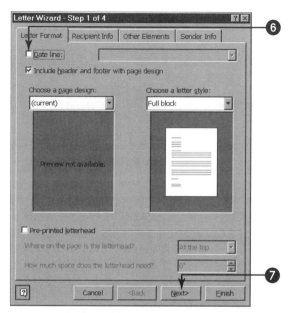

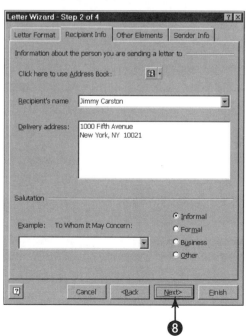

Working with a Contacts List

4

Sending a Letter to a Contact

That's better. Now the window is full size and you can see the entire letter after you type it. Notice that the prompt "Type your text here" is highlighted and appears near the top of the letter. This *dummy* text is a placeholder for the text you're going to type in the letter.

⑮ Type **Dear Jimmy,** (don't forget the comma) and press Enter twice.

⑯ Type the body of the letter as it appears in the accompanying figure. To insert the proper spacing, follow the instructions in the next two steps.

⑰ Click at the end of the date and press Enter four times.

This inserts space between the date and the inside address.

⑱ Click at the end of the last line of the address and press Enter twice.

This inserts space between the address and the salutation.

You've created your first letter to a contact using Outlook and Word's Letter Wizard.

⑲ Select the File menu.

⑳ Choose the Save command.

㉑ Name the file MYLETTER.

Your letter should look like the accompanying figure. The red wavy line beneath *Carston* and *Bronner* suggests that there may be possible spelling errors because these words are proper nouns. To remove the red wavy line, right-click the word and choose Ignore All in the Spelling shortcut menu.

㉒ Click the Close button in the upper-right corner of the Word window to exit the Word program.

To take letter writing one step further, you can even perform a mail merge using your contacts list. A *mail merge* is a word processing feature that enables you to produce form letters, mailing labels, and envelope addresses.

Two files make up a basic merge procedure: the data source file and the main document. The main document contains the

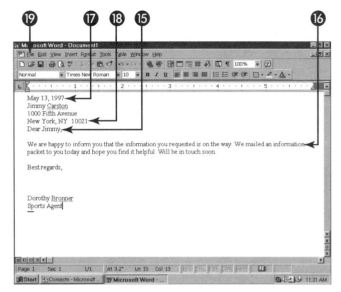

unchanging text and the codes that control the merge. The data source contains the variable information, such as names and addresses, that you want inserted into the main document. If you have created a contacts list in Microsoft Outlook (a component in the Microsoft Office 97 suite), a personal Address Book in Microsoft Exchange (a component of Windows 95), or a contacts list in Schedule+ (a component in the Microsoft Office 95 suite), you can use these records as a data source.

Calling Contacts with AutoDialer

Nowadays it may be considered old-fashioned to let your fingers do the dialing on your phone. Outlook's AutoDialer can dial a contact's phone number automatically. Using AutoDialer, you can call anyone with a business, home, fax, or mobile phone number in your contacts list. You can even create a speed-dial list that contains a list of phone numbers you dial frequently. From this list you can quickly dial numbers. AutoDialer keeps a list of the phone numbers you recently dialed, and you can choose a phone number from this list to dial quickly. If the number you want to dial is not in your contacts list, there's no problem dialing it automatically. Use AutoDialer's New Call command to enter the contact name and phone number and dial straight from the New Call dialog box.

In this exercise you'll let Outlook's AutoDialer do the dialing for you—a cool way to make phone calls.

1 Click the Stephanie Gray contact.

2 Click the AutoDialer drop-down arrow on the Contacts toolbar.

You see the AutoDialer menu.

TIP

If you know you want to dial the first number listed for a contact, then you can simply select the contact and click the AutoDialer button on the Contacts toolbar. Outlook dials the contact's first phone number entry.

3 Choose the business phone number.

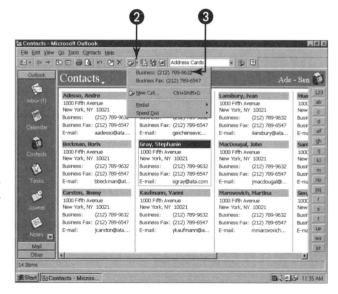

Working with a Contacts List

4

Going to a Contact's Web Page

AutoDialer

Outlook's AutoDialer lets you automatically and quickly dial any phone number for a contact, redial recently dialed numbers, and speed dial any numbers to which you frequently make calls.

The Outlook AutoDialer.

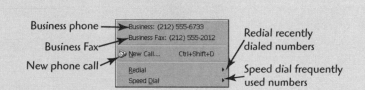

Business phone — Business: (212) 555-6733
Business Fax — Business Fax: (212) 555-2012
New phone call — New Call...   Ctrl+Shift+D
Redial
Speed Dial

Redial recently dialed numbers
Speed dial frequently used numbers

④ Click Start Call.

You'll hear a dial tone momentarily. Then Outlooks dials your contact's phone number.

⑤ After you're connected, you can chat with your contact.

⑥ When you're finished with your phone call, click End Call.

Going to a Contact's World Wide Web Page

Outlook's Explore Web Page feature enables you to go directly to a contact's World Wide Web page. Keep in mind that the contact's Web page address needs to be included in the contact's information, such as `http://www.slugger.com`, before you can explore the Web page. One of your business contacts whom you entered in Outlook has a Web page on the Internet. View that Web page using Outlook, as long as the contact's information contains an Internet address. First you need to add an Internet address to a contact's information.

① Double-click the Ivan Lansbury contact.

② In the Web Page text box, type **www.slugger.com.**

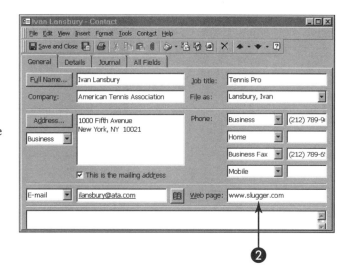

Going to a Contact's Web Page

You need the contact's URL (Uniform Resource Locator) address to specify the Web page address. In this case, www.slugger.com is the URL. A URL is similar to a filename that the Web will use to search and locate the Web page. For the purposes of this exercise, the URL in this step is fictitious. Feel free to enter a real URL to explore one of your favorite Web pages from Outlook.

3 Select the File menu.

4 Click Save.

This saves the Web page address with the contact's information.

5 Outlook automatically inserts http:// in front of the Web page address. HTTP is the protocol information that the Web uses to search and locate addresses.

6 Click the Explore Web Page button on the Contacts toolbar.

Outlook takes you to the Web, searches for the contact's Web page, and then displays it.

7 When you're finished reading the contact's Web page, close the Web browser's window.

You're taken back to the contact's window in Outlook.

8 Click the Save and Close button on the Contacts toolbar to close the contact's window.

FILING AND PRINTING CONTACTS

You can save a contact item as a file in a particular format with Outlook's File Save As command. The file formats let you use a contact in other ways in Outlook. You can also file contacts under different names.

Outlook enables you to preview your contacts list before printing it. When you print your contacts list, you can choose from five print styles to print the contacts exactly the way you want. In this lesson you print a phone directory list.

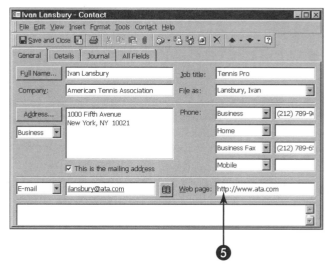

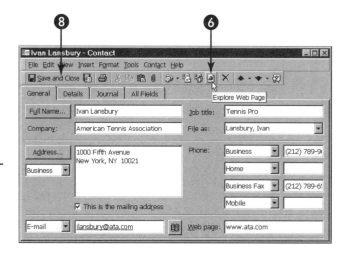

Creating a Unique "File As"

Creating a Unique "File As"

Outlook lets you save a contact item as a file in any of the following formats:

- **Text Only** (*.txt). Converts a contact item into a text file that you can use in an e-mail message or a word processing program (word processing file).

- **RTF Text Format** (*.rtf). Stands for Rich Text Format, a type of file that contains formatting such as bold, italic, underline, and so on. You can use an .RTF file in an e-mail message or a word processing program.

- **Outlook Template** (*.oft). Converts the contact item into a template so that you can create new contact items based on the original contact.

- **Message Format** (*.msg). Converts the contact item into a message format for use with e-mail.

Now save a contact in the Text Only format.

1 Click the Andre Adesso contact to select it.

2 Open the File menu.

3 Click the Save As command.

The Save As dialog box appears.

4 Click the drop-down arrow in the Save as type box.

Outlook displays a list of file formats.

5 Choose Text Only (*.txt).

6 Click Save.

Now you can include this file in an e-mail message, or open the file in a word processing program and use the contact's information in a word processing document.

You just learned how to save an item as a file in a different format to use the item in other ways. Next I'll show you how to use the File As feature to create a unique name for a contact's name and

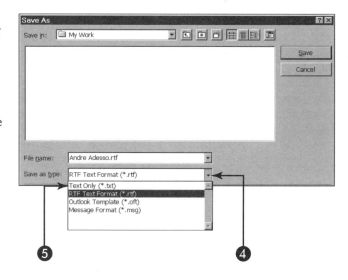

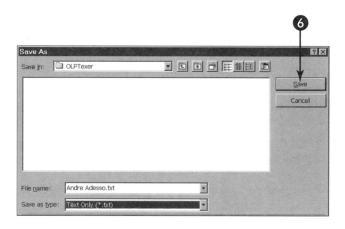

Creating a Unique "File As"

business. Then you can organize your contact items by the File As name. For example, you can use the contact's nickname or the contact's type of business, such as retail, wholesale, agency, or manufacturer.

① Double-click the Andre Adesso contact to open it.

Beneath the Job title field you see the File as field. By default, Outlook displays the contact's full name with the last name first, followed by a comma and the first name. In the File as field you can either type a unique name for the contact and business in the File as text box or choose one from the drop-down list. Take a look at the list.

② Click the File as drop-down arrow.

A list of suggested unique names appears.

In the File as list you have several choices:

- The contact's full name with the last name first, followed by a comma and the first name (default file as name)

- The contact's first and last name

- The company name

- The contact's full name with the last name first, followed by a comma and the first name, followed by the company name enclosed in parentheses

- The company name, followed by the contact's full name with the last name and first name separated by a comma, enclosed in parentheses

③ Choose a name from the list.

④ Click the Save and Close button on the contact's toolbar.

Notice that the unique File as name you specified is the first field that appears in the contact item and is highlighted in a different color, as shown in the accompanying figure. The contact's full name appears beneath the File as name. If you want to, you can sort or group your contacts by their File as name.

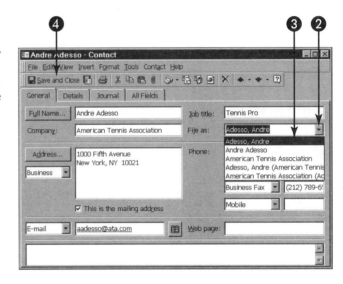

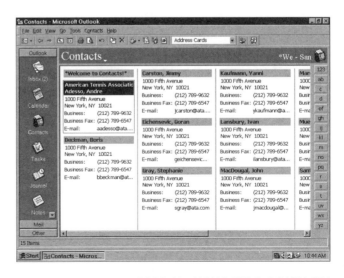

4

Working with a Contacts List

Printing Your Address Book

Printing Your Address Book

In this exercise you learn how to print your Address Book from the Print dialog box. But if you have already set up your print options and are back to Contacts, you can simply click the Print button on the Contacts toolbar to print your Address Book. Before you print the contacts, check them out in Print Preview. In Print Preview you can zoom in and out to enlarge and reduce the contacts in the list you see onscreen. You can also scroll through the pages to see how the page layout of the list will look when printed. Zooming and scrolling are features that you may already have used in Word and Excel's Print Preview. You can print directly from Print Preview, too.

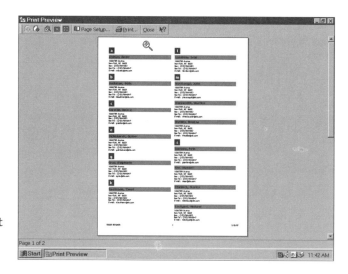

1 Click the Print Preview button (the button with a piece of paper and magnifying glass) on the Contacts toolbar.

You see a preview of how your contacts will look when you print them (see the accompanying figure). Notice that all the contacts fit on Page 1. The mouse pointer is a magnifying glass with a plus sign (+). This mouse pointer indicates that you can zoom in to enlarge whatever portion of the list you want to view. Go ahead and zoom in at the top of the list.

2 Click somewhere at the top of the contacts list.

The contacts at the top of the list are enlarged. The mouse pointer is now a magnifying glass with a minus sign (-). This mouse pointer indicates that you can zoom out to reduce the list to one page again. See the accompanying figure.

3 Click anywhere in the contacts list.

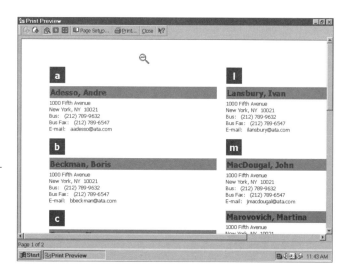

TIP

To scroll through multiple pages in Print Preview, you can use the scroll bars.

4 Select the File menu.

5 Click Print (or press Ctrl+P).

Printing Your Address Book

The Print dialog box pops up, as shown in the figure to the right. This dialog box contains options with which you can control your print jobs. The current printer appears at the top of the dialog box. Make sure the correct printer is selected. To select a different printer, click the Name drop-down arrow and choose a printer from the printer list.

NOTE *You can choose any printing options you want in the Print dialog box. For example, five print styles are available. Next to each style you see a small sample of what the printout will look like when printed. You can choose from Card Style, Small Booklet Style, Medium Booklet Style, Memo Style, and Phone Directory style. Choosing one is a matter of preference and need. If you want, you can print one of each style. Select File ➢ Print to specify the style you want to print for each printout.*

Another printing option is Print Range. For example, select the All Items option to print all the contacts in your contacts list. But what if you want to print only selected items? No problem. Select the first contact in the contacts list, hold down the Ctrl key, and click each additional contact to select more contacts. Select File ➢ Print and choose the Only selected items option in the Print Range area.

To print multiple copies, click the Number of Copies up arrow until you see the number you want. Perhaps you want to print two copies of your contacts list. Click the up arrow until you see 2.

6 Scroll down the Print style list and choose Phone Directory Style.

7 Click OK to start printing your phone directory.

While the contacts are printing, Outlook displays a Printer icon at the right end of the Windows taskbar. To stop a file from printing, double-click the Printer icon to display the print queue dialog box. Then click the filename and select Document ➢ Cancel Printing from the menu bar in the dialog box to cancel the print job. Click the Close button to close the dialog box.

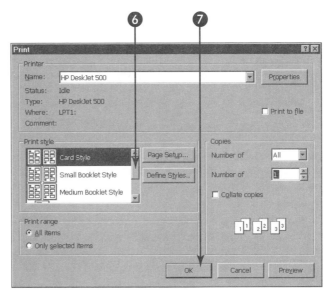

4

Working with a Contacts List

Skills Challenge

Now you have a printout of your first contacts list. How impressive! Pass it around the office to show off your professional-looking phone directory that you created in Outlook.

8 Select all the contacts and then delete them to prepare for the Skills Challenge.

SKILLS CHALLENGE: PUTTING CONTACTS TO GOOD USE

In this final exercise you utilize the contacts in several ways to recap what was covered in this lesson.

1 Import the file named EX04-2.PST.

2 Click Contacts in the Outlook Bar, if necessary.

3 Select a contact.

4 Open the Contacts menu.

5 Choose the New Letter to Contact command.

6 Choose the Date line option.

7 Click the Next button three times. You'll be in the fourth tab in the Letter Wizard dialog box.

 What four tabs appear in the Letter Wizard dialog box?

8 Choose Sincerely yours for the complimentary closing.

9 Click the Finish button.

The Office Assistant pops up and asks if you want to do more with the letter. In this exercise you're only creating a letter.

10 Remove the Office Assistant from the screen.

11 Maximize the Word window.

⑫ Type a salutation and the body of the letter. In this letter, ask your contact to give a presentation at the All Sports Conference.

⑬ Select the File menu.

⑭ Click Save.

⑮ Name the file CONTACT LETTER.

⑯ Exit Word.

⑰ Select a contact.

⑱ Call the contact with AutoDialer.

 2 *How do you redial the last number you called?*

⑲ Open a contact.

⑳ In the Web page text box, type **www.nike.com.**

 3 *What is a more technical name for a Web page address?*

㉑ Open the File menu.

㉒ Choose the Save command.

㉓ Click the Explore Web Page button on the Contacts toolbar to view the contact's Web page.

㉔ When you're finished reading the Web page, return to Outlook.

㉕ Use Print Preview to see the contacts list before printing it.

㉖ Click the Print button on the Print Preview toolbar.

㉗ Choose the Card Style print style.

㉘ Click OK to print your contacts list.

 4 *Can you name the five print styles for printing a contacts list?*

Troubleshooting

TROUBLESHOOTING

You probably know more about working with contacts now, but if you had some questions that came up during this lesson, you may find the answers in the following table.

Problem	Solution
When I selected Contacts ➤ New Letter to Contact, the Letter Wizard didn't appear.	Microsoft Word or the Letter Wizard may not be installed on your computer. Refer to Microsoft's installation instructions to install Microsoft Word and the Letter Wizard.
I dialed a contact and the line was busy.	First click Hang Up. To redial the number, click the AutoDialer drop-down arrow, select Redial, and then choose the number from the Redial list.
Outlook located the wrong Web page for my contact.	Verify that your contact's Web page address is correct, and then type the correct address in the Web page text box in the contact's window.
I would like to see the page layout of my contacts list before I print it.	Click the Print Preview button on the Contacts toolbar, and click the Multiple Pages button on the Print Preview toolbar.

Even if you experience some of these challenges as you learn Outlook, most are not disastrous and resolving them helps you learn more about the program.

WRAP UP

Let's review the things you learned in this lesson. You learned how to

- Send a letter to a contact

- Call contacts using AutoDialer

- Go to a contact's World Wide Web page

- Create a unique "File As"

- Print your Address Book

For more practice, send a letter to a personal contact to stay in touch with him or her. Also, the next time you call a business contact, try using AutoDialer. You can go to a business contact's Web page to see what information you can find on that contact. Print your contact list using all the print styles available.

In the next lesson you're introduced to e-mail in Inbox.

4

Working with a Contacts List

PART III

Handling Outlook E-Mail

When you finish the chapters in this part, you'll know how to connect to your mail delivery service, how to send and receive mail, and how to manage your e-mail.

This part contains the following lessons:

- Lesson 5: Sending E-Mail
- Lesson 6: Receiving E-Mail
- Lesson 7: Managing E-Mail

Sending E-Mail

GOALS

In this lesson you learn these basic skills:

30 MINUTES

- Switching to the Mail toolbar
- Adding a service
- Connecting to your service
- Composing a message
- Sending a message
- Sending RTF messages
- Attaching a file to a message

Switching to the Mail Toolbar

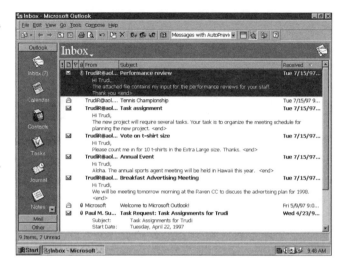

GET READY

To work through these exercises, you need the files named
EX05-1.PST and PICNIC INVITE.DOC from the One Step folder.
When you're finished with these exercises, you will have sent messages
using Outlook's e-mail. The accompanying figure shows messages
after they have been sent.

MAKING THE CONNECTION

There are several ways to set up Outlook to send and receive e-mail.
If Outlook has already been set up to send and receive e-mail, then
check with your administrator to find out how and where e-mail is
delivered. Otherwise, ask your administrator how to configure your
system to send and receive e-mail in Outlook. To configure Outlook,
you need to add a mail-delivery service and then connect to your
service.

Switching to the Mail Toolbar

First import the file named EX05-1.PST from the One Step folder.
This file contains several mail messages. You'll see some icons in the
row above the mail messages. Table 5-1 lists these icons.

TABLE 5-1 MAIL MESSAGE ICONS

Icon	Name	Definition
!	Importance	Indicates whether the message is of high or low importance.
▯	Message type	Shows the type of message.
⚑	Message flag	Shows whether there's a message flag. A message flag indicates that a follow-up action to the message is needed.
📎	Attachment	Shows whether the message has an attached file such as a Word document or Excel spreadsheet.

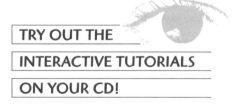

TRY OUT THE

INTERACTIVE TUTORIALS

ON YOUR CD!

Adding a Service

Icon	Name	Definition
From	From	Shows the sender of the message.
Subject	Subject	Displays the subject of the message.
Received ▽	Received	Shows the date and time you received the message.

① Click Inbox on the Outlook Bar.

The Inbox appears in the Information Viewer, and the Inbox coworker appears at the top of the window. The default view for Inbox is set to Messages with AutoPreview. This view lists your mail messages showing the first three lines of each message and several other columns of information. Table 5-1 showed a list of icons you'll see next to your messages.

TIP

You may see a number in parentheses next to the Inbox icon on the Outlook Bar. This number represents the number of unread messages.

② Click the Mail button at the bottom of the Outlook Bar.

As you can see, a group of mail icons appears on the Outlook Bar. The Visual Bonus in the next section shows a figure of the Mail toolbar.

Adding a Service

Before you can send and receive mail, you need to add a service. Follow these steps to add a service:

① Select the Tools menu.

② Choose the Services command.

The Services dialog box opens.

③ Click Add.

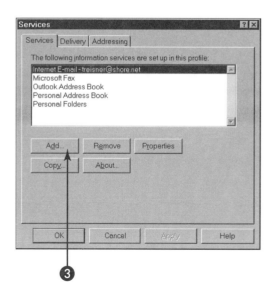

5

Sending E-Mail

Inbox Toolbar and Mail Toolbar

The Inbox toolbar and the Mail toolbar contain the most frequently used tools for performing activities in Outlook's e-mail program. The Inbox toolbar provides buttons for sending, changing, printing, and viewing your mail.

The Inbox toolbar.

The Mail toolbar gives you several tools for viewing your mail in Inbox. A number in parentheses next to the Inbox icon on the Mail toolbar indicates the number of messages you haven't read yet.

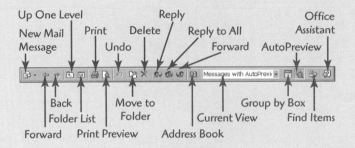

Up One Level
New Mail Message
Print
Undo
Delete
Reply
Reply to All
Forward
AutoPreview
Office Assistant

Back
Folder List
Move to Folder
Group by Box
Current View
Find Items

Forward
Print Preview
Address Book

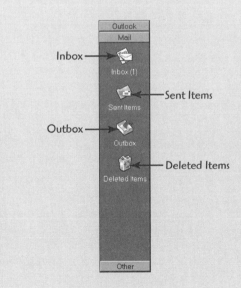

Inbox
Sent Items
Outbox
Deleted Items

The Mail toolbar.

Adding a Service

4 Choose a service. For example, Internet Mail.

5 Click OK.

The Internet Mail dialog box appears. An example of the typical information you would enter in the Mail Account Properties dialog box is shown in the accompanying figure. You see four tabs: General, Servers, Connection, and Advanced. First you'll work with the General tab. You need to enter your full name and e-mail address. An e-mail address has the following format: username@domain.extension. For example, `mfranklin@shore.net`.

6 Enter your name in the Name box.

7 Enter your e-mail address in the E-mail Address box.

Next you enter information in the Mailbox Information section. You need to enter a server name, account name, and password. A server name has the following format: mail.domain.extension. For example, `mail.shore.net`.

8 Enter your mailbox information in the appropriate boxes.

Now you need to enter a protocol for the outgoing and incoming mail servers. A protocol is a code that tells computers how to communicate with each other. An example of a protocol is `relax1.shore.net`.

9 Click the Servers tab.

The Servers tab lets you enter the protocols for the servers and login information.

10 In the Server Information section, type the protocol in the Outgoing Mail (SMTP) text box. Check with your ISP for the correct information to type.

11 In the Incoming Mail (POP3) text box, type the protocol.

In the Login Information section at the bottom of the dialog box, the Logon using option is selected. Now you fill in the logon information.

12 In the Login Information section, enter your account name in the Account Name box.

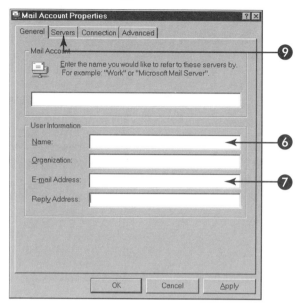

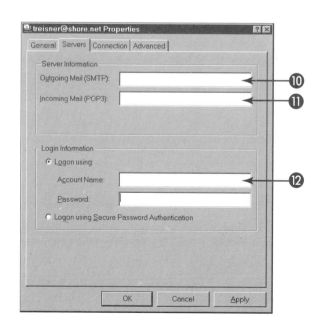

5

Sending E-Mail

Connecting to Your Service

⑬ Enter your password in the Password box.

⑭ Click the Connection tab.

The Connection tab gives you options for connecting to the mail server via the network or the modem.

⑮ In the Connection box, choose the type of connection you want.

If you want to work offline and use Remote Mail, choose the Disconnect when finished sending and receiving option at the bottom of the dialog box.

⑯ Click OK.

⑰ Click OK again.

You can make changes to the connection setting at any time. Just select Tools ➤ Services, choose a mail server, and click Properties.

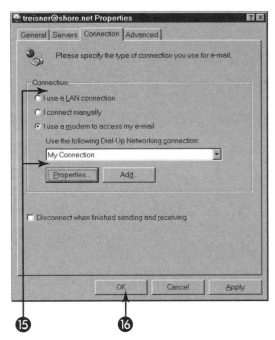

When you start Outlook, you can connect to the server or work offline. If you prefer one method over the other, you can set up an offline or online connection for ongoing use. To do so, click Inbox and select Tools ➤ Services. Choose your mail server, click Properties, and click the General tab. To always start Outlook offline, choose Work offline and use dial-up networking. To specify each time you start whether to work offline or online, select the Choose the connection type when starting option. Click OK. Exit Outlook and then restart Outlook.

▶ Connecting to Your Service

After you add a service, you need to connect to that service. Follow these steps to connect to your service using Dial-Up Networking.

❶ Open My Computer.

❷ Open Dial-Up Networking.

3 Open My Connection.

The Connect To dialog box appears. This dialog box will contain the user name, password, service phone number, and dialing from the location that you typed in. If you want Windows to enter your password automatically, choose the Save password option.

4 Click Connect to connect to your service.

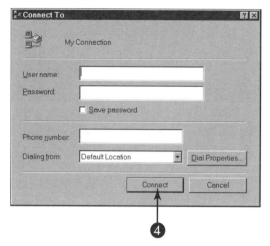

SENDING MAIL

After you have connected to your mail delivery service, you can compose mail, send the mail, and attach a file to a mail message.

If you want to send messages to other users who use the Rich Text Format (RTF), you can easily do this in Outlook. You can set up a contact's e-mail options so that the contact always receives your mail message in Windows Messaging Rich Text Format. An RTF message preserves all formatting such as bold, italic, tabs, and so on. It's useful to use RTF in a message if you need to send highly formatted messages. Also, RTF text looks much prettier than plain text.

Composing a Message

In this exercise you compose a message to a contact.

NOTE

*You can send messages in plain text or Rich Text Format such as bold or italic text. If you send and receive mail over the Internet, make sure the recipients of your mail are using a program that will read Rich Text Format. To set messages to plain-text format, open a contact you want to send messages to in plain-text format. In the E-mail box, double-click the e-mail address. In the Properties dialog box, clear the check box for the option **Always send to this recipient in rich-text format**. To set this option for recipients in your Personal Address Book, open the Personal Address Book, double-click the recipient's name, and then clear the check box for the option **Always send to this recipient in rich-text format**.*

5

Sending E-Mail

Sending a Message

1 Click the New Mail Message button on the Inbox toolbar.

The Message dialog box appears.

2 In the To box, type **Allison Armida.**

TIP *Instead of typing a name in the To box, you can click the To button to insert one or more names from Contacts or your Personal Address Book. You can also click the Address Book button on the Message toolbar to open your Address Book. Before you send a message, Outlook verifies the names you've entered in the To box. If a name is not in the Address Book or in Contacts, or there is more than one possible match, you will see a red wavy or green dashed line under the name. This line is a reminder to verify the name before you send the message.*

3 In the Subject box, type **Research Project.**

4 In the large empty box, type **The research project will start on Monday.**

Now you're ready to send the message. In the next exercise you learn how to send the message and check that it's been sent.

TIP *To add some pizzazz to your message, you can enhance your text with fonts, font sizes, font styles, and colors. You can also align and indent text as well as create a bulleted list. The Format menu gives you all of these options and much more.*

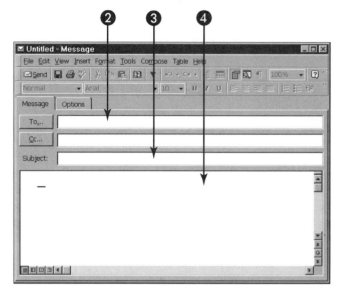

Sending a Message

After you compose a message, the next step is to send the message to the recipient. In this exercise you walk through the steps for sending a message, but you won't be able to actually send the message because the contact is fictitious. If you want to send mail to a real person, change the name in the To box to whatever real name you want.

❶ Click the Send button on the Message toolbar.

Outlook displays a message informing you that the mail has been sent. If Outlook has any difficulty sending the mail, a message will display informing you that there is a problem. Check the Sent Items folder to see what mail has been sent.

❷ Click Sent Items on the Mail toolbar.

The mail that has been sent appears in Sent Items.

If the message was not sent, it will not appear in Sent Items. To look at your message, click Outbox on the Mail toolbar. The Outbox shows the mail with an explanation why it was not sent. If you edit a message in the Outbox and save the changes, Outlook does not send the message automatically. You need to open the message and click the Send button on the Message toolbar.

By default, Outlook saves a copy of messages you send and displays them in Sent Items. If you don't want to save your sent messages, select Tools ➢ Options, and click the Sending tab. Clear the option Save copies of messages in "Sent Items" folder.

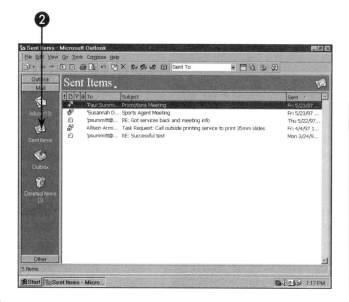

TIP

*Suppose you send a message to the wrong person or you forget to attach a file to the message. It's never too late to recall a message after you send it, provided that you sent the message to recipients who are logged on and using Outlook and who have not read the message or moved the message out of their Inboxes. To recall a message, click Mail on the Outlook Bar, click Sent Items, and open the message you want to recall. Select Tools ➢ Recall This Message and choose Delete unread copies of this message. If you want Outlook to send you a notification that the message has been successfully recalled, choose the **Tell me if recall succeeds or fails for each recipient** option and click OK.*

5

Sending E-Mail

Sending RTF E-Mail Messages

▶ Sending RTF E-Mail Messages

In this exercise you set e-mail messages that you send to a contact to use Rich Text Format.

① Click Contacts on the Outlook Bar, if necessary.

② Open the contact Michael Franklin.

Add Michael's e-mail address to his contact information.

③ In the E-mail address box, type **mfranklin@asm.com.**

④ In the E-mail address box, double-click the e-mail address.

The Properties dialog box for the contact appears.

⑤ Choose the Always send to this recipient in Microsoft Exchange rich-text format option.

⑥ Click OK.

Now you can send an e-mail message to the contact using Rich Text Format.

Keep in mind that most users cannot view rich text messages unless they're using Outlook on the same office network. The formatting gets lost in transit elsewhere.

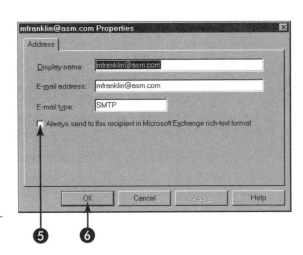

 NOTE *You can also save any Outlook item in RTF. If you'd like to save an e-mail message, contact, or note, saving the item in RTF ensures that it retains the proper formatting. Choose File ➢ Save As and select RTF Text Format in the Save As Type box.*

▶ Attaching a File to a Message

In some cases you may want to attach a file to a message. The PICNIC INVITE.DOC file needs to be sent to a contact. In this exercise you compose a new message and attach the Word document.

Attaching a File

1 Click the New Mail Message button on the Inbox toolbar.

2 In the To box, type **mfranklin@asm.com.**

3 In the Subject box, type **Summer Picnic.**

4 In the large empty box, type a message regarding the summer picnic invitation.

5 Click the Insert File button on the Message toolbar.

The Insert File dialog box appears.

6 Navigate to the PICNIC INVITE.DOC file (in your One Step folder).

7 Double-click PICNIC INVITE.DOC to insert it into your message.

The file appears as an icon with the filename in the message.

8 Click the Send button on the Message toolbar.

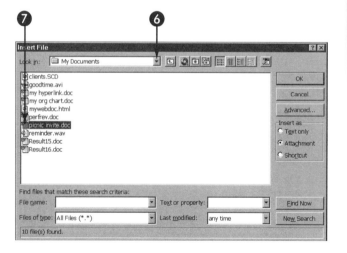

SKILLS CHALLENGE: SENDING E-MAIL

In this review exercise, you practice all the skills you've learned in this lesson about sending e-mail.

1 Compose a message to a contact.

 Which button on the Inbox toolbar creates a new message?

2 Send the message.

 How do you send a message?

3 Check the Sent Items to see the message you've sent.

4 Compose a message to a contact with a file attached to it.

 How do you attach a file to a message?

5 Send the message.

5

Sending E-Mail

Troubleshooting

6 Check the Sent Items to see the message with the attached file you've sent.

TROUBLESHOOTING

Finishing this lesson means that you've grasped many of the skills needed to send e-mail. This table offers solutions to some questions or challenges you may have experienced while practicing these skills.

Problem	Solution
When I start Outlook, a prompt asks me to connect to the server or work offline and always prefer one method over the other.	To set up an offline or online connection for ongoing use, click Inbox. Select Tools ➢ Services. Choose your mail server, click Properties, and click the General tab. To always start Outlook offline, choose Work offline and use dial-up networking. To specify each time you start whether to work offline or online, select the Choose the connection type when starting option. Click OK. Exit Outlook and then restart Outlook.
I can't send e-mail messages.	You must have a modem, a mail-delivery service, and a phone line or a network cable connection to send messages. If you connect to your mail service using a modem, make sure the Dial-Up Networking options are correct. Be sure that only one information service is set for sending e-mail. It's also possible that the server may be down, so just wait and try again. You can also check with your system administrator.

TRY OUT THE
INTERACTIVE TUTORIALS
ON YOUR CD!

Problem	Solution
I'm having problems sending e-mail messages over the Internet.	If you send messages in Rich Text Format over the Internet, the recipients of your messages will receive an attachment named WinMail.dat. If the recipients are using a program that cannot read Rich Text Format, then you need to send mail in plain-text format. Open a contact you want to send messages to in plain-text format. In the E-mail box, double-click the e-mail address. In the Properties dialog box, clear the check box for the option Always send to this recipient in rich-text format.
My messages remain in Outbox and are not sent.	Make sure the correct mail-delivery service is the only service being used to send e-mail messages. Select Tools ➢ Check for New Mail On. Select the services you want to check for new e-mail messages.

WRAP UP

You've practiced several new skills in this lesson. You learned how to

- Switch to the Mail toolbar
- Add a service
- Connect to your service
- Compose a message
- Send a message
- Attach a file to a message

5

Sending E-Mail

Wrap up

If you would like more practice with these skills, try sending e-mail to your coworkers and friends and attach a file to some of the messages.

In the next lesson you learn about receiving e-mail.

Receiving E-Mail

GOALS

In this lesson you learn these basic skills:

- Reading messages
- Replying to a message
- Forwarding a message
- Deleting a message
- Storing mail in a folder
- Sorting and grouping mail
- Viewing mail
- Setting message-handling options
- Finding messages

40 MINUTES

Reading Messages

To work through these exercises, you need the file named EX06-1.PST from the One Step folder. When you're finished with these exercises, you will have replied to messages using Outlook's e-mail. The accompanying figure shows messages after they have been sent.

RECEIVING MAIL

The mail messages you receive appear in Inbox. You can read your messages at any time by selecting a message and opening it. Then you can reply to the message or forward the message to others. If there are any messages you no longer want, you can delete one or more messages.

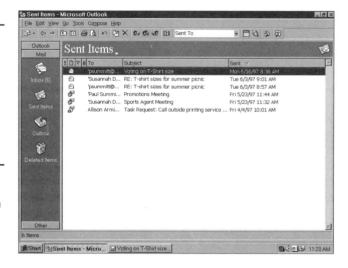

Reading Messages

First import the file named EX06-1.PST from the One Step folder. This file contains several mail messages. In the Message Type column (piece of paper symbol) you see envelope symbols next to the messages. A closed envelope represents a mail message that hasn't been read yet. An envelope with the flap open indicates that the mail message has been opened and read. An envelope with a piece of paper represents a mail message that has a file attached to it.

1 Click a message to select it.

Outlook highlights the message item.

2 Double-click the selected message to open it.

The message window appears. The Reply toolbar appears at the top of the window.

After you read a message, you can do one of several things: close the message and respond to it later, send a reply, or forward the message to someone else. Go ahead and close the message.

3 Click the Close button to close the window.

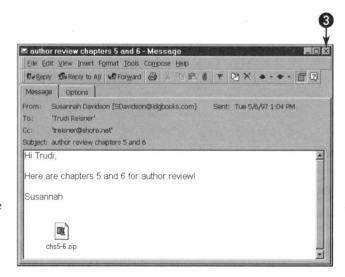

Replying to a Message

VISUAL BONUS

Reply Toolbar

The Reply toolbar contains tools for replying to a mail message.

The Reply toolbar.

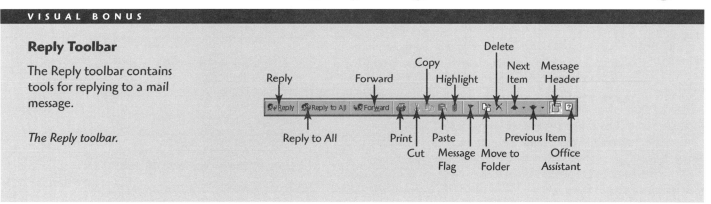

Reply   Forward   Copy   Highlight   Delete   Next Item   Message Header

Reply to All   Print   Cut   Paste   Message Flag   Move to Folder   Previous Item   Office Assistant

Replying to a Message

In this exercise you reply to a mail message.

① Open a message.

If you want to reply to only the sender of the message, you can use the Reply button. If there are names in the To and Cc boxes, and you want to reply to all the names, click the Reply to All button on the Reply toolbar. Go ahead and respond to only the sender in the To box.

② Click the Reply button on the Reply toolbar.

The message window appears. Notice that the To box contains the sender's name, and the Subject box has the subject for the message. The original message appears in the large box at the bottom of the window. The insertion point appears at the top of the large box, indicating where you can begin typing.

③ Type a message in the large box.

④ If you want, you can attach a file to a reply message by clicking the Insert File button on the Message toolbar and selecting the file you want to send. An icon appears in the large box near the message.

⑤ Click the Send button to send the message.

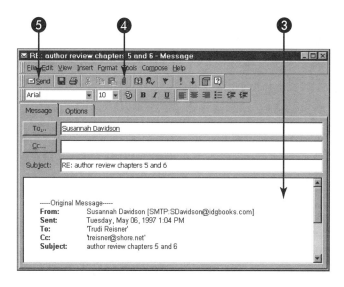

Forwarding a Message

TIP

Suppose you send a message to the wrong person or forget to attach a file to the message. It's never too late to recall a message after you send it, provided you sent the message to recipients who are logged on and using Outlook and who have not read the message or moved the message out of their Inboxes. To recall a message, click Mail on the Outlook Bar, click Sent Items, and open the message you want to recall. Select Tools ➢ Recall This Message and choose Delete unread copies of this message. If you want Outlook to send you a notification that the message has been successfully recalled, then choose the Tell me if recall succeeds or fails for each recipient option and click OK.

Forwarding a Message

In this exercise you forward a message to a contact.

1 Open a message.

2 Click the Forward button on the Reply toolbar.

The message window appears. Notice that Subject box contains the subject for the message. The original message appears in the large box at the bottom of the window.

3 In the To box, type the contact's name.

4 In the large box, type a message above the original message.

5 Click the Send button to forward the message.

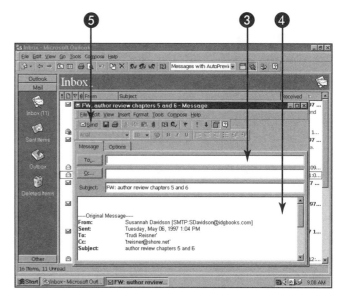

Deleting a Message

You can delete one or more messages that you have accumulated in your Inbox. When you delete a message, Outlook moves the message to the Deleted Items folder. You can do one of two things with the messages in the Deleted Items folder: either retrieve a deleted message or delete a message permanently. When you retrieve a deleted message, you are actually moving the message back to any folder you want to "undelete" it. When you want to delete a message permanently, you must delete it twice—once in the Inbox and again in the Deleted Items folder. Deleting messages permanently creates more space on your hard disk. In this exercise you delete a message, view the deleted message in the Deleted Items folder, and then retrieve the deleted message. You also delete a message permanently.

1 Select a message.

2 Click the Delete button on the Inbox toolbar.

The message disappears from the Inbox.

TIP

> *To delete more than one message in Inbox, select the first message, hold down Ctrl, and click each additional message. Then click the Delete button on the Inbox toolbar.*

3 Click the Deleted Items icon on the Outlook Bar.

You see the deleted message in the Deleted Items folder. Now retrieve the deleted message.

4 Drag the deleted message from Deleted Items to another icon on the Outlook Bar, such as the Inbox or a folder that you created.

5 Click the icon on the Outlook Bar to which you placed the deleted message.

You see the message that you retrieved. Now delete a message permanently.

6 Click the Inbox icon on the Outlook Bar.

7 Select a message that you want to delete.

8 Click the Delete button on the Inbox toolbar.

9 Click the Deleted Items icon on the Outlook Bar.

10 Select the message that you want to delete permanently.

11 Click the Delete button on the Inbox toolbar.

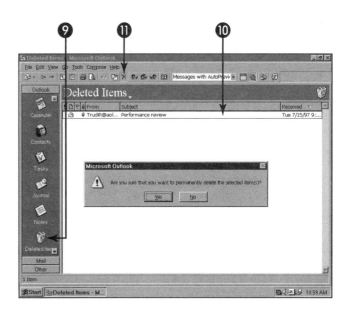

Deleting a Message

Outlook asks you if you want to delete the message permanently.

⑫ Choose Yes.

Outlook removes the message from your hard disk.

TIP *When you exit Outlook, you can have your deleted messages removed automatically. To set this up, select Tools ➤ Options, click the General tab, and choose the Empty the Deleted Items folder upon exiting option. Click OK. Each time you exit Outlook, you're asked if you want to delete the messages in the Deleted Items folder permanently. Choose Yes to delete them.*

TRY OUT THE

INTERACTIVE TUTORIALS

ON YOUR CD!

STORING AND VIEWING MAIL

There are several things you can do in Outlook to organize your mail in Inbox. You can store your mail in any folder in the Folder List or create a new folder and store your mail in it. Sorting, grouping, and viewing your mail in various ways can make it easier and faster to find, especially when you're in a hurry. You can sort your mail by any field in ascending or descending order. Outlook also lets you group your mail in many different ways in ascending or descending order. Another way to organize your mail is to select a view from ten Inbox views.

Initially, Outlook's message-handling options are set up in a certain way, but you can change these options to suit your needs. With the e-mail options, you can specify which service you want Outlook to check for new mail on, what you want Outlook to do when new mail message items arrive, and how to process mail automatically. For the Sending options, you can change options for composing messages, such as the importance and sensitivity, tracking messages, and saving copies of messages in Sent Items. As for the Reading options, you can change options for replying and forwarding messages and moving and deleting open message items. It is recommended that you check with your administrator before you change any message-handling options.

If you're looking for a particular message, Find Items can help you find the message in a snap.

Storing Mail in a Folder

After a while your Inbox accumulates many mail messages. All these messages don't have to stay in the Inbox. Outlook lets you store copies of those mail messages in one or more folders. That way you can keep your messages in more than one place—the Inbox and a specific folder. You may want to store important mail in a folder so that you can refer to the messages in the future. In this exercise you store a mail message in a folder.

❶ Click the Folder List button on the Inbox toolbar.

❷ Select the message you want to store in a folder.

❸ Drag the mail message to a folder in the Folder List.

❹ Click the folder that contains the mail message.

As you can see, the mail message appears in the folder. Next to the folder is a number in parentheses (1) that indicates the number of items in the folder.

❺ Click the Folder List button on the Inbox toolbar to close the Folder List.

Sorting and Grouping Mail

Outlook's Sort and Group features let you organize your messages in the Information Viewer. You can sort your messages by any field in a message (such as To, CC, date) and put the messages in ascending (lowest to highest) or descending (highest to lowest) order. Outlook also enables you to group messages by any field (such as To, Message Flag, Date) to organize the messages into groups. For example, you might want to group your messages by sender or received date. In this exercise you sort your mail messages and group the messages.

❶ Open the View menu.

❷ Choose the Sort command.

The Sort dialog box opens.

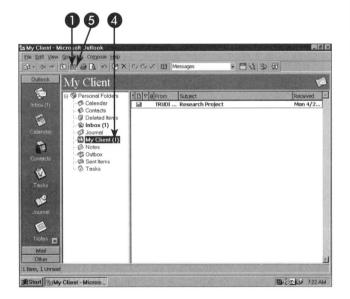

Viewing Mail

③ Choose a field to sort by.

④ Choose Ascending (lowest to highest, such as A–Z or 1–10) or Descending (highest to lowest, such as Z–A or 10–1) order.

⑤ Click OK.

The message items are sorted in the order you specified. Now group the messages.

⑥ Select the View menu.

⑦ Choose the Group By command.

The Group By dialog box opens.

⑧ Choose a group type in the Group items by list; for example, From.

⑨ Choose Ascending or Descending order.

⑩ Click OK.

The message items are grouped by the type you selected.

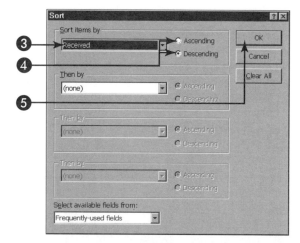

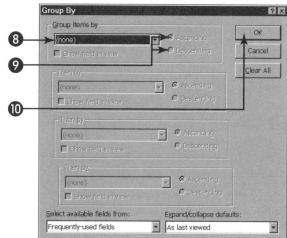

Viewing Mail

Now let's talk about all the Inbox views with which you can organize your mail messages. The default view is Messages with AutoPreview, but there are nine table views that show a list and one timeline view that shows icons to represent mail messages. All the views, except Message Timeline, show the importance, message type, whether there is a message flag, an attachment, and the subject. In this exercise you look at all the Inbox views.

① Click the Current View drop-down arrow on the Inbox toolbar.

② Choose a view from the Current View drop-down list to look at each one of the following views.

- **Messages.** Lists messages with details, as shown in the accompanying figure.

- **Messages with AutoPreview.** Shows messages in a list with the first three lines of the message text.

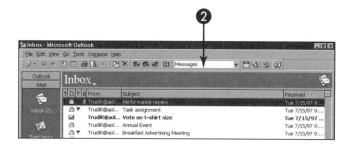

Setting Mail-Handling Options

TIP

A faster way to display all your messages in AutoPreview is to click the AutoPreview button on the Inbox toolbar. To turn off AutoPreview, click the AutoPreview button on the Inbox toolbar again.

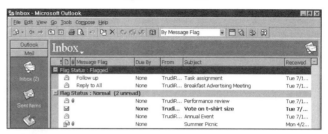

- **By Message Flag.** Grouped by message flags. List includes due date for follow-up action for the message flag, as shown in the accompanying figure.

- **Last Seven Days.** Lists messages that arrived during the last seven days. See the accompanying figure.

- **Flagged for Next Seven Days.** Lists messages that show a message flag for follow-up actions due within the next seven days. See the accompanying figure.

- **By Conversation Topic.** Grouped by subject in a list, as shown in the accompanying figure.

- **By Sender.** Grouped by sender in a list, as shown in the accompanying figure.

- **Unread Messages.** Lists only messages marked as unread.

- **Sent To.** Lists the names of the recipients of the message.

- **Message Timeline.** Shows icons in a timeline arranged in chronological order by date sent.

③ Choose Messages with AutoPreview to return to the default view.

Setting Mail-Handling Options

When you install Outlook and add a mail delivery service, the mail-handling options are set up automatically. However, you can change these options at any time. Take caution with changing these options because you may get some unwanted results. You should check with your administrator before making any changes.

① Open the Tools menu.

Finding Messages

❷ Choose the Options command.

❸ Click the E-mail tab.

You see the Options dialog box with the E-mail tab selected.

❹ In the Check for new mail on section, make sure that only one mail delivery service is selected.

❺ Change any other options if necessary.

❻ Click the Internet E-mail tab.

You see the Internet E-mail options.

❼ By default, Outlook checks for new messages every 15 minutes. You can change the number of minutes to whatever you want at the bottom of the Internet E-mail tab.

❽ Change any options that you want.

❾ Click the Sending tab.

❿ Change any options if necessary.

⓫ Click the Reading tab.

You see the Reading options.

⓬ Change any options if necessary.

⓭ Click OK.

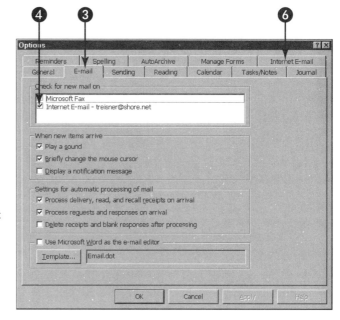

Finding Messages

What if you want to find a message you sent to a client, and the only thing you remember about the message is that you discussed the Tennis for Tots tournament? You can use Outlook's Find Items feature to locate a message in the Sent Items folder that contains the words "Tennis for Tots" in the body of the message.

❶ Click the Find Items button on the Inbox toolbar.

The Find dialog box appears as shown in the accompanying figure. There are several ways to search for a message item: by word, by field, From, Sent To, and Time.

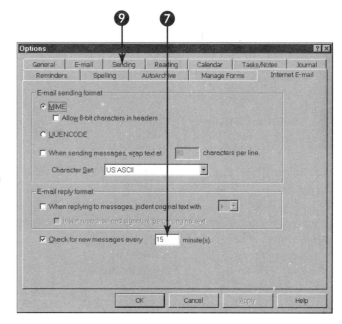

2 Enter or select the search criteria in the Look for box.

3 Click Find Now to find the mail message.

The mail message item appears in a list at the bottom of the dialog box, telling you which folder contains the message.

SKILLS CHALLENGE: READING AND VIEWING E-MAIL

In this review exercise you practice all the skills you've learned in this lesson to receive and reply to e-mail and organize your mail.

1 Read a message.

 1 *How do you read a message?*

2 Reply to a message.

2 *Which tool on the Reply toolbar lets you reply to all names in the To and Cc boxes?*

3 Forward a message.

3 *Which tool on the Reply toolbar lets you forward a message?*

4 Delete a message.

5 Store a mail message in a folder.

6 Sort the mail messages by a particular field in ascending order.

 4 *Which command enables you to sort mail message items?*

7 Group the mail messages by a particular group type.

8 Look at all the Inbox views.

9 Find a message.

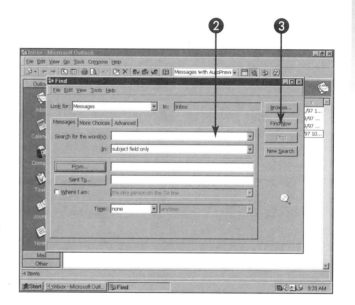

Troubleshooting

TROUBLESHOOTING

Finishing this lesson means you've grasped many of the skills needed to reply to and organize e-mail. This table offers solutions to some questions or challenges you may have experienced in practicing these skills.

Problem	Solution
I can't receive e-mail messages.	You must have a modem, a mail-delivery service, and a phone line or a network cable connection to send messages. If you connect to your mail service using a modem, make sure the Dial-Up Networking options are correct. Be sure that only one information service is set for receiving e-mail. It's also possible that the server may be down, so just wait and try again. You can also check with your system administrator.
I sent a message to the wrong person.	You can recall the message, provided you sent it to recipients who are logged on and using Outlook and who have not read the message or moved the message out of their Inboxes. To recall a message, click Mail on the Outlook Bar, click Sent Items, and open the message you want to recall. Select Tools ➤ Recall This Message and choose Delete unread copies of this message. If you want Outlook to send you a notification that the message has been successfully recalled, choose the Tell me if recall succeeds or fails for each recipient option. Click OK.

Problem	Solution
I tried recalling a message and then sending a replacement message, but it doesn't work.	If you're not on a company intranet, you cannot always recall and replace a message. You can recall or replace a message only to a recipient who uses Outlook and whose message is still unread in Inbox.
I accidentally deleted an important message in Inbox.	You can retrieve a deleted message by clicking the Sent Items icon on the Outlook Bar. Select the message you want to retrieve and drag it to the Inbox icon on the Outlook Bar. Click Inbox on the Outlook Bar to see the message you retrieved.

WRAP UP

You've practiced several new skills in this lesson. You learned how to

- Read messages
- Reply to a message
- Forward a message
- Delete a message
- Store mail in a folder
- Sort, group, and view mail
- Set message-handling options
- Find messages

If you would like more practice with these skills, experiment with replying and forwarding e-mail to your coworkers and organizing your mail in a way that works for you.

In the next lesson you learn about managing mail.

Managing
E-Mail

GOALS

In this lesson you learn these basic skills:

40 MINUTES

- Tracking e-mail messages
- Recalling e-mail messages
- Managing Remote Mail
- Flagging e-mail messages for follow-up activities
- Adding a custom signature
- Creating reusable templates of standard messages
- Using e-mail as a voting tool

Managing Your Mail

GET READY

When you're finished with these exercises, you will have experienced various ways to work with your e-mail messages. The accompanying figure shows a custom signature on a message.

MANAGING YOUR MAIL

In many cases you probably want to know when e-mail messages you send are delivered or read by recipients. If you are on a network and using an Exchange server, Outlook lets you track this information by sending you a notification as each message is delivered or read. The message notifications appear in your message list. The tracking information is recorded on the Tracking tab of the original message. Automatic recording of tracking results is turned on by default, but you can turn off this feature to review each notification before the tracking results are recorded on the Tracking tab. Outlook also lets you automatically delete message notifications in your message list.

You can recall an e-mail message you've already sent to recipients, given that they are logged on to a network, are using an Exchange server, and are using Outlook and have not read the message or moved the message out of their Inboxes. You can even receive a notification about the success of the recall for each recipient.

If you don't use Microsoft Exchange Server or only need to download messages from your Inbox, you can use Outlook's Remote Mail feature to perform those actions. Remote Mail gives you several ways to manage messages and other items from remote locations. You can screen out messages you don't want to download by first downloading the message headers and then downloading the complete messages that you choose. Following are several reasons you may want to use Remote Mail:

- Perhaps you want to reduce the time spent on the phone because you have a second computer at home with a slow modem.

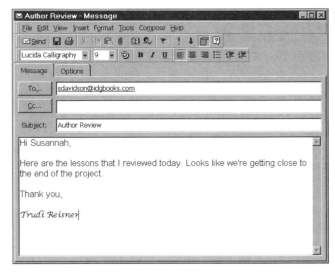

TRY OUT THE
INTERACTIVE TUTORIALS
ON YOUR CD!

Tracking E-Mail Messages

- You may want to retrieve messages for your Inbox only because you connect from an airport or hotel where the telephone access charges are high.

- You also may want to use a server other than Microsoft Exchange Server.

If a message requires follow up, you can flag a message with one of Outlook's message flags. When you send a message, you can flag a message for yourself or the recipient(s) of the message. For example, you might want to flag a message to your attorney to resolve a legal issue. When you flag a message, either of two flags will appear in the Flag Status column in the message list. A red flag indicates that the message is flagged, and a gray flag indicates that the flagged message is complete. When a recipient receives a flagged message, a comment on the purpose of the flag appears at the top of the message. You can also set a due date to appear with the comment.

Tracking E-Mail Messages

You can track e-mail messages you send to recipients and specify several options that let you keep track of the responses to your message. You may want to make the message highly important and personal. You can specify that you want *voting buttons* so that the recipients can accept or reject a request in your message. You can tell Outlook when to deliver the message and specify an expiration date for the message. Also, you can tell Outlook to notify you when the message has been delivered and when the message has been read. In this exercise you set up a new message so that Outlook can track it.

1. Click the New Message button on the Inbox toolbar.

2. Type any message information you want in the message.

3. Click the Options tab.

4. For the Importance option, choose High.

5. For the Sensitivity option, choose Personal.

6. Click the Use voting buttons check box.

   The voting buttons let the recipients accept or reject any request you make in your message.

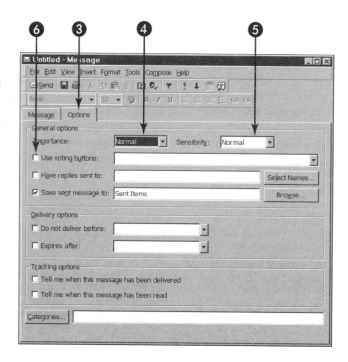

Recalling E-Mail Messages

7 In the Delivery options section, click the Do not deliver before check box.

8 Choose a date.

9 In the Delivery options section, click the Expires after check box.

10 Choose a date.

11 In the Tracking options section, click the Tell me when this message has been delivered check box.

12 In the Tracking options section, click the Tell me when this message has been read check box.

The accompanying figure displays the options you should have entered.

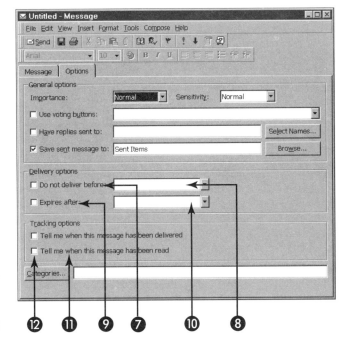

NOTE *To turn off automatic recording of tracking results, select Tools ➢ Options and click the E-mail tab. Clear the Process delivery, read, and recall receipts on arrival check box, and click OK. If you want to review delivered or read message notifications before recording the tracking results, select Tools ➢ Options and click the E-mail tab. Clear the Process requests and responses on arrival check box, and click OK. Perhaps you want Outlook to delete notifications automatically. Select Tools ➢ Options and click the E-mail tab. Select the option Delete receipts and blank responses after processing, and click OK.*

Recalling E-Mail Messages

If you're using Outlook on a company network (intranet), it's never too late to recall a message you've sent. If you're not using Outlook on an intranet, you can't recall the message. In this exercise you recall a sent mail message.

1 In Sent Items, open the message you want to recall.

2 Open the Tools menu.

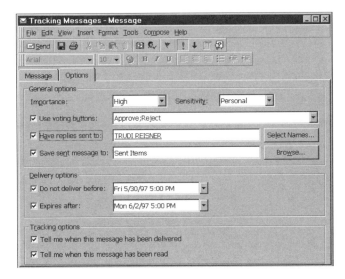

3 Choose the Recall This Message command.

The Recall This Message dialog box appears.

4 Choose the Delete unread copies of this message option.

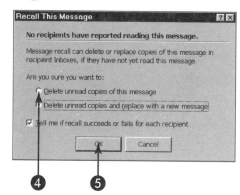

TIP

If you want Outlook to give you notification about the success of the recall, you can select the Tell me if recall succeeds or fails for each recipient option. The recall notification will appear in your message list.

5 Click OK.

Outlook deletes the unread copy of the message.

Managing Remote Mail

To work with Remote Mail, you need to set the options for it in Outlook. If you use Microsoft Exchange Server, make sure a Dial-Up Networking connection has been set up. The Remote Mail options vary, depending on the mail-delivery service you use. For example, if you use Microsoft Exchange Server, you can specify times for Remote Mail sessions or retrieve messages using a filter.

To set options for Remote Mail, from Inbox select Tools ➤ Services and choose a service you want to set up for Remote Mail. Click Properties and choose the options you want, and click OK. Click the Delivery tab and specify where you want your messages delivered. Click the Addressing tab and select the options you want, and then click OK. Exit Outlook and then restart the program.

After you set up your computer for Remote Mail, you'll be ready to use it. Here's what Remote Mail enables you to do:

- Connect and download message headers to weed out the messages you don't want to download

- Mark message headers to download

- Copy and delete messages

- Reconnect and download your messages

Managing Remote Mail

To see how Remote Mail works, start by connecting to Remote Mail.

1 From Inbox, open the Tools menu.

2 Choose Remote Mail.

3 Choose Connect.

The Remote Connection Wizard dialog box appears, as shown in the accompanying figure.

4 Follow the instructions in the Remote Connection Wizard dialog boxes to connect to Remote Mail.

Now you are connected to Remote Mail. When Remote Mail downloads messages, they are placed on your local computer only. When you copy a message, Outlook places a copy of the message on your local computer and leaves a copy on the server. When you delete a message, Outlook removes the message from both your local computer and the server. If you use a docking laptop, downloading the messages is a good idea. Now display the Remote toolbar and mark the message headers to download, copy, and delete.

5 From Inbox, select the Tools menu.

6 Choose Remote Mail.

7 Choose Remote Tools.

The Remote toolbar appears, as shown in the accompanying figure.

8 Select the messages you want to download.

9 Click the Mark to Retrieve button on the Remote toolbar.

TIP

To unmark a message, click the Unmark button on the Remote toolbar. If you want to unmark all messages, click the Unmark All button on the Remote toolbar.

10 Select the messages you want to copy and download.

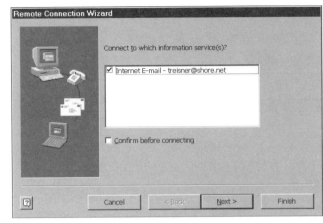

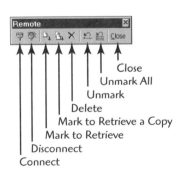

⓫ Click the Mark to Retrieve a Copy button on the Remote toolbar.

⓬ Select the messages you want to delete.

⓭ Click the Delete button on the Remote toolbar.

Flagging E-Mail Messages for Follow-Up Activities

You can flag a message for follow up with a message flag. You can flag a message either for yourself or for the recipient(s) of the message. For example, you may want to flag a message to your boss to respond with a deadline for a project you're going to work on. Outlook displays either of two flags next to a message. A red flag means that the message has been flagged, and a gray flag means that the follow up to the flagged message is complete. The recipient who receives the flagged message sees a comment on the purpose of the flag at the top of the message. You can also assign a due date that will appear with the comment. In this exercise you flag a message for follow up.

❶ Open a message.

❷ Click the Message Flag button on the Message toolbar.

The Flag Message dialog box appears. The Outlook message flags include the following: Call, Do Not Forward, Follow up, For your information, Forward, No response necessary, Read, Reply, Reply to All, and Review. If you want, you can type your own message flag in the Flag text box.

❸ In the Flag drop-down list, choose the type of flag you want.

❹ If you want to assign a due date, choose a date on the calendar in the By box.

❺ Click OK.

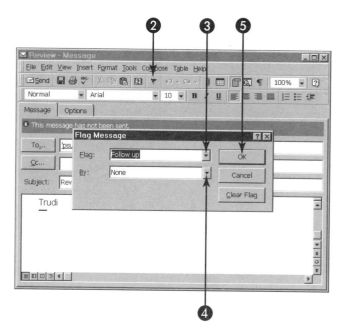

Beyond Mail

TIP

To clear a message flag, open the message and click Message Flag on the Message toolbar. Click Clear Flag and then click OK.

If you set a due date for a flagged message and it is overdue, the overdue flagged message appears in red in the message list. You can change the due date on a message flag. Open the message, click Message Flag on the Message toolbar, and choose a new date in the By box. Then click OK.

To flag a message as completed, open the message, click Message Flag on the Message toolbar, and choose the Completed option. Then click OK.

BEYOND MAIL

Using Outlook's cool AutoSignature feature, you can add a custom signature to your messages or any Outlook item, except a note. For example, you can add your name, job title, and phone number to messages you send. AutoSignature even lets you change the font and alignment for the text in your signature to make it look unique. You can use different formats for individual characters or words in the signature and add bullets. You can set up AutoSignature to add a signature either automatically or manually. The automatic mode inserts a signature in messages you create, reply to, and forward. The manual mode enables you to insert a signature only when you want to.

You can create your own reusable templates from a standard message. For example, you always send your messages with your Web page Internet address and custom signature. Enter this information in a new mail message and save the message as a template file. Then you can create new messages based on that template.

You can use e-mail as a voting tool and ask others to vote in a message. The recipients click a voting button to make their choice and then send the reply to you. Then you can view the vote responses. You can even copy the results of the vote responses to a document in another program such as Word or Excel.

▶ Adding a Custom Signature

Outlook's AutoSignature feature lets you add a custom signature to your messages. For example, you can add your name, job title, and phone number to messages you send. You can even change the font, font size and style (bold, italic, underline), and text alignment (left, center, right) for the text. You can also add bullets to the text. Outlook lets you set up AutoSignature to add a signature automatically or manually. The automatic AutoSignature feature inserts a signature in messages you create, reply to, and forward. The manual AutoSignature feature lets you insert a signature at your discretion. In this exercise you use Outlook's AutoSignature to create a custom signature for later use (manually).

❶ From Inbox, open the Tools menu.

❷ Choose the AutoSignature command.

   The AutoSignature dialog box appears.

❸ Type the text for your custom signature in the box.

❹ Select the text you want to enhance.

❺ Click Font.

❻ Select a font.

❼ Select a font size.

❽ Select a font style.

❾ Click OK.

   The accompanying figure shows an AutoSignature in 9-point Lucida Calligraphy.

❿ If desired, click Paragraph.

⓫ Align the text or add bullets.

⓬ Then click OK.

⓭ Click OK in the AutoSignature dialog box.

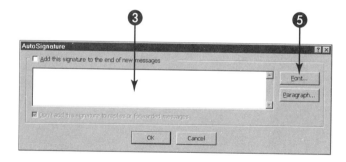

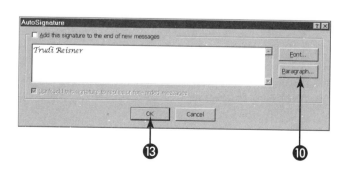

7

Managing E-Mail

Creating Reusable Templates

NOTE *To create a signature for automatic use, from Inbox select Tools ➢ AutoSignature. Select the Add this signature to the end of new messages option. Type the text for your custom signature in the box. Change the font or alignment, or add bullets. If you want to automatically add the signature to messages you reply to or forward, clear the Don't add this signature to replies or forwarded messages check box.*

⑭ Now that you've created a signature, it's time to insert it into a message. Start a new message or reply to a message in your Inbox.

⑮ In the large text box, click where you want the signature to appear.

⑯ Select the Insert menu.

⑰ Choose the AutoSignature command.

Wow! There's your custom signature in a message. The accompanying figure shows an example of a custom signature at the end of a message.

Creating Reusable Templates of Standard Messages

Outlook lets you create reusable templates from messages so that you don't have to type standard information in your messages each time you compose a new message. For example, if you always send your messages with your Internet address, phone number, fax number, and custom signature, then you can enter this information in a new mail message and save the message as an Outlook template. An Outlook template has the file type .OFT. When you compose a new message, you can base it on the Outlook template. In this exercise you create a reusable template from a standard message and then use the template to create a new message.

❶ Create a new message or open any message that contains information you want to store in a template.

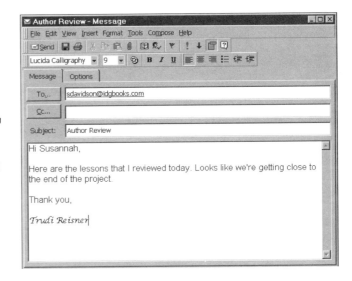

2 Insert your custom signature.

3 Open the File menu.

4 Choose the Save As command.

5 In the File name box, type a name for the template.

6 In the Save as type box, choose Outlook Template.

7 In the Save in box, choose the Outlook folder.

At this point your Save As dialog box should look similar to the one in the accompanying figure.

8 Click Save.

Now create a new message based on the template.

9 In Inbox, open the File menu.

10 Choose the New command.

11 Select Choose Template.

The Choose Template dialog box appears. The General tab shows several Outlook templates for each type of item in Outlook, such as Appointment, Contact, Mail, Post (Notes), Task, and While You Were Out.

12 Click the Outlook tab.

The Outlook tab contains more Outlook templates, including the one you created.

13 Double-click the template you created.

Notice that the new message is based on the template.

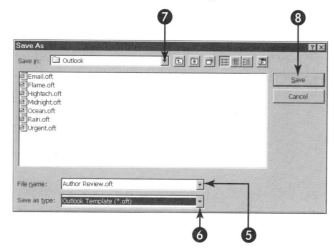

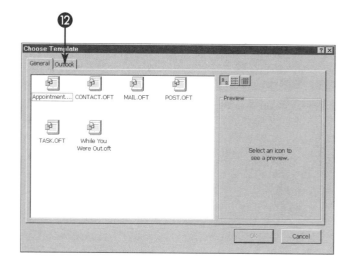

Using E-Mail as a Voting Tool

With Outlook you can add voting buttons to your messages so that recipients can accept, reject, or make a choice in their reply to your request. You can create specific options from which the voter can choose. These options will appear next to the voting buttons in the recipient's message. You can view the voting responses and copy the results to a document in another program such as Word or Excel. All

Using E-Mail as a Voting Tool

Sports Management is giving T-shirts to all employees at the summer picnic. In this exercise you create voting buttons for the T-shirt sizes.

1 Create a message asking your coworkers to vote on T-shirt sizes.

2 Click the Options tab.

3 Choose the Use voting buttons option.

You can use the button names supplied by Outlook by clicking the Select Names button, or you can create your own names. You'll create the voting button names and separate them with semicolons.

4 In the box, type **Small;Large;Extra Large.**

5 Choose the Save sent message to option.

The vote responses will be recorded on the Options tab in this saved message, so it's a good idea to jot down the folder name in which you are storing the saved message. For example, the Sent Items folder is where you'll look for the vote responses.

6 Click Send on the Message toolbar to send the message.

Next you'll view the vote responses to the message.

7 Click Sent Items on the Outlook Bar.

8 Open the original message that contains the vote.

9 Click the Options tab.

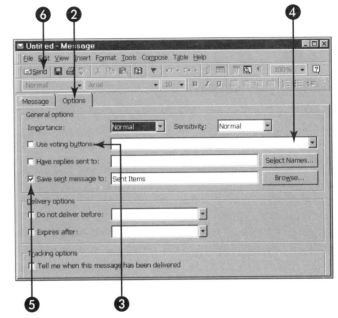

TIP *If you want to keep all the voting responses, make sure the **Delete receipts and blank responses after processing** check box is not checked off on the E-mail tab in the Options dialog box. If you want Outlook to delete the voting responses automatically, be sure the **Delete receipts and blank responses after processing** option is selected.*

You can copy the voting responses to another Outlook item, such as a task, or to a document in another program, such as Word or Excel. First select the responses you want to copy. Click and drag over the rows in the list, or select the first response, hold down Ctrl, and click each additional response. Select Edit ➤ Copy, switch to a text box in the Outlook item or the other program, and select Edit ➤ Paste.

SKILLS CHALLENGE: MANAGING E-MAIL

In this review exercise you practice all the skills you've learned in this lesson to manage your mail.

1 Track a message.

 Where can you view the tracking results?

2 Recall a message you've already sent.

 Which command lets you recall a message?

3 Flag a message for follow up.

 What are the two types of message flags?

4 Add a custom signature.

 Which command enables you to add a custom signature?

5 Create a reusable template from a standard message.

6 Send a voting message to coworkers that asks them to vote on three entrees being served at the summer picnic.

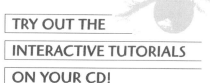

**TRY OUT THE
INTERACTIVE TUTORIALS
ON YOUR CD!**

TROUBLESHOOTING

Finishing this lesson means you've grasped many of the skills needed to manage e-mail. This table offers solutions to some questions or challenges you may have experienced in practicing these skills.

Wrap up

Problem	Solution
I couldn't recall a message that I sent.	There can be several reasons for this. You may not be able to recall the message, depending on who you are sending it to. Usually this option works only if you are connected to a local area network and an Exchange server.
I can create a custom signature using only the Word mail editor and not Outlook.	You've selected Word as your mail editor. Deselect it in the E-mail tab of the Options dialog box, and you'll be able to create a custom signature.

WRAP UP

You've practiced several new skills in this lesson. You learned how to

- Track e-mail messages

- Recall e-mail messages

- Manage Remote Mail

- Flag e-mail messages for follow-up activities

- Add a custom signature

- Create reusable templates of standard messages

- Use e-mail as a voting tool

If you would like more practice with these skills, create a template for your personal e-mail and add a custom signature.

The next lesson introduces you to Calendar.

PART IV

Managing Your Schedule

The lessons in this part show you how to use Calendar and work with appointments, events, and meetings.

This part contains the following lessons:

- Lesson 8: Using the Calendar
- Lesson 9: Viewing Your Schedule
- Lesson 10: Planning a Meeting

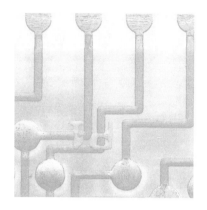

Using the Calendar

55 MINUTES

GOALS

This lesson introduces you to ways you can use Outlook's Calendar to create your own personal schedule, including the following:

- Adding appointments and events
- Adding an appointment with multiple time slots
- Scheduling an event on multiple days
- Setting recurring appointments
- Scheduling a contact
- Changing an appointment's time
- Rescheduling an appointment
- Setting and removing a reminder
- Deleting an appointment

Adding Appointments

To run through this lesson, you need the files EX08-1.PST and EX08-2.PST from the One Step folder. When you finish the last exercise in this lesson, you will have produced a schedule that should look like the accompanying figure.

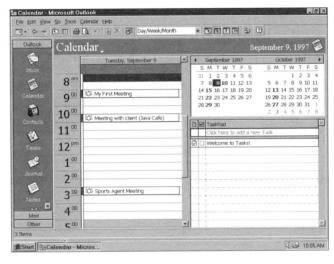

SCHEDULING APPOINTMENTS AND EVENTS

Do you tote around a Day-Timer® book during the day? Do you have a desk or wall calendar at home marked up with appointments, events, birthdays, anniversaries, holidays, meetings, and so on? What if you lost your Day-Timer®? Unfortunately, you could lose it, and you might be totally lost without it. Why not track your schedule electronically with Outlook's Calendar to computerize your business and personal schedule in one location?

With Calendar you can schedule and keep track of all your daily activities and even set up meetings. You can fill in daily and weekly appointments and events in your schedule. For example, you might want to track interviews, meetings, doctor and dentist appointments, and events such as birthdays, anniversaries, and conferences.

▶ Adding Appointments

The time schedule in Calendar displays a 24-hour day from 12:00 a.m. to 11:00 p.m. By default, an alarm rings to remind you of an appointment. That way you don't miss the appointment. You can also remove the reminder if you don't want to be interrupted while you're working on the computer.

How does Outlook define an appointment? An appointment is an activity for which you specify a block of time in Calendar that doesn't involve inviting other people or resources. By default, a scheduled appointment marks a time slot as busy. There are other ways to mark an appointment to show others who view your Calendar how blocks of time are scheduled. Blocks of time are marked, viewed, and displayed in Calendar, as listed in Table 8-1.

TRY OUT THE

INTERACTIVE TUTORIALS

ON YOUR CD!

TABLE 8-1 CALENDAR'S BLOCKS OF TIME

Show Time As	How Time Is Viewed by Others	How Time Slot Is Displayed
Busy	Unavailable	Blue border around white time slot
Free	Available	White
Tentative	Available	Light blue
Out of office	Unavailable	Purple

Outlook lets you schedule all your appointments and events in your own Calendar, and others can grant you permission to schedule or make changes to appointments in their calendars. You can even schedule private appointments that you don't want others to see. Outlook displays a private appointment in your schedule with a key symbol next to it. Only you can access your private appointments; not even someone you gave permission to access your folders.

Import the EX08-1.PST file from the One Step folder. This file is a schedule containing some appointments that are already set up. There are a few ways to add appointments and events:

- Click the New drop-down arrow on any Outlook toolbar and choose Appointment.

- Click the New Appointment button on the Calendar toolbar.

- In Calendar, type the appointment information into a time slot in the schedule.

In this exercise you add an appointment to the schedule using one of the methods described earlier.

1 Import EX08-1.PST.

The accompanying figure shows the Calendar after you import the file. Nothing will look different on your Calendar, unless the current month in Calendar coincides with the dates that the appointments and events were scheduled for this exercise.

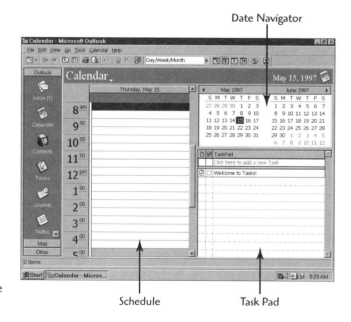

Date Navigator

Schedule

Task Pad

Adding Appointments

② Click the New Appointment button on the Calendar toolbar.

The Appointment window opens. The appointment's name is untitled until you save the appointment.

TIP *If you prefer using the keyboard over the mouse, when you're in Calendar you can use Ctrl+N to select Calendar ➤ New Appointment. If you're in another Outlook component, you can use Ctrl+Shift+A to select the New Appointment command.*

③ In the Subject text box, type **Meeting with client.**

④ Press Tab.

⑤ In the Location text box, type **Java Café.**

Leave the start date as is, but change the meeting time.

⑥ Click the Start time (currently 9:00 AM) drop-down arrow to display the time options.

TIP *If you select a time slot that contains a scheduled appointment and open the New Appointment window to add a new appointment, Outlook displays a warning message at the top of the window. This message informs you that there is a conflict with another appointment in Calendar. To remedy this, you can change either the existing or new appointment's time.*

⑦ Choose 11:00 AM.

TIP *If you already know the start and end time dates and times, you can simply type them into the appropriate Start time and End time text boxes. For faster start and end time entry, try using Outlook's AutoDate feature. For example, you can type **next Wednesday** or **noon** instead of typing a date or time.*

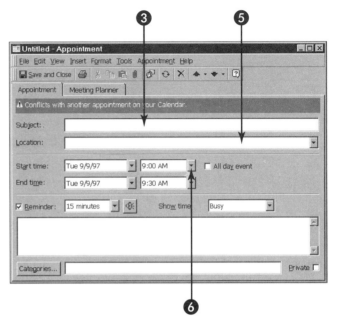

Notice the End time is 11:30 AM. By default, Outlook sets half-hour appointments unless otherwise specified. The reminder is set at 15 minutes by default. This means the reminder alarm will ring 15 minutes prior to your appointment to alert you, no matter what program you're working in on your computer. Also notice the Show time option is Busy, which is also the default setting. This means the block of time for the appointment you just scheduled is considered to be unavailable.

8 Click the Save and Close button on the Appointment toolbar.

The appointment appears in the 11:00 AM time slot with its location enclosed in parentheses. The reminder symbol, a bell, appears next to the appointment. See the accompanying figure.

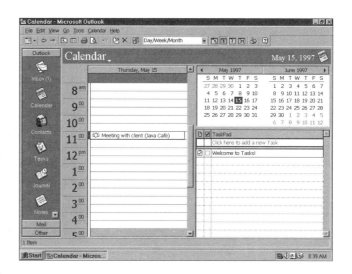

Adding Events

What is considered an event? An *event* is an activity that lasts 24 hours or longer. For example, you can schedule an event such as a three-day conference, your summer vacation, or a seminar. Events such as birthdays and anniversaries occur every year on a specific date and last for one day. Events and annual events don't take up blocks of time and appear at the top of the dates in Calendar. An event that displays at the top of the schedule is called a *banner* by Microsoft. A banner can spread out over multiple days. Events are considered to be free time and appear in white to others viewing your calendar.

Your client's birthday is coming up, and your assignment is to add that event to the schedule. Adding appointments and events are similar processes.

1 Click 3 in the October month calendar to select October 3.

2 Click the New Appointment button on the Calendar toolbar.

3 In the Subject text box, type **Client's birthday.**

4 Click the All day event check box.

Now that you've told Outlook to schedule an event, Outlook removes the Start and End time boxes. This happens because an event takes up an entire 24-hour day. Therefore, you don't

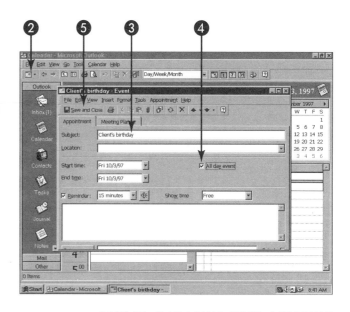

Adding Events

need to specify any start and end times for an event. Also, notice that the Show time option is Free, which means that the blocks of time of that day are still available.

Leave the reminder set to 15 minutes.

⑤ Click the Save and Close button on the Appointment toolbar.

Your client's birthday is noted at the top of the schedule beneath the date, as shown in the accompanying figure. This event is called a banner because it stretches across the top of the day's schedule like a real banner or streamer.

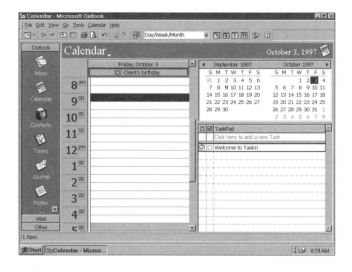

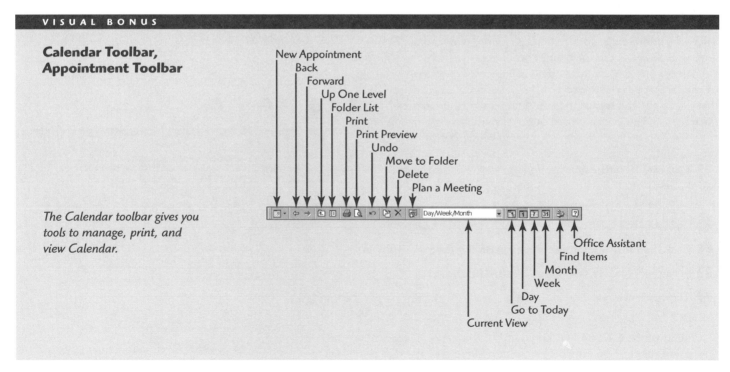

VISUAL BONUS

Calendar Toolbar, Appointment Toolbar

New Appointment
Back
Forward
Up One Level
Folder List
Print
Print Preview
Undo
Move to Folder
Delete
Plan a Meeting

The Calendar toolbar gives you tools to manage, print, and view Calendar.

Office Assistant
Find Items
Month
Week
Day
Go to Today
Current View

Adding an Appointment

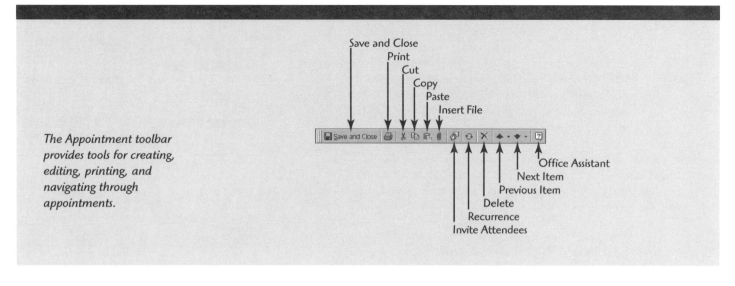

Save and Close
Print
Cut
Copy
Paste
Insert File

The Appointment toolbar provides tools for creating, editing, printing, and navigating through appointments.

Office Assistant
Next Item
Previous Item
Delete
Recurrence
Invite Attendees

Adding an Appointment with Multiple Time Slots

Often an appointment may take more than a half hour (default time). You can add an appointment with multiple time slots to reserve as much time as you want in the schedule. In this exercise you add an appointment for a Public Relations Workshop that requires two hours of time in the schedule.

❶ Click 10 in the September calendar to select September 10.

❷ Click 1:00 PM in the schedule.

❸ Drag down to the 3:00 PM time slot.

The 1:00 PM to 3:00 PM time slots (inclusive) are highlighted.

❹ Type **Public Relations Workshop** in the highlighted area.

❺ Click in any time slot.

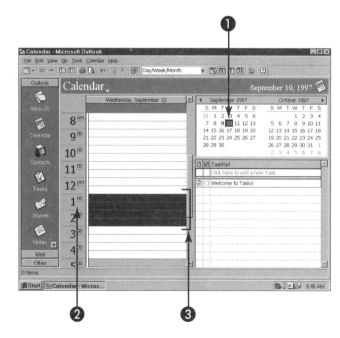

You see the new appointment in multiple time slots with a reminder, as shown in the accompanying figure.

After you type an appointment in a slot, be sure to click in a different time slot if you're planning to add another appointment. If you click in the time slot you just filled or press Enter, and you add another appointment by clicking the New Appointment button on the Calendar toolbar, Outlook will display a warning message in the Appointment window. This message informs you that there is a conflict in the schedule. At this point you can select a different time or day to remove the warning message.

Scheduling an Event on Multiple Days

What if you need to schedule an event such as a conference that lasts for more than one day? That's easy to do in Outlook. In this exercise you schedule an event on multiple days.

① Click the New Appointment button on the Calendar toolbar.

② In the Subject text box, type **All Sports Conference.**

③ In the Location text box, type **Boston Convention Center.**

④ Click the All day event check box.

⑤ Click the Start time date drop-down arrow to display the month calendar.

⑥ Choose Fri 9/12/97.

⑦ Click the End time date drop-down arrow to display the month calendar.

⑧ Choose Sun 9/14/97.

Notice that the Show time option is Free and the Reminder is set to 15 minutes. These options are fine for the conference. Your event information should look like the accompanying figure.

⑨ Click the Save and Close button on the Appointment toolbar.

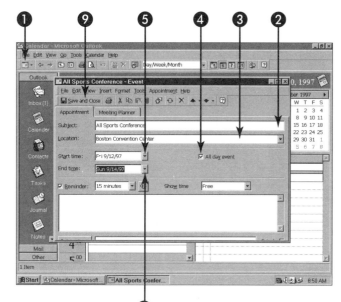

⑩ Click 12 on the September calendar.

In your schedule, take a look at the first day of the conference noted in a banner at the top, beneath the date.

⑪ Click 13 on the September calendar to see the second day of the conference.

⑫ Click 14 on the September calendar to see the last day of the conference.

Setting Recurring Appointments

You can also schedule recurring appointments. For example, if you have a weekly staff meeting on Monday at 1:00 p.m., then Outlook can schedule that meeting as a recurring appointment on that weekday and time slot into the near future or for as long as you like.

As a sports agent, you're required to attend the obligatory weekly staff meeting on Monday at 1:00 p.m. Because this meeting needs to be written in stone in your schedule for a long time into the future, schedule this meeting as a recurring appointment. With a recurring appointment, each meeting is scheduled week after week until you tell Outlook to stop scheduling them. That way you won't have to manually add this meeting to your schedule every week, one at a time.

① Click 15 in the September month calendar.

② Click the New Appointment button on the Calendar toolbar.

③ In the Subject text box, type **Weekly Staff Meeting.**

④ In the Location text box, type **Stadium Conference Room.**

⑤ For the Start time, choose 1:00 PM.

⑥ For the End time, choose 2:00 PM.

⑦ Click the Recurrence button (a button with two arrows, one curving up and left and the other curving down and right) on the Appointment toolbar.

The Appointment Recurrence dialog box opens. There are three major categories of options in this dialog box: Appointment time, Recurrence pattern, and Range of recurrence.

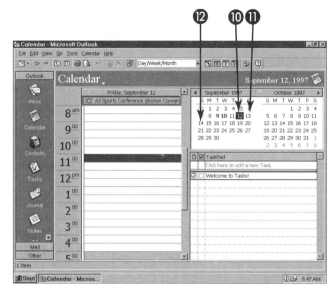

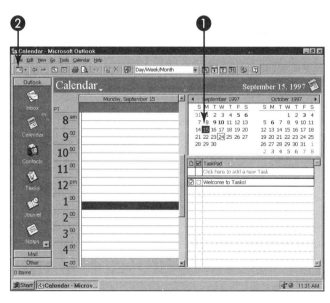

Scheduling a Contact

The information in the Appointment time section indicates that the appointment is from 1:00 PM to 2:00 PM and is for one hour. For this exercise the information is correct, so you can leave it alone.

The Recurrence pattern is weekly and recurs every week on Monday. Again, this information is fine for this example.

For the Range of recurrence, the default option is No end date. For the purposes of this exercise, keep in mind that when a sports agents starts to travel, the staff meeting time may need to be changed periodically. Change the Range of recurrence to end on a specific date.

8 In the Range of recurrence section, choose End by and leave the date Mon 11/17/1997.

9 Click OK.

In the Weekly Staff Meeting appointment window, about halfway down, you see an information message stating the recurring appointment information.

10 Click the Save and Close button on the Appointment toolbar.

Notice that the recurring appointment in the 1:00 PM to 2:00 PM block of time has a reminder and a recurrence symbol (one arrow curving up and left, another arrow curving down and right) next to it, as shown in the accompanying figure.

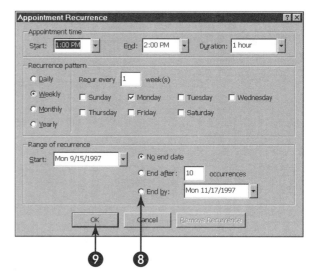

Scheduling a Contact

If a contact is already set up in Outlook, you can quickly schedule that contact into your calendar. One of your potential clients, a golfer, wants to meet with you to discuss a golf tournament. Other potential clients from your contacts list can be invited to this meeting, too. But for now, go over to Contacts and schedule that golfer for a meeting. When you schedule a contact for a meeting, Outlook sends the appointment to the contact as an e-mail message. The contact can then add the appointment to his or her schedule.

1 Click Contacts on the Outlook Bar.

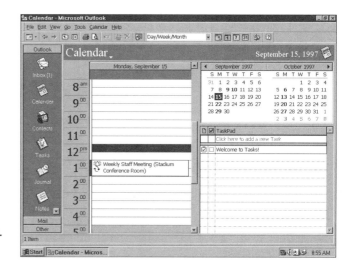

2 Click Nick Farina to select the contact.

3 Click and drag Nick Farina onto Calendar in the Outlook Bar.

Outlook displays a meeting window with the contact's e-mail address in the To box.

4 In the Subject text box, type **Players Tournament Meeting.**

5 In the Location text box, type **Palmetto Country Club.**

6 For the Start time date, choose September 24.

7 For the Start time, choose 6:00 AM.

Your contact window should look like the figure at the bottom of this page.

At this point, you would click the Send button on the Meeting toolbar to send this e-mail message to set up the meeting with your contact. But in this exercise, just close the window and save the meeting information.

8 Click the Close button in upper-right corner of the Meeting window. The Microsoft Outlook dialog box appears.

9 Choose Yes in the dialog box.

Outlook asks you if you want to send the message.

10 Choose No.

Now look at the meeting you scheduled in Calendar.

11 Click Calendar on the Outlook Bar.

12 On the September calendar, click 24.

Notice the More Appointments icon just above 8 AM in the schedule. The More Appointments icon indicates that there are more appointments at the top of the schedule (in this case, before 8 AM).

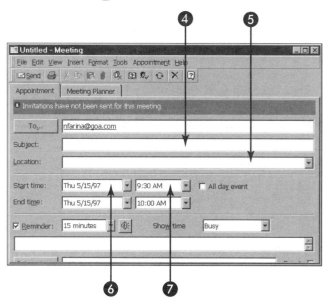

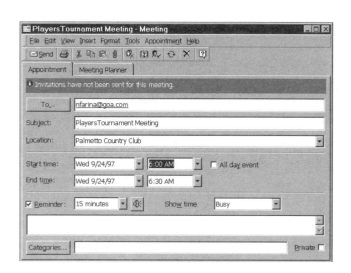

Changing an Appointment's Time

⑬ Use the vertical scroll bar to the right of the schedule to scroll up until you see the meeting.

The figure at the bottom of this page shows the meeting with a reminder and a meeting icon (two faces).

CHANGING APPOINTMENTS

Sometimes you'll want to change an appointment. Frequently, you'll need to change the start and end time for an appointment or reschedule it to a different date and time.

Before you can change any appointment, you need to know how to select and open appointments. To select an appointment, click it in the schedule. To open an appointment's window, double-click the appointment in the schedule.

With Outlook you can't forget about your appointments because an alarm rings to remind you of an appointment. Also, Outlook displays the Reminder dialog box. From this box you can dismiss, postpone, or open the appointment.

You typically let Outlook remind you of an appointment, but there may be some cases when you don't want to be reminded. For example, you may have an early morning appointment before you get to the office, and you won't be at your computer to be reminded. Why bother with a reminder? You can remove the reminder at any time.

If an appointment gets canceled, you can delete an appointment from Calendar with just one click. Outlook also offers the Undo command to restore deleted items. Another level of security is the Deleted Items feature that holds all your deleted items until you decide to get rid of them, as explained earlier in Lesson 2.

Changing an Appointment's Time

Outlook lets you change an appointment's date and time whenever you want. There are two ways you can do this:

- Open the appointment and select a new date and time.

- Drag the appointment to a different date and time slot in the schedule.

More Appointments icon

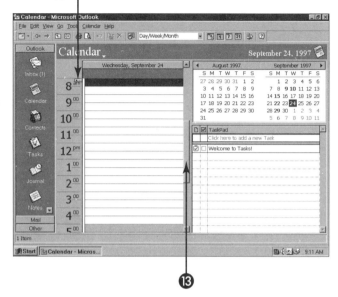

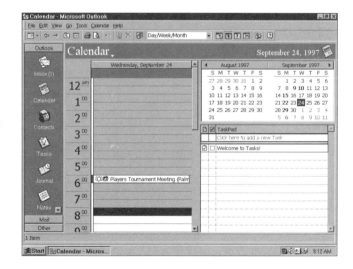

Changing an Appointment's Time

The meeting time with your client has been changed to an earlier time that morning. Follow these steps to change the appointment's time:

❶ In the month calendar, display the current month (where you scheduled the meeting with your client).

Notice that the days in the month calendar that have appointments appear in bold.

❷ Click September 9 in the current month calendar.

❸ Double-click *Meeting with client* at 11:00 a.m.

❹ In the Start time box, choose 10:30 AM.

❺ Click the Save and Close button on the Appointment toolbar.

The appointment appears in a new time slot, as shown in the accompanying figure.

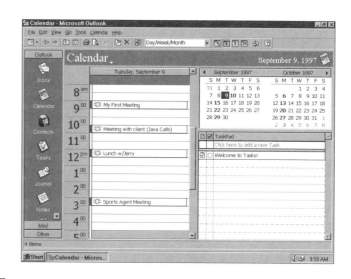

TIP

To change an appointment's time quickly, you can move the mouse pointer to the left side of a time slot for an appointment. The blue vertical bar on the left side of the time slot is called the left-move handle. The mouse pointer changes to a four-headed arrow. Drag the appointment by its left-move handle to the new location. You can move the appointment to a different time slot on the same day, or you can even move the appointment to a different day in the same time slot by dragging it to a day on the month calendar.

Now change the appointment to 10:00 a.m. using the mouse.

❻ Point to the blue vertical bar on the left side of the appointment in the 10:30 a.m. time slot.

The mouse pointer changes to a four-headed arrow, as shown in the accompanying figure.

❼ Drag the appointment up to the 10:00 a.m. time slot.

The appointment appears in the new time slot.

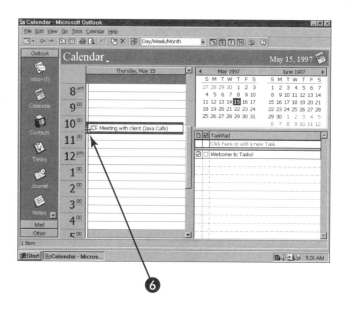

Rescheduling an Appointment

Rescheduling an Appointment

Suppose the date or date and time have changed for an appointment. No problem. You can easily reschedule an appointment. Your client has a conflict during lunch on Tuesday, but lunch on Wednesday is okay. In this exercise you make that change.

1 Scroll to the September calendar.

2 Click 9 on the September calendar.

3 Double-click Lunch w/Jerry at 12:00 p.m.

4 For the Start date, choose Wed 9/10/97.

5 Click the Save and Close button on the Appointment toolbar.

6 Click 10 on the September calendar.

The rescheduled appointment should appear like the one in the accompanying figure.

Setting and Removing a Reminder

By default, the reminder is always set to ring an alarm 15 minutes before your appointment. However, you can set the reminder to a different time interval or remove it if you don't need it.

The restaurant at which you're having lunch with your client is 20 minutes away from your office. You've never been there before and have been given directions. It would be nice to be reminded a half hour before lunch so that you can drive there and have an extra ten minutes for possibly getting lost. In this exercise you change the reminder setting to 30 minutes for the lunch appointment.

1 Double-click Lunch w/Jerry in the 12:00 p.m. time slot.

In the Reminder section, there are three options you need to know about. The Reminder check box lets you turn the option on or off. The Reminder time box enables you to set the reminder time (the default time is 15 minutes). The Reminder Sound button lets you change the reminder sound that plays (the default sound is a ringing bell). See the accompanying figure.

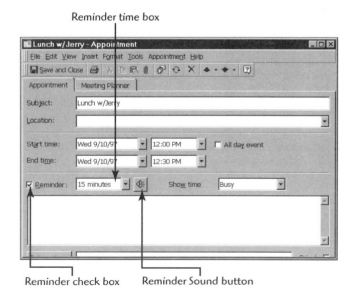

Reminder time box

Reminder check box   Reminder Sound button

2 In the Reminder section, choose 30 minutes.

3 Click the Save and Close button on the Appointment toolbar.

NOTE *You can customize the reminder sound that plays. Click the Reminder Sound button (a button with a bell on it) in the Appointment window. Click the Browse button, switch to the directory that contains sound files, and select the sound you want. Then click OK.*

Now delete the reminder for the Public Relations Workshop.

4 Double-click Public Relations Workshop.

5 Click the Reminder check box.

6 Click the Save and Close button on the Appointment toolbar.

Notice that the bell that was next to the workshop appointment has disappeared. From this day forward you will not be reminded about this appointment.

When Outlook reminds you about an appointment, event, or meeting, your computer plays a ringing bell sound and the Reminder dialog box appears, as shown in the accompanying figure. A reminder gives you three choices:

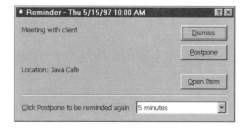

- **Dismiss.** Click the Dismiss button to close the reminder, and you won't be reminded again.

- **Postpone.** Choose an amount of time in the Postpone time box at the bottom of the dialog box, and then click the Postpone button to display a reminder again.

- **Open Item.** Click the Open Item button to open the item and change any reminder settings.

Deleting an Appointment

When you no longer need an appointment, you can delete it. Your boss has informed you that one of the weekly staff meetings has been canceled. In this exercise you wipe out an appointment altogether.

Deleting an Appointment

1 Click 6 on the October calendar.

2 Select Weekly Staff Meeting at 1:00 p.m.

3 Click the Delete button on the Calendar toolbar.

Because this is a recurring appointment, Outlook asks if you want to delete all occurrences or just the selected one. Because you selected an appointment before starting the deletion, Outlook defaults to the Delete this one option, which is what you want.

4 Click OK.

Outlook deletes the appointment and removes it from the schedule. Also, the 6 in the October calendar is no longer bold, indicating that no appointments are scheduled for that day.

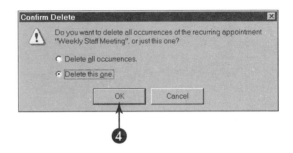

Confirm Delete

Do you want to delete all occurrences of the recurring appointment "Weekly Staff Meeting", or just this one?

○ Delete all occurrences.

⊙ Delete this one.

[OK]   [Cancel]

4

TIP

To delete more than one appointment simultaneously, select the first appointment, hold down the Ctrl key, and select each additional appointment. Then click the Delete button on the Calendar toolbar.

SKILLS CHALLENGE: SCHEDULING APPOINTMENTS

This exercise gives you hands-on experience with reviewing all the skills you've mastered in this lesson. You schedule and change appointments in a new Calendar schedule stored in EX08-2.PST.

1 Import EX08-2.PST.

2 Add an appointment for an advertising meeting on today's date at 9:00 a.m.

 Identify the three ways to add an appointment.

3 Add an event for your own birthday.

 What is the difference between an appointment and an event?

Schedule an appointment for a two-hour tennis workshop tomorrow.

 Schedule a tennis seminar as an event on a Saturday and Sunday.

 Set a recurring appointment for a monthly promotional meeting.

 What are the three major categories of options you can set for a recurring appointment in the Appointment Recurrence dialog box?

 Schedule one of your contacts for a meeting tomorrow.

 Change the time for the Advertising meeting to 10:00 a.m.

 Reschedule the tennis workshop to next week.

 What are your choices when the Reminder dialog box appears?

 Reset the reminder time for the advertising meeting to 30 minutes.

 Remove the reminder from the tennis workshop appointment.

 Delete one of the monthly promotional meetings.

TROUBLESHOOTING

Finishing this lesson means that you now know how to add appointments and events needed to produce a schedule. Also, some of the Calendar tools and procedures you've explored are the tools that Outlook has to offer in its other components. This table offers solutions to several issues you may have encountered while working on these skills.

Problem	Solution
The Inbox is currently displayed and I would like to add an appointment to my schedule.	Click the New drop-down arrow on the Inbox toolbar, and choose Appointment or press Ctrl+Shift+A.

continued

Wrap up

Problem	Solution
When I tried to add a new appointment, Outlook displayed a warning message informing me of a conflict with another appointment in Calendar.	You selected an existing appointment before creating the new one. You can change either the existing or new appointment's time.
The Reminder dialog box appeared to remind me of an appointment that was in the past.	You didn't turn on your computer when the appointment was scheduled. Reschedule or delete the appointment.
I scheduled the wrong time for an appointment I have tomorrow.	Click the left side of the appointment's time slot. When you see a four-headed arrow, move the appointment to the correct time slot.

WRAP UP

You've had hands-on experience with quite a few skills in this lesson. You learned how to

- Add appointments and events
- Add an appointment with multiple time slots
- Schedule an event on multiple days
- Set recurring appointments
- Schedule a contact
- Change an appointment's time
- Reschedule an appointment
- Set and remove a reminder
- Delete an appointment

If you want to become more proficient with these skills, create a schedule for the next month to include your business and personal appointments and events.

The next lesson introduces you to more Calendar features that help you view the schedule in various ways.

Viewing Your Schedule

45 MINUTES

GOALS

This lesson presents you with a variety of ways to view your schedule and customize Calendar, including the following:

- Looking at a day schedule
- Viewing a week schedule
- Glancing at a month schedule
- Viewing discontinuous days
- Changing months
- Showing two time zones
- Customizing your Calendar view
- Setting permissions for others to access your calendar

Changing Calendar Views

GET READY

For this lesson you need the files EX09-1.PST and EX09-2.PST stored in the One Step folder.

When you complete the exercises in this lesson, you will have viewed a month schedule like the one shown in the accompanying figure.

CHANGING CALENDAR VIEWS

By entering all your appointments and events in Calendar, you create a professional-looking schedule. The next logical step is to find out what you've scheduled and where things are. With Calendar's Date Navigator you can quickly and easily find and view information in your schedule. By making use of the tools on the Calendar toolbar, you can navigate to any date in Calendar.

No more leafing through pages and flipping back and forth between pages in your Day-Timer® or desk calendar. No need to turn those month pages over on a wall calendar to fish around for appointments, events, and holidays. Those days are over, literally, when you have Calendar. Viewing today's schedule and any particular day, week, or month is made virtually effortless in Calendar. The power of the Date Navigator is only a click away.

In Calendar you can view single days as well as multiple days. The multiple days can be continuous or discontinuous days. *Continuous days* are contiguous days in a row, one day following the next without any breaks—Monday, Tuesday, Wednesday, and so on. You can select the days you want to see, and Outlook shows you a schedule for only the days you selected.

Discontinuous days are days not in a row—any group of days not necessarily adjacent to each other. An example of discontinuous days is Monday, Wednesday, and Saturday. Discontinuous days don't have to be in the same week or month, or even year. This view is handy when you're planning to take a long weekend off and want to see at a glance what you have planned for Monday and Friday.

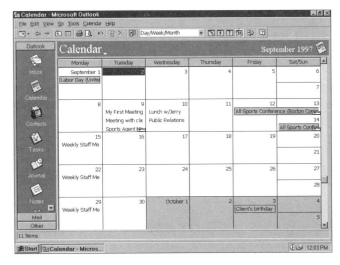

TRY OUT THE

INTERACTIVE TUTORIALS

ON YOUR CD!

Looking at a Day Schedule

For this exercise you need to import the EX09-1.PST file from the One Step folder. This file contains the schedule you worked with in the previous lesson. Your boss has asked you to check next Monday's schedule to see if you're free for a breakfast meeting. Until you see it for yourself, you may not believe how easy it is to view a particular day in Calendar.

① Import the file called EX09-1.PST. Be sure to select the Import from a personal folder file (.pst) option when you import the file.

② Click 15 in the September 1997 calendar.

You can tell which day is selected in the month calendar because it's highlighted in a different color. Your schedule shows that you have a weekly staff meeting at 1 p.m. You are free for an early breakfast! Now check today's schedule.

③ Click the Go to Today button on the Calendar toolbar.

Outlook always lets you know what the current day is in the month calendar because it is enclosed in a black box. When you go to today's date, the current day appears in blue on the month calendar. Notice that the Day button on the Calendar toolbar is still selected, even though you clicked the Go to Today button.

④ Using the vertical scroll bar next to the day schedule, scroll down through the day to see if there are any night appointments.

⑤ Scroll up to the top of the day schedule (8 a.m.).

TIP

If you accidentally select the wrong day on the month calendar, just click the day you want to view that day's schedule.

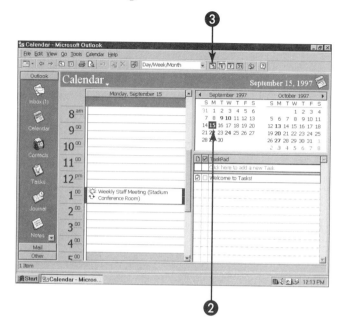

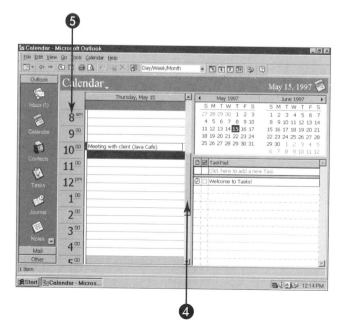

Viewing a Week Schedule

Viewing a Week Schedule

You're probably wondering what a week schedule looks like. Perhaps you would like to attend some of your client's practice games. In this exercise you view the schedule for the second week of September.

1 Scroll to the September 1997 calendar, if you're not already there.

You can click any day of the week to tell Outlook which week you want to view. For this exercise, choose September 8.

2 Click 8 in the September calendar.

3 Click the Week button on the Calendar toolbar.

The week looks busy, so you'll need to attend those practice games on a different week. On the right in the month calendar, notice that all the days of the selected week are highlighted. On the left you see two columns with appointments and events for an entire week. The first column starts with Monday at the top, followed by Tuesday and Wednesday. At the top of the second column is Thursday, ending with Saturday and Sunday. The day you selected in Step 2 (to specify which week you wanted to see) is highlighted in the week schedule.

TIP

If you unintentionally select the wrong week, click a day in the month calendar for the week you want to see, and then click the Week button on the Calendar toolbar.

When you're viewing an entire week, Outlook won't stop you from making changes to an appointment. Click the appointment and use the editing functions—overtype, insert, and delete—to make the changes.

If you want to move an appointment in week view, move the mouse pointer to the left edge of the appointment, and you'll see the mouse pointer change to a four-headed arrow. Drag the appointment to the new location.

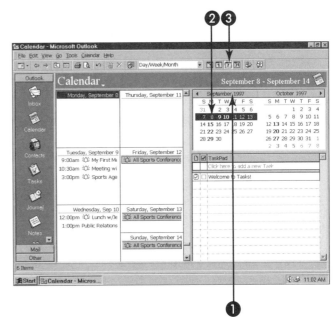

Glancing at a Month Schedule

Glancing at a Month Schedule

Until now you've seen bits and pieces of the whole monthly calendar—a particular day, today's schedule, and a week's schedule. In this exercise you view the whole month and nothing but the whole month.

1 Click the Month button on the Calendar toolbar.

The Information Viewer now contains a month schedule as shown in the accompanying figure. Notice that each week starts with Monday on the left and goes across to Saturday and Sunday on the far right. The last selected day appears in blue. In the last week you see the first few days of the following month. All-day events appear in a gray box.

Also, in the lower-right corner of a few calendar items is a light-yellow rectangle with a down arrow followed by three dots. This symbol indicates that a calendar item doesn't fit in the current view. For example, Sports Agent on September 9 doesn't show all the text for this calendar item. Take a look at the rest of that item.

2 For Tuesday, September 9, click the Go to This Day icon next to Sports Agent.

You're back to the familiar day schedule and can now see the entire item.

TIP

If you happen to select the wrong month, click the left and right arrows at the top of the month calendars to scroll to the month you want, and then click the Month button on the Calendar toolbar.

Another way to scroll through the months is to use the vertical scroll bar on the right side of the Information Viewer. Scroll up to see previous months, and scroll down to see the following months.

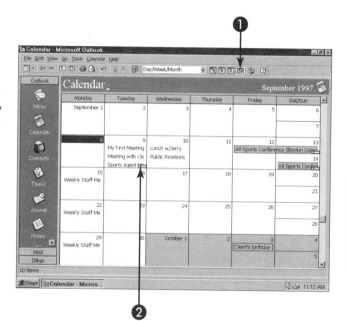

Viewing Discontinuous Days

Viewing Discontinuous Days

Discontinuous days are days not in a row on the calendar. You select the days you want to view, and Outlook displays the multiple discontinuous days next to each other on the left side of the Information Viewer. Viewing discontinuous days works in day and week view, but not in month view. Your client would like to know if you are free on three particular days to attend his practice games. In this exercise you select and view three discontinuous days—a multiple-day schedule.

1 Select September 29.

2 Hold down Ctrl and select October 6.

3 Hold down Ctrl and select October 8.

Outlook displays the day schedule for three discontinuous days. It looks like you're free to attend two practice games on October 6 and 8.

4 Click September 9 to return to a single-day schedule.

CUSTOMIZING CALENDAR

Outlook gives you plenty of ways to change months and view specific dates in your schedule. Choose any one of the methods most convenient for you, depending on where you are in Calendar and where you want to go to today. The methods for changing months and viewing specific dates include the following:

- Click the left and right arrows on the month calendars to move to previous and next months.

- Use the vertical scroll bar to display previous and next months.

- Select the Go ➢ Go to Date command or press Ctrl+G to go to a specific date in a certain view.

The Go to Date command is handy when a date is either far back in time or way into the future, and you don't want to scroll all that distance in Calendar.

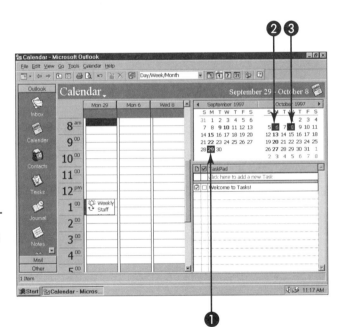

Outlook figured you would eventually get around to setting up Calendar exactly the way you want it, and it invented some tools to help you customize Calendar to suit your needs. In the following exercises you learn how to show two time zones, add holidays to your calendar, and set permissions for others to access your calendar. Many more customization options are possible, and you'll see what they are in Exercise 7 and the Visual Workout later in this lesson.

Changing Months

Suppose you want to look back at what you planned earlier in the year, or you want to make some plans for the future. How can you change the months in Calendar? With just a mouse click. Follow these steps:

❶ Click the left arrow in the upper-left corner of the month on the left side until you see December 1996.

Clicking the left arrow displays the previous month. The last day you select is selected in each month to which you scroll. For example, you selected September 9, 1997 in the previous exercise, and Outlook highlights the ninth of each month you scroll through. Notice that January 9, 1997 is selected in the accompanying figure.

❷ Click the right arrow in the upper-right corner of the month on the right side until you reach January 1998.

Clicking the right arrow displays the next month. Notice that January 9, 1998 is selected in the accompanying figure.

 TIP

For faster scrolling through the months, click the left or right arrow with the left mouse button and hold down until you see the month you want.

What if you know exactly what day you want to see? Then you're ahead of the game because Outlook has the Go to Date command that lets you instantly go to a specific date in a specific view. Go to July 4 and see what's happening on that day.

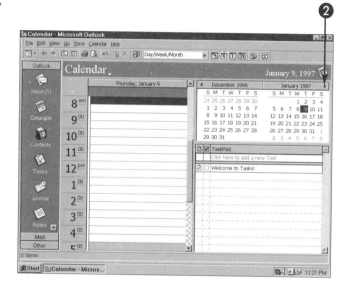

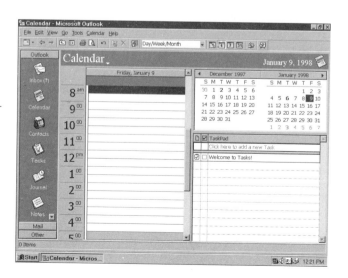

Showing Two Time Zones

3 Open the Go menu.

4 Choose the Go to Date command or press Ctrl+G.

The Go to Date dialog box appears with the last date and view selected. In this dialog box you can specify the date and view you want. The date appears in the month, day, year format (July 4, 1998). You can type a date in the same format or use slashes or hyphens.

5 In the Date box, type **7/4/98**, replacing the text you see in the box.

Three views are available in the Show in list: Day Calendar, Week Calendar, and Month Calendar. Stick with the Day Calendar option.

6 Click OK.

Outlook immediately brings you to the Day Calendar for July 4. As you can see, there are no plans for a July 4 that falls on a Saturday.

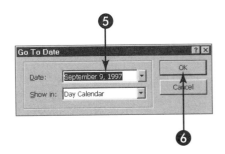

Showing Two Time Zones

By default, Outlook displays one time zone on the left side of the Day schedule in Calendar. However, you can display two times zones, one next to the other, on the left side of the Day schedule. Your contacts are located in all parts of the United States, and there may be times when you want to see what time zone they're in. In this exercise, you're on the East Coast and will be flying to the West Coast to see your client for the July 4 weekend. Eastern Time is already displayed along the left side of the Day Calendar, but you need to see Pacific Time, too. Your first time zone may be different than the one in this exercise. Try showing a second time zone.

1 Open the Tools menu.

2 Choose the Options command.

The Options dialog box opens with the Calendar tab already selected.

3 Click the Time Zone button at the bottom of the dialog box.

You see the Time Zone dialog box.

④ For the current time zone, type **ET** in the Label box, for example, or the appropriate label for your time zone.

The label ET, which stands for Eastern Time, shows at the top of the Eastern Time zone column in the Day Calendar.

⑤ Choose the Show an additional time zone option.

⑥ For the second time zone, type **PT** in the Label box, for example, or the appropriate label for the time zone of your choice.

The label PT, which stands for Pacific Time, shows at the top of the Pacific Time zone column in the Day Calendar.

⑦ Click the Time drop-down arrow.

⑧ Scroll up the list and choose a time zone. For example, Pacific Time (US & Canada), Tijuana.

⑨ Click OK to close the Time Zone dialog box.

⑩ Click OK again to close the Options dialog box.

Your schedule now contains two time zones going down the left side of the Day Calendar. Now add an appointment for your flight to the West Coast.

⑪ Click and drag from 8 AM to 3 PM Eastern Time to select six hours of time.

⑫ Type **Flight to west coast** and press Enter.

Now it's easy to see that your direct flight will arrive at 12 p.m. Pacific Time, as shown in the accompanying figure.

TIP

*To return to one time zone, select Tools ➢ Options and click the Calendar tab (if necessary). Next, click the Time Zone button, choose the **Show an additional time zone** option to remove the check mark, and click OK.*

⑤   ④

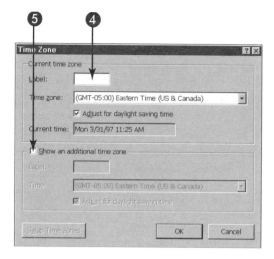

Additional Time Zone   Current Time Zone

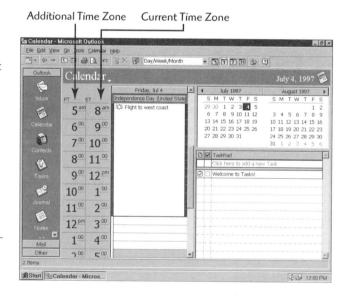

9

Viewing Your Schedule

Customizing Calendar View

Customizing Calendar View

The default Calendar view that you've seen up until now is the Day/Week/Month view. However, there are several other Calendar views you might want to use, depending on what you need to see in your Calendar at any given time. You can pick from any of these six Calendar views:

- **Day/Week/Month.** Shows appointments, events, and meetings for single or multiple days, weeks, or for an entire month. This view also shows a list of tasks. You may feel most comfortable with this view because it's similar to a paper calendar or planner.

- **Active Appointments.** Displays a list of all appointments and meetings starting with today and running into the future. Shows details including the subject, start and end times, location, categories, and whether there's an attachment and whether it's a recurring Calendar item.

- **Events.** Lists all events with their details, such as the subject, start and end times, location, categories, and whether there's an attachment and whether it's a recurring Calendar item.

- **Annual Events.** Lists events that happen once a year with their details, such as the subject, start and end times, location, categories, and whether there's an attachment and whether it's a recurring Calendar item. These annual events may include birthdays and anniversaries.

- **Recurring Appointments.** Displays a list of recurring appointments and their details, including the subject, start and end times, location, categories, and whether there's an attachment and whether it's a recurring Calendar item.

- **By Category.** Shows a list of all Calendar items grouped by category and their details, such as the subject, start and end times, location, categories, and whether there's an attachment and whether it's a recurring Calendar item.

You'll take a look at all the views in this exercise. Then you can refer to the Visual Bonus in the next section to see four of the Calendar views.

① Click the Current View drop-down arrow on the Calendar toolbar.

You see a list of six Calendar views.

② Choose Active Appointments.

Outlook displays a dialog box asking if you want to discard the current view settings because they had been changed.

③ Choose OK.

The Active Appointments view appears in the Information Viewer. The Calendar items are sorted by start date. This view displays the subject, location, start and end times, recurrence pattern, and categories.

By default, holidays do not appear in Calendar, but you can add them to Calendar whenever you want. To add holidays, you need to select Tools ➢ Options and click the Calendar tab. Next, click the Add Holidays button, choose one or more countries for which you want to add their holidays, and click OK. Outlook imports the holidays for each country you selected. Finally, click OK. The holiday appears at the top of a Calendar day, just beneath the date.

Where do those categories such as Holidays and Gifts come from? By default, the holidays are assigned to the Holidays category. The Calendar items assigned to the Gifts category were set up previously for the purposes of this lesson. But you already learned how to assign contacts to categories in an earlier lesson on Contacts. It works the same way with Calendar appointments and events. By assigning an appointment or event to a category, you can better organize your Calendar items. When you add or edit a Calendar item, click the Categories button in the lower-left corner of the Appointment window, choose one or more categories, and click OK.

④ Scroll down to the bottom of the list to see all the active appointments.

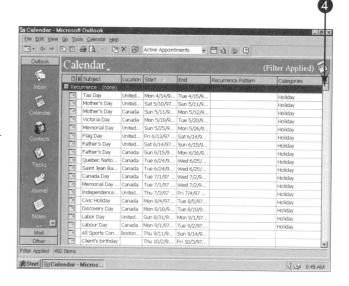

9

Viewing Your Schedule

Customizing Calendar View

5 From the Current View list, choose Events.

As you can see, the Events view gives you the subject, location, recurrence date, duration, recurrence pattern, and categories.

6 From the Current View list, choose Annual Events.

The Events and Annual Events views show you the same columns of information in the same order. The only difference is that only annual event items appear in this view.

7 From the Current View list, choose Recurring Appointments.

The items are ordered by week, month, and year. You see the subject, location, recurrence pattern, recurrence start and end dates, and categories.

8 From the Current View list, choose the last view option, By Category.

Next to the Holidays and Gifts categories is a button with a plus sign (+) indicating that you can expand each category list.

9 Click the plus sign (+) button next to Gifts and Holidays to expand both lists.

This shows all the items assigned to the Gifts categories and all the United States and Canadian holidays.

10 From the Current View list, choose Day/Week/Month to return to that paper calendar look.

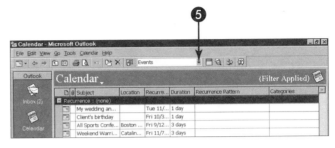

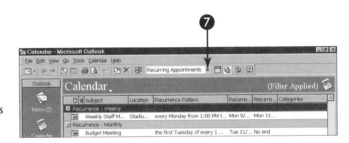

Calendar Views

Outlook gives you more ways than one to view Calendar. Click the Current View drop-down arrow on the Calendar toolbar, and then choose a view that suits your fancy.

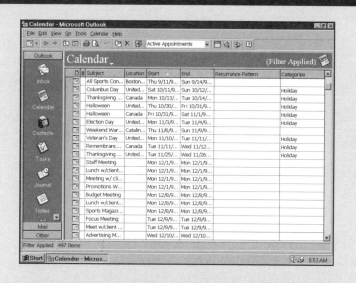

Active Appointments.

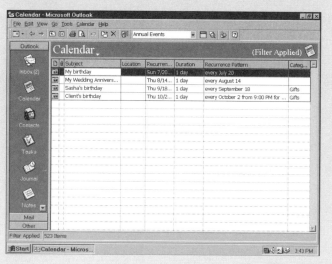

Annual Events.

continued

9

Viewing Your Schedule

Recurring Appointments.

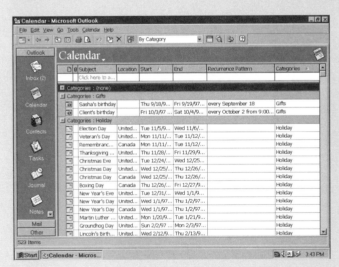

By Category.

▶ *Letting Others Access Your Calendar*

Why would you want to give others access to your calendar? You may
want to share your schedule with others when you're going to be out
of the office for a while—you're at a meeting outside the office, at a
conference, or on vacation.

1 Click the Folder List button on the Calendar toolbar.

2 Right-click the Calendar folder.

3 From the shortcut menu, choose Properties

4 Click the Permissions tab.

5 Click the Add button.

6 In the Type name or select from list box, type the name of a
person in your office for whom you want to set different
permissions.

7 Click the Add button.

8 Click OK.

9 In the Names box, click the name you just added.

10 In the Roles box, choose Author.

11 Click OK.

Now that person has access to your calendar. With the author
role, he or she will be able to read and create items, as well as
change and delete items you create.

SKILLS CHALLENGE: VIEWING A BUSY SCHEDULE

This review exercise gives you plenty of practice with viewing a
schedule that you picked up in this lesson. You use the schedule you
worked with in earlier exercises.

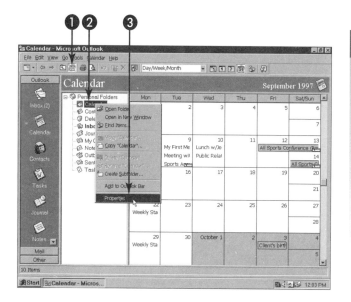

Troubleshooting

1. Import EX09-2.PST.

2. View the Day Calendar for December 1.

3. Look at today's schedule.

4. Look at a Week Calendar for the second week of December.

5. Look at a Month Calendar for December.

    How do you change months?

6. View Monday, December 8; Wednesday, December 10; and Friday, December 12.

    Can you identify the two types of multiple days that you can view in Calendar?

7. Look at a Day Calendar for November 6.

8. Scroll to January 1998.

9. Show two time zones: Eastern Time and Hawaii.

    How do you change the order in which time zones appear in Calendar?

10. Add Canada's holidays to Calendar.

     How do you import holidays to Calendar?

11. Give permission to someone in your office to access your calendar in the Reviewer role (read-only).

TROUBLESHOOTING

Finishing this lesson shows that you've learned how to view a schedule in a variety of ways and how to customize Calendar. This table offers explanations for several issues you may have come across when stepping through these skills.

Wrap up

Problem	Solution
I added an appointment and now I can't find it.	Click the Find Items button on the Calendar toolbar, type the appointment subject, and click Find Now.
I selected the wrong day and now I'm viewing the wrong week in a Week Calendar.	Click the day you want in the Month Calendar, and click the Week button on the Calendar toolbar.
I imported some holidays that I no longer want in Calendar.	For each holiday you don't want, click the holiday and click the Delete button on the Calendar toolbar.
I am showing two time zones and now want to display one time zone.	Select Tools ➢ Options and click the Calendar tab (if necessary). Click the Add Holidays button, choose the Show an additional time zone option to remove the check mark, and click OK.

WRAP UP

In this lesson you've learned some new skills. You learned how to

- Look at a day schedule
- View a week schedule
- Glance at a month schedule
- View discontinuous days
- Change months
- Show two time zones
- Customize your Calendar view
- Set permissions for others to access your calendar

9

Viewing Your Schedule

Wrap up

If you want more practice with these skills, experiment with all the views and customize Calendar to suit your business and personal needs.

In the next lesson you work with the Meeting Planner, which takes the hassle out of meeting planning.

Planning
a Meeting

GOALS

This lesson shows you how to set up a meeting in Outlook and includes the following:

- Entering the attendees
- Choosing a meeting start time and end time
- Specifying the meeting location
- Sending a memo to attendees
- Viewing the meeting planned on the schedule
- Planning a meeting when you're not on a company network

Setting Up a Meeting

GET READY

For this lesson you need the EX10-1.PST file from the One Step folder. When you're finished with the exercises in this lesson, you will have planned a meeting, as shown in the accompanying figure.

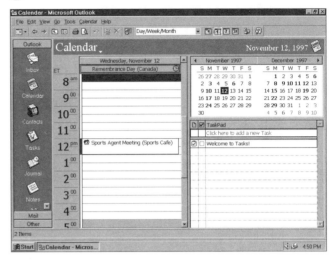

SETTING UP A MEETING

In Lesson 9 you learned about adding two types of items in Calendar—appointments and events. There is one more type of item in Calendar that you need to know about—meetings. In Calendar you can use Meeting Planner to plan a meeting from start to finish.

There are many benefits to automating the process of planning a meeting with Outlook's Meeting Planner. For starters, you can eliminate paper memos that announce a meeting. You can reduce the number of phone calls that go back and forth between yourself and meeting attendees to discuss schedule conflicts. You can also avoid the possibility of those memos getting lost in interoffice mail.

There are four major steps to setting up a meeting:

① Specify the attendees.

② Determine a start and end time and check for any schedule conflicts.

③ Specify a location.

④ Send a memo to each attendee inviting him or her to the meeting.

Meeting Planner works with Microsoft Exchange to figure out a person's schedule. If you invite coworkers to a meeting, Microsoft Exchange checks each coworker's schedule for his or her availability. Microsoft Exchange also tells you whether the person's time is scheduled as *tentative, busy,* or *out of the office.* If schedule conflicts exist, you can reschedule the meeting to a different date and/or time. If there are no schedule conflicts, you can keep the meeting date as planned. To notify the meeting attendees, you can set up the meeting as an appointment in Calendar and send this appointment information in a memo to each attendee. After you set up the

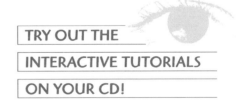

TRY OUT THE

INTERACTIVE TUTORIALS

ON YOUR CD!

meeting, you can always make changes to it. You can add and remove attendees and change the date, time, and location.

Entering the Attendees

You'll be working with the EX10-1.PST file from the One Step folder. This file contains the schedule from exercises you've worked with before. Your boss has asked you to hold a sports agent meeting and invite two sports agents. For the purposes of this lesson, you're going to invite two of your coworkers. Your first task is to enter the meeting attendees.

1 Import the file called EX10-1.PST. Be sure to choose Import from a personal folder file (.pst) when you import the file.

2 Make sure you're online and connected to your company network or the Microsoft network and Microsoft Exchange.

3 Click the Plan a Meeting button (a calendar with two people's heads) on the Calendar toolbar.

Outlook opens the Plan a Meeting dialog box. In this dialog box you can enter the attendees and determine a meeting time. At the top of the All Attendees list, your name or the computer user's name appears in the first box. The second box contains *Click here to add attendee.* This is where you enter the first attendee.

4 In the All Attendees list, click in the second box and type a coworker's name.

5 Press Enter.

6 Type a second coworker's name and press Enter.

Now you should have three attendees, including yourself (or whatever person's name appears in the first attendee box). The next step is to choose a meeting start and end time.

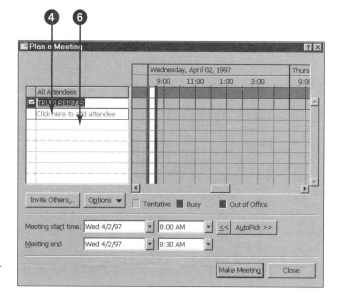

TIP

If you no longer want an attendee, you can remove the name by selecting it and pressing the Delete key. Poof! It's gone.

Choosing a Meeting Time

▶ Choosing a Meeting Start and End Time

In this exercise you choose a meeting start and end time according to meeting attendees' availability. The time grid on the right side of the Plan a Meeting dialog box shows you the meeting date and time you choose and if there are any schedule conflicts.

Beneath the time grid are colors that identify how an attendee's time is scheduled. Tentative is light blue, Busy is dark blue, and Out of Office is purple. If an attendee's block of time is free, you'll see that the block of time is clear or has no color. If the schedule is unknown because you're not online or the attendee's schedule has not been set up, then the block of time has diagonal lines.

1 In the Meeting start time month calendar, choose Wed 11/12/97.

2 In the Meeting start time drop-down list, choose 9:00 AM.

3 In the Meeting end drop-down list, choose 10:00 AM.

4 Microsoft Exchange checks the attendees' availability only if you're connected to an Exchange server. Are both of your coworkers available? If the answer is yes, then tell Outlook where the meeting will be held.

5 If the answer is no, then move the vertical bars (green and purple bars) to choose a different meeting time by dragging them to a new location on the time grid.

▶ Specifying the Meeting Location

Now you need to tell Outlook the meeting location. Follow these steps:

1 Click the Make Meeting button at the bottom of the Plan a Meeting dialog box.

The Meeting dialog box appears. The Appointment tab is selected. Isn't this deja vu? This tab looks just like the Appointment dialog box you've used before to enter your appointments. You can enter a name for the meeting, specify

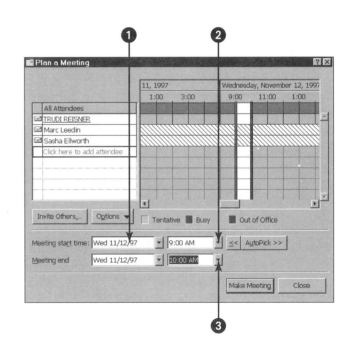

the meeting location, and verify or change the meeting start and end date and time.

If you would like to add or delete attendees or change the meeting date and/or time, click the Meeting Planner tab in the Meeting dialog box. Then you can make the necessary changes.

② In the Subject text box, type **Sports Agent Meeting.**

③ Press Tab.

④ In the Location text box, type **Sports Café.**

Now that you've given the meeting a name, notice that it appears in the title bar of the Meeting dialog box. You've also told Outlook the meeting location. For a meeting appointment, the Reminder option is not selected and the Show time option is set to Busy.

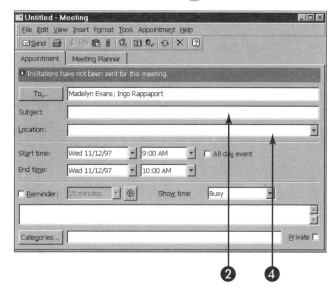

10

Planning a Meeting

The Meeting Planner

When you plan a meeting in Calendar, you need to fill in a couple dialog boxes. The Plan a Meeting dialog box lets you enter the attendees and choose a start and end meeting date and time. The Meeting dialog box lets you name the meeting and specify a meeting location.

The Meeting Planner.

All Attendees

Options

Invite Others

Meeting start time

Meeting end

Date and time grid

Tentative

Busy

Out of Office

AutoPick

Make Meeting

Sending a Memo

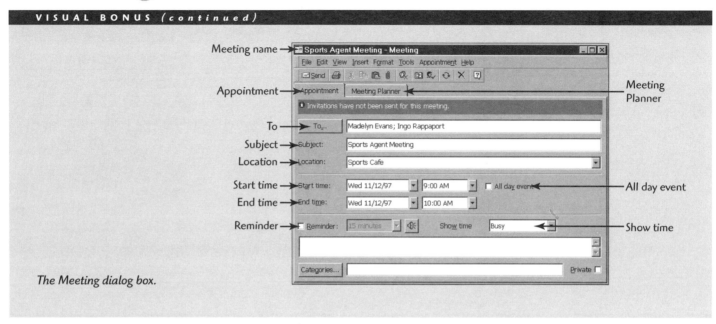

Meeting name →
Appointment →
To →
Subject →
Location →
Start time →
End time →
Reminder →

← Meeting Planner
← All day event
← Show time

The Meeting dialog box.

Sending a Memo and Responding Automatically

Notice the information message at the top of the Appointment tab that reads *Invitations have not been sent for this meeting* (see the accompanying figure). This message reminds you that you haven't sent invitations to the meeting. All it takes is one click of a button to send a memo to each meeting attendee. Click the Send button on the Meeting toolbar. This sends a memo regarding the meeting to all attendees who are invited. Outlook sends these memos through Microsoft Exchange to the appropriate people if they are connected to the Exchange server. Your coworkers will receive this memo in their mailboxes.

If there is a problem with any of the names to which you're sending the memo, then Outlook displays the Check Names dialog box. The message in the box informs you that Microsoft Windows Messaging doesn't recognize a name. You can either create a new address or change the address, as shown in the figure on the next page.

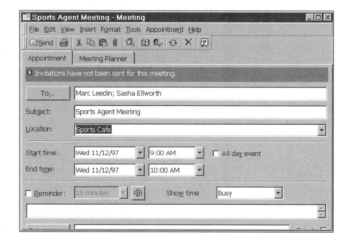

Outlook can respond automatically to a meeting invitation. You can specify how you want Outlook to respond to a meeting invitation, such as accept or decline meeting requests. To do so, follow these steps:

1 Open the Tools menu.

2 Select Options.

3 Click the Calendar tab.

4 Click the Advanced Scheduling button. The Advanced Scheduling dialog box appears.

5 If you want to automatically accept meeting invitations, click the Automatically accept meeting requests and process cancellations check box. Outlook accepts the invitation automatically, places the meeting in Calendar, and sends an acceptance to respond to the invitation. If you want to decline meeting invitations when there is a conflict with another appointment on your schedule, click the Automatically decline conflicting meeting requests check box.

6 Click OK.

7 Click OK again in the Options dialog box.

VIEWING AND PLANNING A MEETING VIA E-MAIL

After you set up a meeting with Meeting Planner, you are able to view the meeting in Calendar. A meeting item looks like a regular appointment on the schedule except for two things: The meeting has a meeting icon and doesn't have a reminder.

Keep in mind that all the people you invite to the meeting must be using Microsoft Outlook and Microsoft Exchange on a network to know about the meeting. If you are not using Outlook on a company network or Microsoft network and are not using other Microsoft Exchange servers, you can still plan a meeting with Meeting Planner. Use the New Meeting Request command in Calendar to send meeting invitations through e-mail. These invitations are sent as regular e-mail messages.

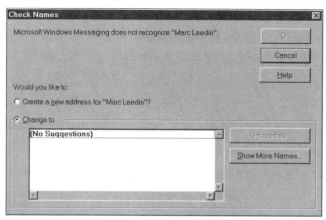

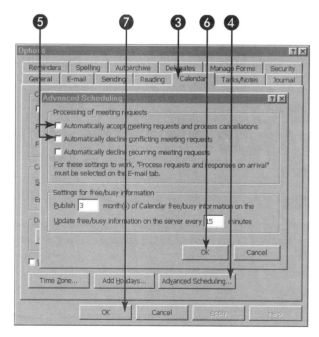

10

Planning a Meeting

Viewing the Meeting

Viewing the Meeting Planned on the Schedule

The meeting has been planned and the memos have been sent, but you need to look at the meeting planned on the schedule.

1 In Calendar, scroll to November 1997 in the Month Calendar.

2 Click 12 in the November calendar.

Your schedule should now look like the accompanying figure. The Sports Agent meeting at the Sports Café is scheduled at 12:00 p.m., as indicated by a Meeting icon (with two people's heads).

3 Double-click the meeting to open it.

4 Click the Meeting Planner tab.

On the Meeting Planner tab, the Show attendee status option is selected. You see three columns of information regarding the meeting you planned: Name, Attendance, and Response. This information shows you the responses that are tracked by Meeting Planner.

5 Click the Close button to close the Meeting dialog box.

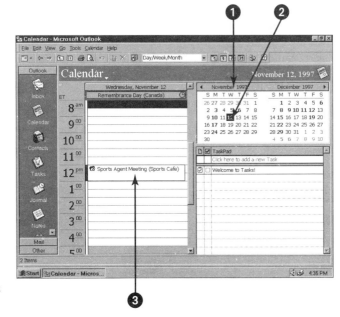

Planning a Meeting When You're Not on a Company Network

If you're not connected to a company network or the Microsoft network and other Microsoft Exchange servers, you can still plan a meeting with Meeting Planner. Instead of sending the meeting invitations over the network as you did earlier in this lesson, you can send e-mail messages to the invitees via Outlook's electronic mail system. In this exercise you plan a meeting with some All Sports Management clients not connected to your company network.

1 In Calendar, click 19 on the November calendar.

2 In Calendar, select Calendar.

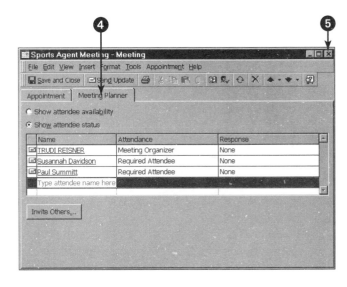

③ Select New Meeting Request (or press Ctrl+Shift+Q).

The Untitled–Meeting dialog box appears.

④ In the To text box, type a contact name.

⑤ In the Subject text box, type the subject for the meeting.

⑥ In the Location text box, type the location of the meeting.

⑦ Choose a start time.

⑧ Choose an end time. In this example, November 19, 1997 from 9:00 AM to 10:00 AM are the start and end times.

⑨ Click the Meeting Planner tab.

⑩ Click the Invite Others button.

The Select Attendees and Resources dialog box opens.

⑪ Click the contact you want to invite.

⑫ Click the Required button to choose each additional contact.

⑬ Click OK.

⑭ Click the Send button on the Meeting toolbar.

You have now sent meeting invitations to the contacts as e-mail messages. After you send the invitations, Meeting Planner tracks responses to your invitations. Let's check the responses.

⑮ Double-click the meeting to open it.

⑯ Click the Meeting Planner tab.

SKILLS CHALLENGE: PLANNING A MEETING

In this final exercise you get to review the meeting planning skills that you learned in this lesson. You use the schedule you've worked with in earlier exercises.

 1 *What are the four major steps involved when planning a meeting?*

❶ Click the Plan a Meeting button on the Calendar toolbar.

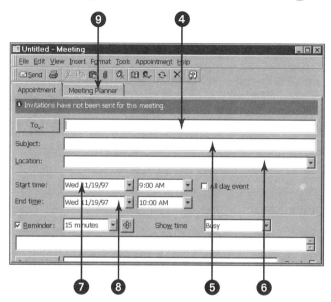

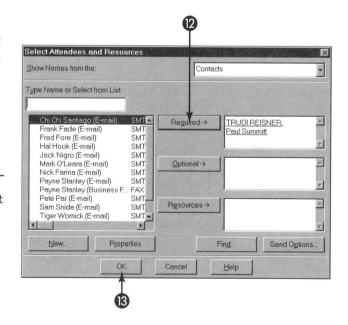

2 Enter three coworkers in the Attendees list.

> **2** *How do you remove an attendee?*

3 Choose a meeting start date and time.

4 Choose a meeting end date and time.

> **3** *Can you describe the colors and pattern that indicate the block of time for a person's schedule?*

5 If there are no schedule conflicts, click the Make Meeting button to continue. If there are conflicts, choose a different time.

6 Name the meeting Holiday Party Planning Meeting.

7 Specify Valencia Country Club for the meeting location.

8 Send a memo to the attendees.

9 Take a look at the meeting on your schedule.

> **4** *In Calendar, what does a meeting icon look like on the schedule?*

TRY OUT THE
INTERACTIVE TUTORIALS
ON YOUR CD!

TROUBLESHOOTING

Completing this lesson demonstrates that you've grasped the concepts and procedures to set up professional meetings. This table offers solutions to several problems you may have encountered when going through these skills.

Problem	Solution
There is a schedule conflict with one of my coworkers.	Choose a different meeting time by dragging the green and purple vertical bars to a new location on the time grid.
Outlook will not send a memo to the meeting attendees and informs me that the names might be incorrect.	You can either create a new address or change the address.

Problem	Solution
After I set up a meeting with Meeting Planner, I remembered that two more coworkers need to be at the meeting.	Double-click the meeting item on your schedule in Calendar, type the attendees' names in the Attendees list, click the Make Meeting button, and send the additional attendees a memo.
The location of the meeting that I planned has been changed.	Double-click the meeting item on your schedule in Calendar, click the Appointment tab, change the location, and send a memo to all attendees.

WRAP UP

Before you turn to the next lesson, remember the new skills you learned in this lesson. You learned how to

- Enter the attendees

- Choose a meeting start time and end time

- Specify the meeting location

- Send a memo to attendees

- View the meeting planned on the schedule

If you want more practice with these skills, plan a staff meeting and invite the coworkers in your department.

In the next lesson you learn how to create tasks in Outlook.

10

Planning a Meeting

Managing Tasks

You learn about using the Task list in this part, as well as how to create tasks and how to view and track tasks in various ways.

This part contains the following lessons:

- Lesson 11: Creating a Task List
- Lesson 12: Viewing and Tracking Tasks

Creating a Task List

40 MINUTES

GOALS

This lesson introduces you to setting up columns in your documents, and you learn the following skills:

- Entering tasks

- Creating a regenerating task

- Prioritizing a task

- Assigning status to a task

- Assigning a due date to a task

- Assigning a task to a contact

Entering Tasks

GET READY

In this lesson you will be working with the files EX11-1.PST, EX11-2.PST, and EX11-3.PST that are stored in the One Step folder. When you've completed the exercises in this lesson, you will have created a Task list such as the one shown in the accompanying figure.

CREATING TASKS

Outlook can help you stay focused during the day by managing your to-do list in Tasks. This Task list helps you organize tasks and projects that are significant to the various dates and appointments on your schedule. You can build lists of daily things you need to do and items you must work on to complete a project. Any item you enter in the Task list is called a task. Outlook's Tasks works like a simple project-management program—it tracks your tasks, recognizes your scheduling conflicts, and helps you stay on track with your ongoing projects.

Before you read any further, you need to know what tasks and projects are. A *task* is a specific duty you need to perform as part of your work responsibilities or projects. Some examples of tasks are completing a form, making a phone call to a contact, scheduling a doctor's appointment, and fixing a piece of equipment. A *project* is a larger goal that you need to complete and can include several tasks. For example, reviewing the budget, preparing an annual report, giving a performance review, writing a book, and designing a brochure are some projects that you might need to accomplish.

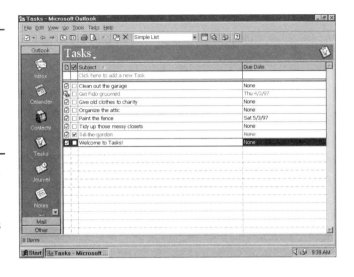

Entering Tasks

There are three types of tasks you can add to the Task list: a task that can occur once, a recurring task, and a regenerating task. In this exercise you enter a task that can occur once. One example of a task that occurs once is creating overheads for a sales presentation. In Outlook, both tasks and projects can have specific end dates. An *end date* is the date by which the work must be completed. Often, tasks and projects have vague start dates or work schedules, and typically they are not added as appointments in Calendar. Instead, tasks and

TRY OUT THE
INTERACTIVE TUTORIALS
ON YOUR CD!

appointments appear in Tasks and in a special TaskPad in the lower-right side of Calendar.

You'll be working with the EX11-1.PST file from the One Step folder. This file contains several tasks for a spring-cleaning project. There are several ways to add tasks:

- Click the New Task button on the Task toolbar.

- From anywhere in Outlook, click the New drop-down arrow on the toolbar and choose Task.

- Type the task directly into Tasks.

Your mission is to add another task to the project. To do this, follow these steps:

1 Import the file called EX11-1.PST.

In Outlook's Tasks you see a Task list in Simple List view. The first column contains task icons that represent a task type. A new task icon has a clipboard with a red check mark. You'll see other types of task icons as you progress through this lesson. The second column shows whether the task has been completed. The task item names appear in alphabetical order (descending) in the Subject column. The last column contains due dates. At the top of the Subject column is the message *Click here to add a new Task*. This is where you'll add the new task.

2 Click where it says *Click here to add a new Task*.

The insertion point appears in the box where you're going to type the task entry.

3 Type **Tidy up those messy closets.**

4 Press Enter.

You've created a task that occurs once. A task that occurs once is added to the Task list. Items in the list appear in alphabetical order from the bottom of the list to the top. The new task you entered moves down the Task list to appear in alphabetical order, while existing tasks shift accordingly.

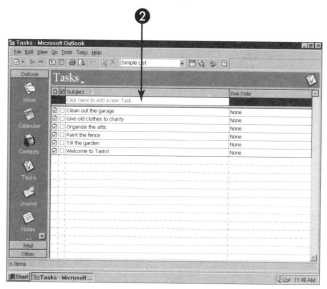

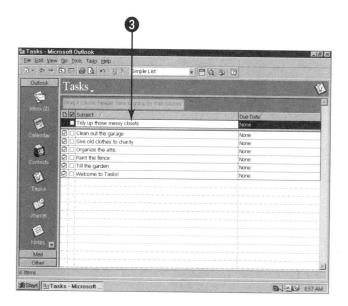

Entering Tasks

TIP

If you decide that you no longer want a task, there's no need to worry. Just click the task to select it, and then click the Delete button on the Task toolbar.

The task items that you add to the Task list appear alphabetically in descending order in the Subject column, by default. To arrange the items alphabetically in ascending order, just click the Subject heading at the top of the column. Click the Subject heading again to switch back to alphabetical in descending order.

You can easily navigate among tasks as you would in any Microsoft Office application, such as a Word document, Excel worksheet, or PowerPoint slide. Table 11-1 lists the navigation keys you can use to move around a task list.

TABLE 11-1 NAVIGATION KEYS IN TASKS

To Move	Press
Up one task	↑
Down one task	↓
To the first task in the Task list	Ctrl+Home
To the last task in the Task list	Ctrl+End
To the next page in the Task list	PgDn
To the previous page in the Task list	PgUp

After you enter tasks, you'll find that editing them is easier than you think. Already knowing how to edit text helps you edit tasks in a snap. You can edit the text in tasks the way you normally would for any other text—insert, overtype, and delete.

Creating a Regenerating Task

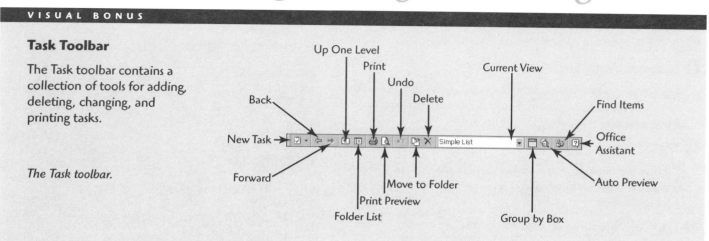

Task Toolbar

The Task toolbar contains a collection of tools for adding, deleting, changing, and printing tasks.

The Task toolbar.

Labels: Up One Level, Print, Undo, Delete, Current View, Back, Find Items, New Task, Office Assistant, Forward, Move to Folder, Auto Preview, Print Preview, Folder List, Group by Box

Creating a Regenerating Task

Now that you've entered a task that can occur once, let's discuss the other two types of tasks: recurring and regenerating. A *recurring task* repeats at regular intervals, such as daily, weekly, monthly, or yearly. An example of a recurring task is sending your boss a weekly status report every Friday. A recurring task appears in the Task list and is arranged alphabetically from the bottom to the top of the list. A *regenerating task* repeats based on the completion date. An example of a regenerating task is filing your paperwork (a chore you probably don't relish) after one week has passed since the last time you filed. Or perhaps you want to get the dog groomed after one month has gone by since his last grooming. Regenerating tasks are added to the Task list one at a time. When you mark a regenerating task complete, the next occurrence of the task appears in the Task list. You usually take your dog to get groomed once a month. Add this chore as a regenerating task.

❶ Click the New Task button on the Task toolbar.

The Task dialog box appears.

❷ In the Subject box, type **Get Fido groomed.**

❸ Click the Recurrence button on the Task toolbar.

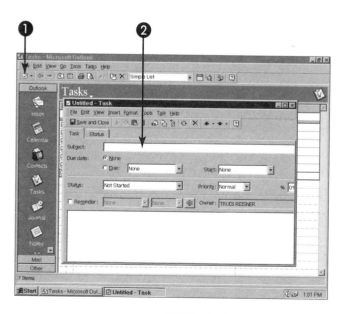

Prioritizing a Task

The Task Recurrence dialog box opens.

④ In the Recurrence pattern section, choose Monthly.

⑤ Choose the Regenerate new task option.

The frequency for regenerating the new task is set to 1 month after each task is completed. Because the dog gets groomed once a month, leave the option as is.

⑥ Click OK.

Notice the message at the top of the Task dialog box. It tells you when the regenerating task is due and how often the task will be regenerated.

⑦ Click Save and Close on the Task toolbar.

The new regenerating task appears in the Task list. In the task type column, you see a recurrence task icon that contains a clipboard with a red check mark and a gray box with two curving arrows. Notice the due date in the Due Date column.

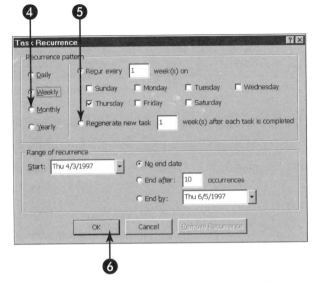

Prioritizing a Task

To organize your tasks, you can choose a priority. The three priority levels you use to prioritize a task are Low, Normal (default), and High. You assign a priority to a task to show its level of importance. Priority is useful when you want to sort tasks by how important they are.

You just bought a new sports car and you need to clean out your two-car garage to accommodate the car. Choose a high priority for the *Clean out the garage* task because it's more important than the other tasks in the list.

① Click *Clean out the garage* to select the task.

② Double-click the selected task.

③ Click the Priority drop-down arrow.

④ Choose High.

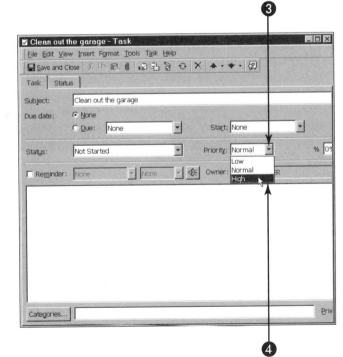

5 Click Save and Close on the Task toolbar.

You won't be able to see the priority in the Simple List view, but you can see it in the Detailed List view. Switch to that view now.

6 Click the Current View drop-down arrow on the Task toolbar.

7 Choose Detailed List.

Take a look at the second column that has an exclamation point (!) as the column heading. This is the priority column. Next to *Clean out the garage* is a red exclamation point (!) in the priority column, indicating a high priority.

A low priority displays a blue down arrow in the Priority column. A normal priority doesn't show any symbol in the Priority column.

8 From the Current View list, choose Simple List.

TIP *If you want to change the priority, repeat the steps in this exercise and choose Low, High, or Normal.*

ASSIGNING TASK ELEMENTS

Some of the cool things you can do with a task include assigning status to a task, assigning a due date to a task, and assigning a task to a contact.

Assigning Status to a Task

Assigning a status to a task can help you track the task whether you or someone else will be performing the task. The five status options include Not Started, In Progress, Completed, Waiting on someone else, and Deferred. You can even get status reports from people assigned to tasks. A status report keeps you informed about the status of a task and appears as a mail message in your Inbox. The status is displayed on a status report sent by the person performing the task to the person who assigned the task.

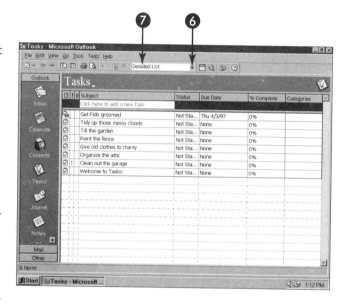

Assigning a Due Date to a Task

After you've worked so hard to finish tilling the garden, you definitely want to show that this task has been completed. In this exercise you assign the Completed status to *Till the garden*.

1 Select *Till the garden*.

2 Open the selected task.

3 In the Status drop-down list, choose Completed.

TIP *Another way to show that a task has been completed is to click the check box in the Completed column (second column) for the task in the Simple List view.*

4 Click Save and Close on the Task toolbar.

Notice that *Till the garden* has been crossed off, and in the second column, the Completed column, you see a check mark in the check box. These two visual changes indicate that the task has been completed. See the accompanying figure.

NOTE *To track the status of a task that you either have been assigned to or have assigned to someone else, you can send and receive status reports. Assigning a task to a contact is discussed later in Exercise 6. To send a status report, click the Send Status Report button on the Task toolbar. You receive a status report as a mail message in Inbox.*

Assigning a Due Date to a Task

To better organize your tasks, it's a good idea to assign a due date to some or all of your tasks. That way, a task will have a specific due date and start date so that you can monitor how long it takes to perform the task. By assigning a due date to a task, you are giving the task a specific end date, which makes it easier to set up a work schedule to accomplish the task to meet that due date. In this exercise you assign a due date to *Paint the fence*.

1 Select *Paint the fence*.

Assigning a Task to a Contact

2 Open the selected task.

3 In the Due date section, choose Due.

4 Click the drop-down arrow in the date box.

5 Choose next Saturday.

6 Click Save and Close on the Task toolbar.

In the figure at the bottom of this page, notice the due date in the Due Date column for *Paint the fence*.

TIP

To specify a due date quickly, select the task in Simple List view and click the box in the Due Date column for the task. Next, click the drop-down arrow in the Due Date box and choose a date.

Assigning a Task to a Contact

Another neat thing you can do in Tasks is assign or delegate a task to a contact. Then you can use Internet Mail or Microsoft Fax to send the contact a memo with the assigned task information in it. As your coworker works on the task, he or she can keep you apprised by changing the status for the task and sending you a status report via Internet Mail or Microsoft Fax. You'll receive the status report for a task in your Inbox.

A coworker friend of yours has volunteered to help you paint the fence. The EX11-2.PST file contains a partial list of your coworkers at All Sports Management. You need to import this list into Contacts before you assign a task to a coworker. You also need to be online so that you can send a message to the contact telling him or her about the assigned task.

1 Click Contacts in the Outlook Bar.

2 Delete all the contacts.

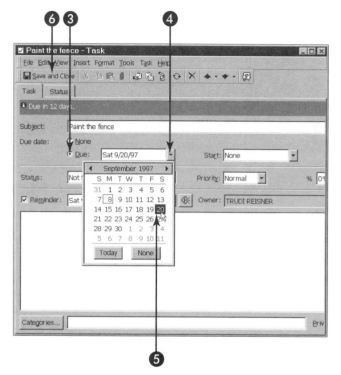

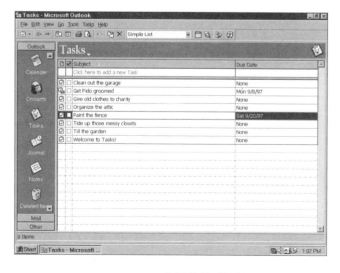

11

Creating a Task List

Assigning a Task to a Contact

3 Import EX11-2.PST. Your screen should look like the accompanying figure.

Michael Franklin is the contact used in this exercise.

4 Click Tasks in the Outlook Bar.

5 Right-click *Paint the fence.*

6 From the shortcut menu, choose Assign Task.

The Task dialog box opens, but it looks a little different from the usual Task dialog box—it looks like a memo. Above the Subject line is a To line. You can type the body of the memo in the box at the bottom of the dialog box.

7 In the To box, type **Michael Franklin.**

TIP *If you don't remember a contact's full name or how to spell it, you can select a contact from a list. Just click the To button in the Task dialog box. Choose the type of name list you want, such as Contacts or Personal Address Book. Double-click a name to which you want to assign a task.*

8 In the Start section, choose a start date. For example, next Saturday.

Take a look at both options near the bottom of the dialog box. They are selected by default. One option keeps an updated copy of the task on your Task list. The other option sends you a status report when the task is completed.

9 Click in the empty box at the bottom of the dialog box.

10 Type a message to the contact.

11 Click Send on the Task toolbar to send the message to the contact.

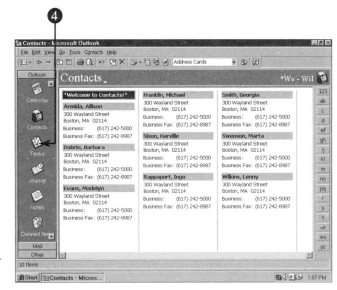

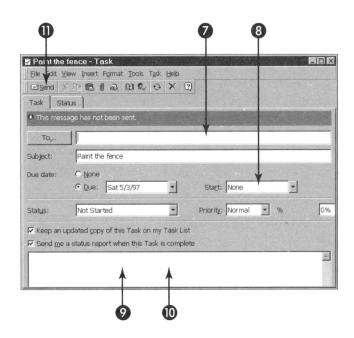

TIP

Assigning a task to a contact while you're in Simple List view and using the shortcut menu is not the only way to assign a task. When you create or edit a task, you can assign that task to a contact while you're in the Task dialog box. Just click the Assign Task button on the Task toolbar.

SKILLS CHALLENGE: CREATING TASKS FOR A WORK PROJECT

This final exercise provides a recap of the task skills you learned in this lesson. You use a Task list that contains tasks for preparing the All Sports Management presentation to a potential client.

TRY OUT THE

INTERACTIVE TUTORIALS

ON YOUR CD!

1 Delete all the tasks in the Task list.

2 Import EX11-3.PST.

3 Add the following task: **Get client's TV commercials video.**

    What are the three ways to add a task?

4 Add a regenerating task for getting a haircut monthly.

    What is a regenerating task?

5 Assign the High priority option to *Create overheads with Microsoft PowerPoint.*

6 Show that the task *Call travel agent for airline tickets* has been completed.

    What are the two ways to assign the Completed status to a task?

7 Assign a due date to the *Get financials from Accounting* task.

Troubleshooting

 4 What are the two ways to assign a due date to a task?

8 Assign the *Call outside printing service to create 35mm slides* task to a contact, and send him or her a memo regarding the task.

9 Delete all the tasks.

TROUBLESHOOTING

Now that you're finished with this lesson, you've probably learned a lot about tasks—enough to make it easier to create tasks and assign priority, status, and due dates to them. This table offers solutions to several problems you may have encountered when acquiring these skills.

Problem	Solution
I added a task and the Task list items appear alphabetically in descending order. I would like to see the items in alphabetical order.	Click the Subject column heading in the Simple list view.
I would like to delete a few tasks that I no longer need in my Task list.	Click the first task to select it, hold down the Ctrl key, and click each additional task you want to delete. Then click the Delete button on the Task toolbar. To restore these deleted task items, immediately click the Undo button on the Task toolbar.
I want to send a status report to the person who assigned a task to me.	Be sure that you're online, choose a status for the task, and then click the Send Status Report button on the Task toolbar.

Problem	Solution
When I assigned a task to a contact and sent a memo to the contact, Outlook displayed an error message informing me that the memo couldn't be sent.	Make sure you're online when you need to send a memo to a contact regarding a task.

WRAP UP

Before leave this lesson, let's review the new skills you learned in this lesson. You learned how to

- Enter tasks

- Create a regenerating task

- Prioritize a task

- Assign status to a task

- Assign a due date to a task

- Assign a task to a contact

If you want more practice with these skills, experiment with creating your own tasks for a business or personal project.

In the lesson coming up, you are shown how to view and track tasks in Outlook.

Viewing and Tracking Tasks

GOALS

This lesson demonstrates how you can view and track tasks, and you learn these skills:

45 MINUTES

- Changing task views
- Viewing tasks with TaskPad
- Sorting tasks
- Grouping tasks
- Moving tasks
- Tracking the status of tasks
- Sending a task status report
- Recording billing information for a task

Changing Task Views

GET READY

For this lesson you need the files EX12-1.PST and EX12-2.PST from the One Step folder. When you're finished with the exercises in this lesson, you will have viewed tasks with TaskPad in Calendar, shown in the accompanying figure.

VIEWING TASKS

After you add tasks to your Task list, Outlook gives you two places to view and track your tasks: Tasks and Calendar. In Tasks you can switch to eight different views to list the tasks and display their details. In Calendar you can track tasks with TaskPad. Calendar provides six TaskPad views: all tasks, today's tasks, active tasks for selected days, tasks for the next seven days, overdue tasks, and tasks completed on selected days. Viewing tasks in Calendar can help you and others who view your schedule grasp the task information quickly.

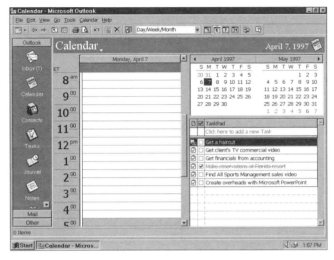

Changing Task Views

In this exercise you'll use the EX12-1.PST file from the One Step folder. This file contains tasks for an All Sports Management presentation. Following is a list of all the task views and what'll you see in each view:

- **Simple List.** Lists all tasks, showing only the subject and due date. This is the same view you see in Calendar's TaskPad (the default TaskPad view).

- **Detailed List.** Lists all tasks with their details, such as task type, priority, attachments, subject, status, due date, % complete, and categories.

- **Active.** Lists all active or incomplete tasks. The details are task type, priority, attachments, subject, status, due date, % complete, and categories.

- **Next Seven Days.** Lists tasks due within the next seven days. Their details include task type, priority, attachments, subject, status, due date, % complete, and categories.

TRY OUT THE

INTERACTIVE TUTORIALS

ON YOUR CD!

- **Overdue.** Lists overdue tasks with their details, such as task type, priority, attachments, subject, status, due date, % complete, and categories. Uh-oh! It might be time to take some tasks off your plate.

- **Assignment.** Shows a list of assigned tasks, grouped by the person to whom you assigned tasks, with details about them. The details shown include task type, priority, attachments, subject, owner, due date, and status.

- **By Category.** Shows a list of tasks that you assigned to categories, grouped by categories. The details displayed are task type, priority, attachments, subject, status, due date, % complete, and categories.

- **By Person Responsible.** Shows a list of tasks grouped by the person responsible for the task. The details include task type, priority, attachments, requested by, owner, due date, and status.

- **Task Timeline.** Displays a timeline that shows what tasks are due relative to other tasks. You can view a daily, weekly, or monthly timeline. Just click the Day, Week, or Month button on the Calendar toolbar.

NOTE

What are attachments? An attachment is a file you can attach to an Outlook item such as a task. It can be a file you created in Word, Excel, or another program. Perhaps someone sent you a file attached to a mail message. For example, a Microsoft Excel document might contain a budget spreadsheet that could help you complete a task on gathering financial information for a budget meeting. To insert a file into a task item, open the task, select File ➢ Insert, locate and choose the file, choose an Insert As option, and click OK.

By default you see the Simple List view. Your job in this exercise is to change task views and look at the information that Outlook displays in each view.

1 Import the file called EX12-1.PST.

Changing Task Views

Notice that you're in Simple List view, as shown in the accompanying figure. You see all tasks with the subject and due date.

2 Click the Current View drop-down arrow on the Task toolbar.

3 Choose Detailed List.

Outlook displays the Detailed List view with task type, priority, attachments, subject, status, due date, % complete, and categories.

4 From the Current View list, choose Active Tasks.

As you can see, the incomplete tasks appear in the list with task type, priority, attachments, subject, status, due date, % complete, and categories.

5 From the Current View list, choose Next Seven Days.

Now you see tasks that are active for the next seven days with task type, priority, attachments, subject, status, due date, % complete, and categories.

6 From the Current View list, choose Overdue Tasks.

Outlook shows you the overdue tasks with task type, priority, attachments, subject, status, due date, % complete, and categories.

7 From the Current View list, choose By Category.

If you assign a task to one or more categories, you'll see those tasks in this list. Also, you'll see the task type, priority, attachments, subject, status, due date, % complete, and categories. To expand a list, click the plus sign (+) button next to a category, and Outlook shows you the tasks assigned to that category. To collapse a list, click the minus sign (−) button next to a category.

Completed / Task type / Subject / Due Date

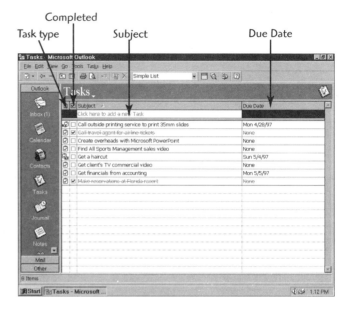

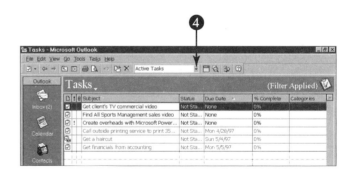

NOTE

In earlier lessons you learned how to assign contacts and appointments to categories. You can also organize your tasks by category. You categorize a task

Changing Task Views

the same way you do contacts and appointments. When you add or edit a task item, click the Categories button in the lower-left corner of the Task dialog box, choose one or more categories, and click OK.

8 From the Current View list, choose Assignment.

The tasks you assign to others appear in the list. Notice they are grouped by the persons to whom you assigned the task. You also see the details, such as task type, priority, attachments, subject, status, due date, % complete, and categories.

9 From the Current View list, choose By Person Responsible.

The tasks with the persons responsible for them are shown in the list. They are grouped by the persons responsible for the task. Notice the details: task type, priority, attachments, subject, status, due date, % complete, and categories.

10 From the Current View list, choose Task Timeline.

Here is a timeline that shows what tasks are due relative to other tasks. This view is visual and contains graphics, making it easy to see the tasks on your schedule. By default you see a daily timeline with the month and year at the top and the tasks with their task type icons beneath the dates. If a task has been scheduled for more than one day, you'll see a timeline bar above the task name. You can use the horizontal scroll bar to scroll through the timeline. Now return to Simple List view.

11 From the Current View list, choose Simple List.

In the Visual Workout that follows, you'll see illustrations and more detail on several Task views.

Task Views

By default, the current Task view is Simple List, but there are eight other views. You were introduced to these views earlier in this lesson. Here are some of the views you may be using a lot more than others.

Detailed List View.

Priority — Task type — Attachments — Subject

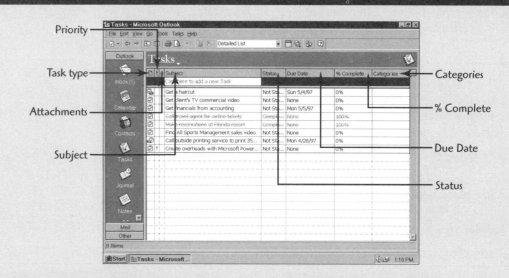

Categories — % Complete — Due Date — Status

Assignment.

Priority — Task type — Attachments — Subject

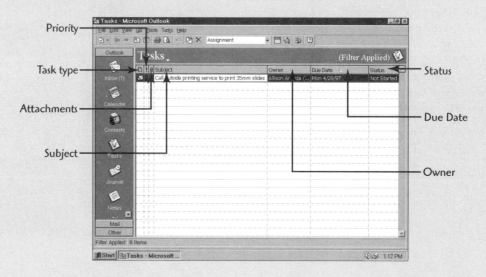

Status — Due Date — Owner

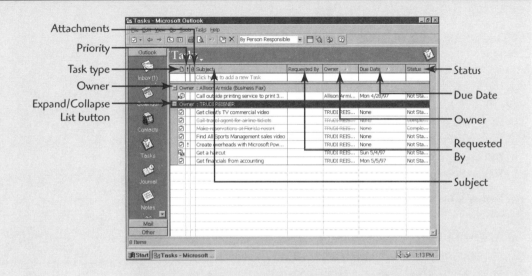

Attachments
Priority
Task type
Owner
Expand/Collapse List button

Status
Due Date
Owner
Requested By
Subject

By Person Responsible.

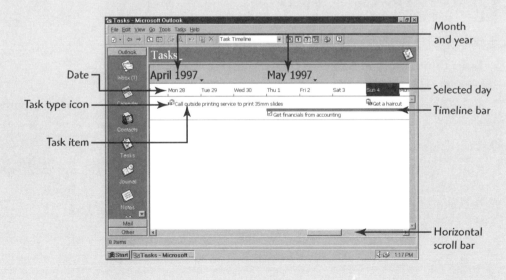

Date
Task type icon
Task item

Month and year
Selected day
Timeline bar

Horizontal scroll bar

Task Timeline.

Viewing Tasks with TaskPad

Viewing Tasks with TaskPad

The TaskPad appears in the lower-right side of the schedule in Calendar to help you track tasks. Some of the task views you saw in Tasks are the same as the TaskPad views in Calendar. The views that look the same in both places are Today's Tasks (default), Overdue Tasks, and Tasks for the Next Seven Days. When you choose TaskPad View on the View menu, Outlook gives you a submenu of TaskPad choices:

- **All Tasks.** Lists all tasks, showing only the subject and due date. This is the same view you see in Tasks's Simple List view.

- **Today's Tasks.** Lists only today's incomplete tasks (default view).

- **Active Tasks for Selected Days.** Lists only the active tasks for the days you select on the calendar.

- **Tasks for the Next Seven Days.** Lists tasks due within the next seven days.

- **Overdue Tasks.** Lists overdue tasks.

- **Tasks Completed on Selected Days.** Shows only the completed tasks for the days you select on the calendar.

In this exercise you'll look at the tasks using some of those TaskPad views.

1 Click Calendar on the Outlook Bar.

Notice that the tasks appear in the lower-right corner of the schedule (see the accompanying figure). This area is called the TaskPad. There are three columns on the TaskPad: task type, completed, and task subject. By default, Outlook shows you today's tasks on the TaskPad.

TIP

*Not only can you view tasks on the TaskPad, but you can add tasks to your Task list, too. To add a task while in Calendar, click where it says **Click here to***

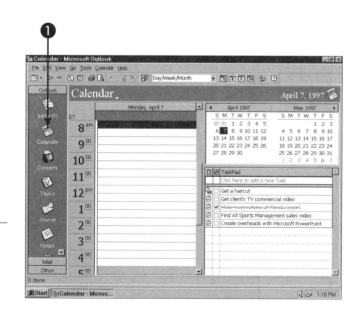

Viewing Tasks with TaskPad

add a new Task, *beneath TaskPad. Type the new task and press Enter. You can also click the New drop-down arrow on the Calendar toolbar and choose Task.*

2 Open the View menu.

3 Select the TaskPad View command.

4 Choose All Tasks.

All tasks appear on the TaskPad. When you opened the TaskPad View submenu, you may have seen the menu item Include tasks with no due date, which had a check mark next to it. This option tells Outlook to display tasks with no due date on the TaskPad. If you choose the option and turn it off, the check mark next to the menu item disappears, and Outlook will display only tasks with a due date.

Now select two days on the calendar and see what tasks need to be done on those selected days.

5 Click 1 on the May calendar.

6 Hold down Ctrl and click 2 on the May calendar.

TIP

You can select the dates before or after you select the Active Tasks for Selected Days TaskPad view.

7 Open the View menu.

8 Choose the TaskPad View command.

9 Choose Active Tasks for Selected Days.

Outlook displays only the tasks that are active for the days you selected. Next, take a look at the completed tasks on two different days.

10 Click 4 in the April calendar.

11 Hold down Ctrl and click 7 in the April calendar.

12 Open the View menu.

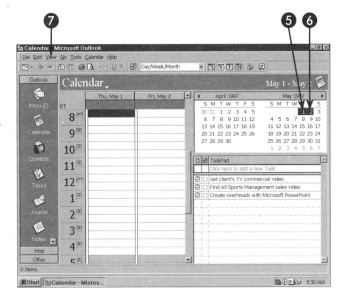

12

Viewing and Tracking Tasks

PART V: MANAGING TASKS **205**

Sorting Tasks

⓭ Select TaskPad View.

⓮ Choose Tasks Completed on Selected Days.

Notice that there are some completed tasks for those selected days. Finally, return to the All Tasks view.

⓯ Open the View menu.

⓰ Select TaskPad View.

⓱ Choose All Tasks.

Now that you've seen how easy it is to track tasks using TaskPad, let's examine how to sort tasks in the next exercise.

WORKING WITH TASKS

There are several ways to change the order of the tasks. You can sort, group, and move tasks. If you need to sort your tasks in a certain way, Outlook lets you sort by any field in the Task list. You can group tasks by a particular field in the Task list. An easy way to organize your tasks is to move them around in the Task list and the TaskPad to put the tasks in the order in which you want to work on them.

Outlook lets you track the status of tasks to see how a task is coming along and how near it is to completion. You can even record important billing information for a task to keep track of how much time you spend on a job.

Sorting Tasks

Outlook allows you to sort your tasks by any field in the Task list. For example, you may want to sort by subject, due date, status, priority, and a host of other fields. Sorting comes in handy if you assign priorities to your tasks when you create them (as shown in Lesson 11, Exercise 3). Then you can sort the tasks by priority.

❶ Click Tasks in the Outline Bar.

❷ Open the View menu.

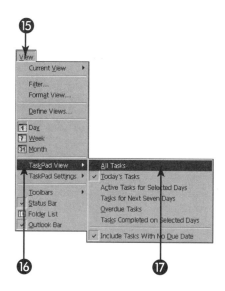

❸ Choose the Sort command.

The Sort dialog box opens.

❹ In the Sort items by drop-down list, choose a field by which you want to sort the tasks.

❺ Choose either the Ascending (low to high, such as A–Z or 0–9) or Descending (high to low, such as Z–A or 9–0) option.

If sorted by more than one field, choose either the Ascending or Descending order option in the Then by section.

❻ Click OK.

Outlook sorts the tasks in the order you specified.

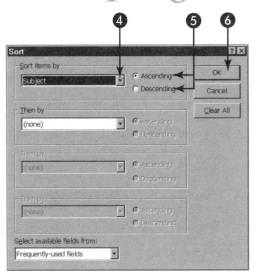

TIP

To unsort the tasks, all you need to do is select View ➤ Sort, click the Clear All button, and click OK. Unsorting tasks enables you to move each task up or down in the list.

Grouping Tasks

You can group your tasks to arrange them into categories. For example, you might want to group by start date or completion date. In this exercise you group the tasks by a particular field to better organize them.

❶ Open the View menu.

❷ Select the Group By command.

The Group By dialog box appears.

❸ In the Group items by drop-down list, choose a field for which you want to group the tasks.

❹ If you want to group by more than one field, choose a field in the Then by drop-down list.

❺ Choose either the Ascending (low to high, such as A–Z or 0–9) or Descending (high to low, such as Z–A or 9–0) option.

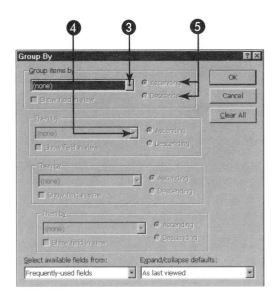

Moving Tasks

If grouped by more than one field, choose either the Ascending or Descending order option in the Then by section.

6 Click OK.

Outlook groups the tasks according to the field you chose.

TIP *You can ungroup the tasks at any time. All you need to do is select View > Sort, click the Clear All button, and click OK. Ungrouping tasks enables you to move individual tasks up and down in the list.*

Moving Tasks

The tasks you enter may not appear in the order you want, but that isn't a problem. You can move tasks up and down in the Task list as well as the TaskPad. You simply drag a task to a new location in the list as shown in the accompanying figure. If your tasks are grouped or sorted, Outlook does not allow you to change the order of the tasks by moving individual tasks up or down in the list. In this case, before you attempt to move any tasks, be sure to unsort or ungroup them. In this exercise you unsort and ungroup the tasks first. Then you move tasks up and down in the Task list.

1 Open the View menu.

2 Choose the Sort command.

3 Click the Clear All button.

4 Click OK.

5 Open the View menu.

6 Choose Group By.

7 Click the Clear All button.

8 Click OK.

9 Point to a task in the Task list.

10 Drag the task up the list to a new location.

Horizontal line with arrows

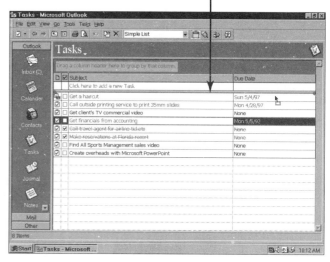

When you drag a task in the list, you'll see a red horizontal line with red arrows at each end. The line and arrows show you exactly where the task will be inserted when you drop it.

⑪ Point to any task in the Task list.

⑫ Drag the task down the list to a new location, as shown in the accompanying figure.

Tracking the Status of Tasks

After you assign or delegate a task to someone, you can track how it's coming along and how near it is to completion. The task recipient to whom you assigned the task can send you a message to tell you that he or she accepted the task and the status of the task. You can view the acceptance task message in your Inbox. All this is done through the Microsoft Exchange Server. Before you track a task, make sure you're on a network connected to the Microsoft Exchange Server and that you're online.

Earlier in Lesson 11, you assigned a task to a contact. For the purposes of this exercise, ask a coworker to send a task request to you. Then track the status of the task assigned to you by the coworker. In this exercise you'll complete the task and return it to the sender.

❶ Click the Inbox icon on the Outlook Bar.

A task assigned to you by a coworker appears in your Inbox.

❷ Double-click the Task Request message from your coworker.

Now you see a Task Request message window, as shown in the accompanying figure. The sender included a copy of the task as an attachment in the e-mail message. You can open the task and then copy the task to your own Task list. That way, you can continue to receive progress updates on the task. You can also send a copy of the task to coworkers so that they can see how work on the task is coming along.

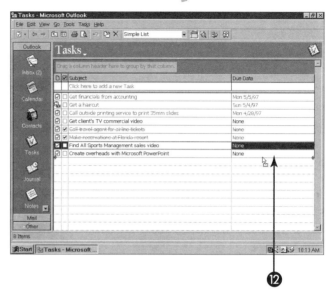

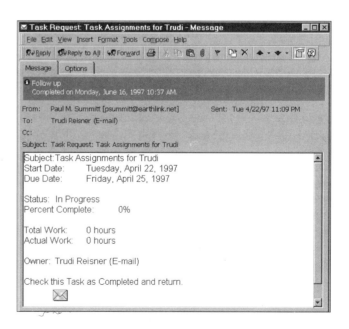

12

Viewing and Tracking Tasks

Tracking the Status of Tasks

3 Double-click the task attachment in the e-mail message box to open the task.

The Task window opens and contains two tabs, Task and Status. Outlook displays the Task tab by default.

4 In the Status section, choose a status from the Status list box.

5 In the % box, type a progress percentage.

6 Click the Status tab.

The Status tab lets you fill in the number of estimated and actual hours for the project.

7 In the Total work box, type the number of estimated hours for the entire project.

Outlook converts the number of hours you enter to a number of days, based on a conversion factor of 8 hours per day and 40 hours per week.

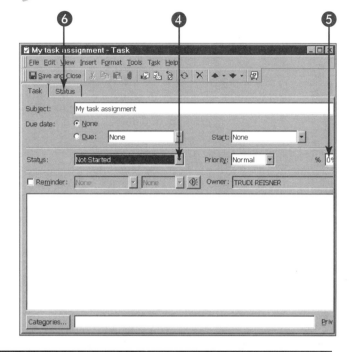

DELEGATE ACCESS

Outlook also enables you to give others access to your Task list so that they can create task items and respond to task requests for you. This type of permission is called *delegate access*. It's like having an assistant in your office to manage your paper mail and to which you delegate work. In Tasks, you can add delegates who already have permission to send on your behalf. You cannot add new delegates in Outlook. This Delegate Access feature can only be obtained through the Microsoft Exchange Server. You need to determine the level of access you want the delegate to have. For example, if you give permission to a delegate to access your folders, the delegate automatically has access to the personal items in the folders. You can give permission for the delegate to have access to your Inbox so that he or she can reply to your mail for you. A delegate can also respond to task requests that are sent to you. To grant a person any level of access means that person has send-on-behalf-of permissions.

Given that your mail is delivered to a personal folder and not a mailbox on the Microsoft Exchange Server, here's how you can add delegates. These delegates must already have permission to send mail for you. Select Tools ➢ Options, click the Delegates tab, and choose a level of access you want for the delegate.

After you've given permission to the delegate, you can send a task request to that delegate and keep track of that task. Keep in mind that these delegate functions do not work unless you are on a local area network.

8 In the Actual work box, type the number of hours actually worked on the project.

9 Click the Save and Close button on the Task toolbar.

Sending a Task Status Report

When you have some progress on the task to report, you can send a status report to anyone who is involved with the task. In this exercise you send a task status report.

1 Double-click the task for which you want to send a status report.

2 Click the Send Status Report button on the Task toolbar.

You see the Task Status Report window. If the task is assigned to you, the names of the people on the update list are already filled in. In this case, you can skip to Step 4. If the task is not assigned to you, proceed to the next step.

3 In the To and Cc boxes, fill in the recipient names.

4 Click the Send button to send the status report.

Recording Billing Information for a Task

If you want to keep track of the time you spend on a job that involves one or more tasks, you can record billing information in order to bill your client. For example, Outlook can track a task using billing information such as the total work hours, actual work hours, and even mileage. You need to record billing information for each task involved in the job.

1 Double-click the task for which you want to record billing information.

This opens the task, and you see two tabs: Task and Status. You'll be working with the Status tab.

2 Click the Status tab.

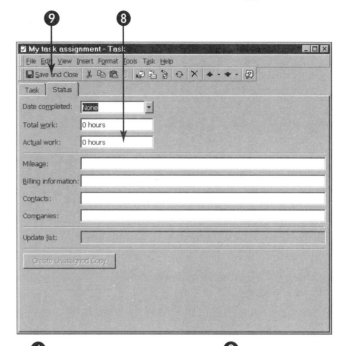

Recording Billing Information

❸ In the Total work box, type the number of estimated hours for the entire task.

Outlook converts the number of hours you enter to a number of days, based on a conversion factor of 8 hours per day and 40 hours per week.

TIP

You can change the hours–per–day conversion factor, if desired. Select Tools ➤ Options and click the Tasks/Notes tab. Type a new number in either the Hours Per Day box or the Hours Per Week box.

Then click OK.

❹ In the Actual work box, type the number of hours actually worked on the task.

Again, Outlook converts the number of hours you enter into days.

❺ In the Mileage box, type the number of miles you traveled on a task.

❻ In the Billing information box, enter the hourly fee or account name or number.

❼ In the Contacts box, fill in any contact names involved with the task.

❽ In the Companies box, type any company names for which you want to keep information. Your screen should now look similar to the accompanying figure.

❾ Click the Save and Close button.

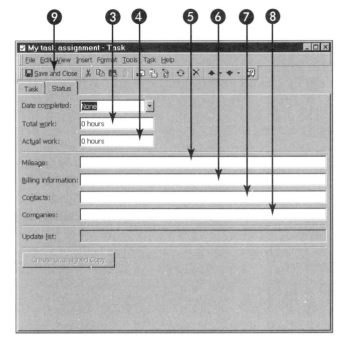

SKILLS CHALLENGE: VIEWING AND TRACKING TASKS

This final exercise reviews the skills you've learned for viewing and tracking tasks. You have been asked to view the tasks for the All Sports Management summer picnic project.

1 Import the EX12-2.PST file.

2 Switch to all the different task views and see which view you like best for your daily work.

 How do you change task views?

3 Use the TaskPad in Calendar to see all the different TaskPad views.

 How do you show completed tasks for selected days on the TaskPad in Calendar?

4 Sort the tasks by priority.

5 Group the tasks by any field you want.

6 Unsort the tasks.

7 Ungroup the tasks.

8 Move a task to the top of the Tasks list.

9 Move another task to the bottom of the Tasks list.

10 Track the status of a task.

 Where do you see a recipient's acceptance of a task assigned to him?

11 Send a task status report.

12 Record billing information for a task.

TROUBLESHOOTING

Now that you've completed this lesson, you've accomplished viewing and tracking tasks. This table offers solutions to several problems you may have encountered when learning these skills.

Wrap up

Problem	Solution
The TaskPad has disappeared from Calendar.	You may have resized other elements in Calendar such as the Folder List, appointment area, Date Navigator, or Outlook Bar. First make sure the Outlook window is maximized. Then move the mouse pointer to any border on an element, and drag in any direction that will reveal the TaskPad again.
An assigned task is not being updated in my Task list.	When you completed the task request, you may not have selected the Keep an updated copy of this task on my task list option. Open the assigned Task and check off this option.
I just read a task update message in my Inbox, but it disappeared.	When a task acceptance message appears in your Inbox, Outlook updates the task in your Task list and then deletes the message for you.
I'm not able to move my tasks up or down in the Task list.	If you have sorted or grouped tasks, you cannot move tasks in the list. You need to click Clear All in the Sort and Group By dialog boxes to clear the settings.

WRAP UP

You've practiced some new skills in this lesson. You learned how to

- Change task views
- View tasks with TaskPad
- Sort tasks
- Group tasks
- Move tasks

- Track the status of tasks

- Send a task status report

- Record billing information for a task

    If you want more practice with these skills, create your own tasks for planning a holiday party, delegate the tasks, and then track them.

    In the next lesson you get to record, change, and view journal entries in Outlook's Journal to track the things you do in Outlook and Microsoft Office.

PART VI

Working With Outlook Components

This part shows you how to use Journal and Notes, as well as how to manage Outlook components and items.

This part contains the following lessons:

- Lesson 13: Creating a Journal
- Lesson 14: Creating Notes
- Lesson 15: Working with Advanced Outlook Components

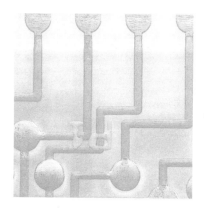

Creating a Journal

GOALS

In this lesson you learn how to record journal entries, including the following skills:

35 MINUTES

- Recording journal entries automatically
- Recording journal entries manually
- Recording a communications activity manually
- Opening a journal entry
- Changing a journal entry
- Moving a journal entry
- Deleting a journal entry
- Locating an event
- Switching journal views

Recording Entries Automatically

GET READY

For this lesson you need the EX13-1.PST file from the One Step folder. When you've completed the exercises in this lesson, you will have created a journal such as the one shown in the accompanying figure.

RECORDING JOURNAL ENTRIES

In Outlook, you can record interactions with important contacts, Outlook items such as e-mail messages, important files, appointments, tasks, or notes. You might record all the activities that have to do with a contact so that you can bill that contact for time and labor spent on a project. The Journal feature lets you record information that you want to keep together in one place.

You can record journal entries a couple ways: automatically and manually. The activities you can automatically record in Journal include an e-mail message, meeting request, meeting response, task request, and task response. You can manually record any of the activities that can be automatically recorded.

You can also automatically or manually record a document created in any of the following programs: Microsoft Access, Microsoft Excel, Microsoft Office binder, Microsoft PowerPoint, Microsoft Word, and any other Microsoft Office-compatible programs. For example, while you're working on a legal brief document in Word, you might want to record the time you spent working on it in order to bill your client.

Another way to use Journal is to manually record any activity that is not an Outlook item. Suppose you had a conversation about a current project with someone in your car pool, or perhaps you sent a memo to a business associate. You can manually record these activities in Journal. After you record your journal entries, you can make changes to them as well as move and delete them at any time.

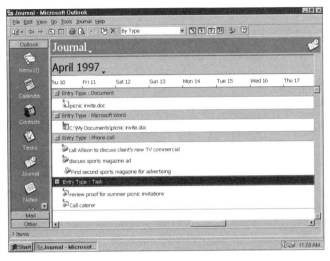

TRY OUT THE

INTERACTIVE TUTORIALS

ON YOUR CD!

Recording Journal Entries Automatically

You can record activities and Microsoft documents automatically in Journal. Some of these activities include an e-mail message, meeting

request, meeting response, task request, and task response. The
Microsoft documents you can record automatically are Word
documents, Excel spreadsheets, and PowerPoint slide shows.

For this exercise you'll use the EX13-1.PST file from the One
Step folder. This file contains the sports agent's journal entries. Your
job is to set up Outlook so that journal entries for some contacts are
recorded automatically.

1 Import the file called EX13-1.PST.

As you can see, there are journal entries in Journal. The Journal
toolbar is located at the top of the Journal. Keep in mind that
whenever you want to switch to Journal, you can just click
Journal on the Outlook Bar.

2 Open the Tools menu.

3 Choose the Options command.

The Options dialog box appears with the Journal tab selected.
In the Automatically record these items section, you can tell
Outlook which items you want to record automatically. Choose
some of them now.

4 In the Automatically record these items section, choose Task
request.

5 In the same section, choose Task response.

You probably don't want to record items for all the contacts you
have. Next, tell Outlook which contacts you want to record
items for.

6 In the For these contacts list, choose Allison Armida.

7 Choose Lenny Wilkins from the same list.

Take a look at the Also record files from section. Notice that all
the Microsoft programs are checked off, which indicates that
Outlook will record any work that you do in these programs.

8 Click OK.

From now on, when you make a task request, respond to a task
request, or work on any Microsoft documents for the contacts

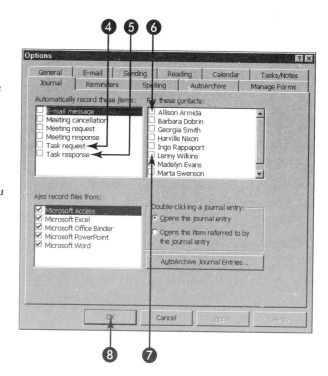

13

Creating a Journal

Recording Entries Manually

you selected, Outlook will record the time spent on the item in Journal.

> **TIP**
>
> *To turn off automatic recording of journal entries for a contact, select Tools ➤ Options and click the Journal tab. Choose the contact to remove the check mark in the check box. Click OK.*

Recording Journal Entries Manually

You can manually record any of the Outlook activities that can be automatically recorded. In addition, you can record an activity for a communications activity, including a phone call, a remote session such as going online and surfing the Internet, or a fax. Also, you can manually record an event such as a birthday, anniversary, seminar, or a conference. Other activities you can record manually include an appointment, a contact, and a note. You can also record a Microsoft document or non-Outlook items such as a conversation with a client, a letter you send to a client, or anything else you may want to record manually. In this exercise you record a phone call manually.

① Click the New Journal button on the Journal toolbar.

The Journal Entry dialog box appears. From here you can enter the journal entry information and start the timer to record the entry manually.

② In the Subject box, type **Find second sports magazine for advertising.**

The default Entry type is Phone call, which is just what you want for this exercise. However, you can choose from a wide variety of entry types that includes communications, events, Outlook activities, and Office documents.

③ In the Contact box, type **Allison Armida.**

Be sure the start date and time are correct. If necessary, choose the date and time you want to start recording. If you want to start recording immediately, you can just type **now** in the Start date and time boxes.

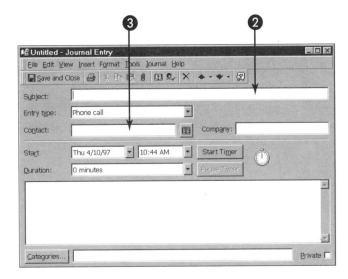

4 Click the Start Timer button.

Outlook starts the timer and begins to track the duration of your journal entry. At this point, you'd call Allison and discuss a second sports magazine for advertising.

5 In the large empty box at the bottom of the Journal Entry dialog box, type a note to yourself regarding the outcome of the phone call.

6 When you're finished talking on the phone, click the Pause Timer button.

The elapsed time is displayed in the Duration box. Your screen should look similar to the accompanying figure.

7 Click Save and Close on the Journal toolbar.

You have manually recorded an item in your journal. The journal entry is saved and added to your Journal. The journal entries are grouped by entry type. Each entry type has a plus sign (+) button for expanding the entry type list.

8 Click the plus sign (+) button next to Phone call. The plus sign turns to a minus sign (−), and you see the entries underneath.

Notice that your new entry appears at the bottom of the list. Outlook lists journal entries in chronological order with the most recent entry at the bottom.

Another way to record a journal entry manually is to open the Outlook item you want to record. Then select Tools ➢ Record in Journal, choose a start date and time, and start the timer.

You can make changes to a journal entry at any time. Just open the entry and choose the options you want. Click Save and Close to save your changes.

NOTE *You can record a Microsoft document manually. To do so, locate the document by using Outlook, My Computer, or Windows Explorer. Next, drag the document's icon to the Journal icon on the Outlook Bar. Outlook opens a journal entry dialog box for the document, and the filename appears in the Subject box. You can start the time and*

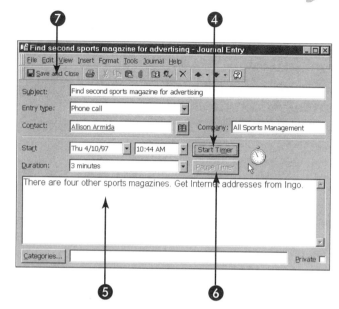

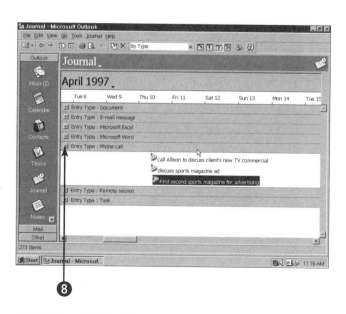

13

Creating a Journal

begin working on the document. When you're finished with the document, pause the timer. This entry will appear in Journal in two groups: Document and a Microsoft program such as Access, Word, Excel, or PowerPoint.

If you need to manually record an activity for a contact, just open the contact, click the Journal tab, click the New Journal Entry button, and fill in the journal entry information.

Recording a Communications Activity Manually

Outlook lets you manually record communications activities such as a phone call, a remote session such as connecting to another computer and downloading a file, going online and surfing the Internet, or a fax. In this exercise you learn how to manually record sending a fax.

1 Click the New Journal button on the Journal toolbar.

The Journal Entry dialog box appears.

2 In the Subject box, type **Sending a fax.**

3 In the Entry type drop-down list, click Fax.

4 In the Contact box, type **Allison Armida.**

Be sure the start date and time are correct. If necessary, choose the date and time you want to start recording. If you want to start recording immediately, you can just type **now** in the Start date and time boxes.

5 Click the Start Timer button.

Outlook starts the timer and begins to track the duration of your journal entry. At this point, you'd send the fax to Allison.

6 In the large empty box at the bottom of the Journal Entry dialog box, type a note to yourself about the fax you've sent.

7 When you're finished faxing, click the Pause Timer button.

The elapsed time is displayed in the Duration box.

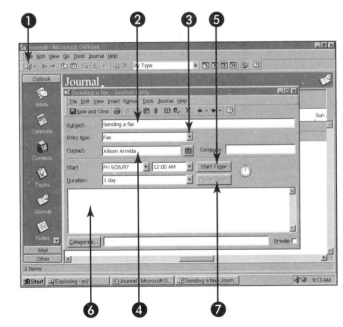

Recording a Communications Activity

Journal Toolbar

The Journal toolbar in Journal provides tools for the most frequently used Journal commands. From this toolbar you can record, view, and change journal entries.

The Journal toolbar.

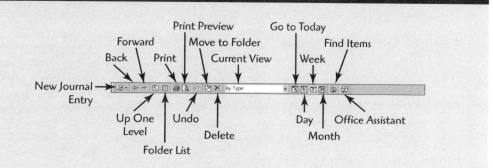

New Journal Entry

Back — Forward — Print — Print Preview — Move to Folder — Current View — Go to Today — Week — Find Items

Up One Level — Undo — Delete — Folder List — Day — Month — Office Assistant

⑧ Click Save and Close on the Journal toolbar.

You have manually recorded a communications item in your journal. The journal entry is saved and added to your Journal. The journal entries are grouped by entry type. Each entry type has a plus sign (+) button for expanding the entry type list.

⑨ Click the plus sign (+) button next to Fax.

Notice that your new entry appears at the bottom of the list. Outlook lists journal entries in chronological order with the most recent entry at the bottom.

WORKING WITH JOURNAL

After you record journal entries, you may want to make some changes to them. The following exercises show you how to open a journal entry, change or move the entry, and delete the entry. You'll also learn how to locate an event and how to switch views in Journal.

Opening a Journal Entry

▶ Opening a Journal Entry

Before you make any changes to a journal entry, you need to know how to open an entry. It's very simple to do. Just follow these steps:

1 In Journal, double-click a journal entry.

Outlook displays the Journal Entry dialog box, as shown in the accompanying figure.

What if you have an item or attachment (such as a Microsoft Word document) within a journal entry, and you need to open that item? Here's how you can open an item within a journal entry.

2 In Journal, double-click a journal entry that contains the item you want to open.

Outlook displays the Journal Entry dialog box. You see an item icon in the large box at the bottom of the dialog box.

3 Double-click the item icon.

Outlook displays the item, as shown in the figure at the bottom of this page.

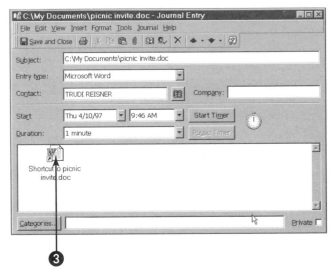

▶ Changing a Journal Entry

Once you record a journal entry, it's never too late to change the entry. You can add more information; delete any text you want; type over existing information; and cut, copy, and paste text.

1 In Journal, double-click a journal entry.

Outlook displays the Journal Entry dialog box, as shown in the accompanying figure.

2 Make any necessary changes by typing or using delete, cut, copy, and paste.

3 Click the Save and Close button on the Journal toolbar.

This saves the changes you made.

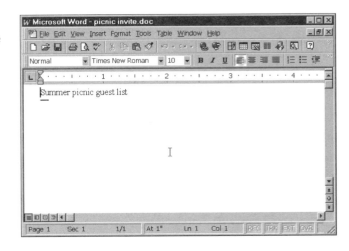

Moving a Journal Entry

Some of your journal entries have a start time, and it's possible to accidentally record one of these entries in the wrong place in the timeline. For example, if you create a task for yourself to organize your desk drawers next week, and instead you start the project tomorrow, the start time will still be next week. The duration time you record in Journal will be correct, but the entry will be in the wrong week. In a case such as this one, you can move the entry and the recorded duration to the correct start date.

NOTE *When you move a journal entry, Outlook doesn't change any information about the item, document, or contact to which the entry refers. It just moves the entry to a different time slot on the timeline.*

❶ In Journal, double-click a journal entry you want to move.

Outlook displays the Journal Entry dialog box.

❷ Specify a new start date.

❸ Specify a new time.

❹ Click the Save and Close button on the Journal toolbar.

This saves the changes you made, as shown in the accompanying figure.

Deleting a Journal Entry

Outlook's Journal can accumulate many journal entries when you record items and documents automatically and manually on a regular basis. To clean out the journal entries you no longer want, you can just delete them. For example, you may want to delete the journal entries you are creating in this lesson, as well as any other ones with which you're practicing. In this lesson you delete one journal entry.

❶ In Journal, click a journal entry you want to delete.

This selects the journal entry, which appears highlighted in a different color.

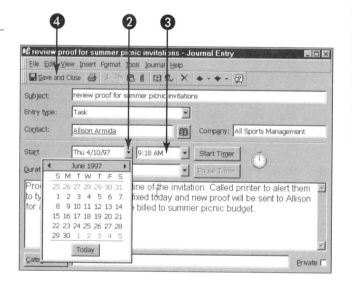

Locating an Event

② Click the Delete button on the Journal toolbar.

The journal entry disappears. The remaining entries adjust accordingly in Journal's list.

TIP *To delete more than one journal entry in Journal, first select the journal entries you want to delete. To select adjacent journal entries, click the first entry, hold down Shift, and click the last entry you want to select. If the journal entries are not adjacent, click the first entry, hold down Ctrl, and click each additional journal entry you want to select. Finally, click the Delete button on the Journal toolbar.*

Locating an Event

In this exercise you learn how to locate an event with the Find Items command. In an earlier lesson you used the Find Items command to locate a contact. In this exercise you locate the journal entry for calling the caterer.

❶ Click the Find Items button on the Journal toolbar.

Outlook displays the Find dialog box. The Look for box and In box already contain Journal because you're currently in Journal. But you can change to any Outlook component by choosing one from the Look for drop-down list. Also, notice the Journal Entries tab is currently selected.

② Type **call caterer** in the Search for the word(s) box.

❸ Click Find Now.

Outlook displays the journal event in a list at the bottom of the Find dialog box. From here you can open the event.

TIP *If Outlook doesn't find what you're searching for, the message **There are no items to show in this view** appears in the list at the bottom of the Find dialog box. Verify your search criteria, and then enter the correct search criteria to search again.*

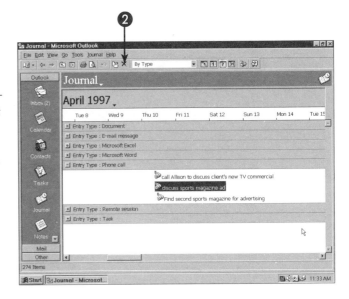

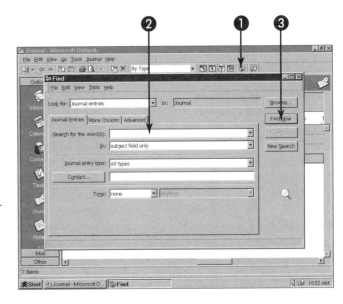

④ Double-click a journal entry item in the list.

At this point you can make changes to the event. But for your purposes, close everything because you're finished finding items.

⑤ Click the Close button in the upper-right corner of the journal entry window.

⑥ Click the Close button in the upper-right corner of the Find dialog box.

Switching Journal Views

Outlook has several Journal views that you can select from the Current View list box on the Journal toolbar. Some of the views are timeline views; you saw the Task Timeline view earlier in Lesson 12. The other views are filtered table views. A *filtered table view* shows some fields and hides others. Following is a list of the Journal views and their description:

- **By Type.** Shows a timeline grouped by type of item, such as Document, Message, Remote Session, or Phone Call.

- **By Contact.** Shows a timeline grouped by contact name.

- **By Category.** Displays a timeline grouped by categories. You can assign journal entries to one or more categories just as you would categorize contacts, appointments, and tasks.

- **Entry List.** Lists journal entries with details, such as item type, whether an item has an attachment, subject, start, duration, contact, and categories. You can sort by any field in the list except Categories.

- **Last Seven Days.** Lists journal entries filtered by Date for entries created in the last seven days.

- **Phone Calls.** Lists journal entries filtered by Type for phone calls.

By default, Journal is set to the By Type view. In this exercise you switch to several other Journal views.

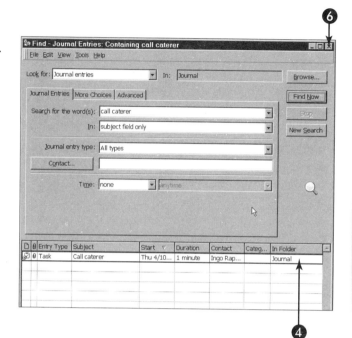

Skills Challenge

1 Click the Current View drop-down arrow on the Journal toolbar.

2 Choose By Contact.

If you see a message informing you that the current view settings have been changed, choose the first option to discard the view settings, and then click OK.

3 Click the plus sign (+) button for each entry type to expand each list.

4 Scroll to the right to see the rest of the long entries.

The accompanying figure shows the journal entries for all the contacts.

5 From the Current View list, choose Entry List.

The accompanying figure shows all the items that have been entered into the journal and the details about them.

6 From the Current View list, choose Phone Calls.

All the phone call journal entries appear in the list, including the details. See the accompanying figure.

7 From the Current View list, choose By Type to return to the default view.

SKILLS CHALLENGE: RECORDING JOURNAL ENTRIES

In this review exercise you practice the journal skills you've picked up in this lesson. Your mission is to record journal entries for the All Sports Management advertising campaign.

1 Import EX13-2.PST.

2 Assign a task to a contact to review the advertising budget. This task request will be recorded automatically.

 Which command do you use to set up recording journal entries automatically?

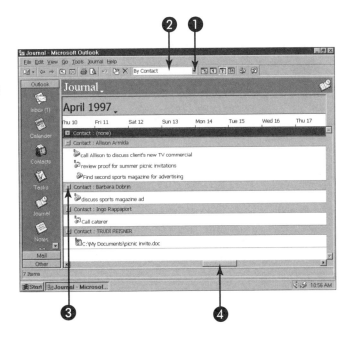

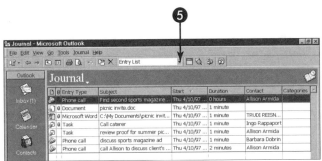

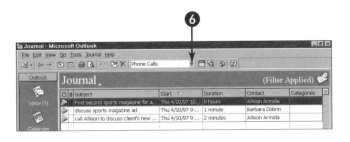

3 Record a phone call to a photographer manually.

 2 *How can you tell Outlook to start manually recording the item immediately?*

4 Manually record the activity on one of your Word documents.

 3 *What are the two ways to record an item manually?*

5 Open a journal entry.

6 Add more information to the journal entry.

7 Save and close the journal entry.

8 Move a journal entry to a different place on the timeline.

9 Delete one journal entry.

10 Locate the journal entry for the advertising budget task request.

11 Switch to all the different Journal views.

 4 *Which Journal views list all the entries recorded in Journal?*

TRY OUT THE

INTERACTIVE TUTORIALS

ON YOUR CD!

13

Creating a Journal

TROUBLESHOOTING

Now that you're finished with this lesson, you've successfully created a journal. This table offers solutions to several problems you may have run into when learning these skills.

Problem	Solution
I tried to record the activity on my Microsoft Word document automatically, but the entry doesn't appear in Journal.	First make sure that Microsoft Word is installed on your computer. Then choose Tools ➤ Options and click the Journal tab. In the Also record files from section, choose the Microsoft Word option and click OK.

continued

Wrap up

Problem	Solution
I tried to record a task automatically, but I can't find it in Journal.	You can record a task manually in Journal, but not automatically.
The start date and time recorded for a journal entry is incorrect.	Open the journal entry and change the start date and time.
I recorded the wrong journal entry.	Select the journal entry and click the Delete button on the Journal toolbar.

WRAP UP

Take a look at the new skills you've practiced in this lesson. You learned how to

- Record journal entries automatically
- Record journal entries manually
- Record a communications activity manually
- Open a journal entry
- Change a journal entry
- Move a journal entry
- Delete a journal entry
- Locate journal entries
- Switch journal views

If you want more practice with these skills, record all the phone calls you make to clients for billing purposes. The next lesson gets you acquainted with Outlook's Notes feature so that you can create electronic sticky notes.

Creating Notes

GOALS

This lesson shows you how to use Outlook's Notes features and highlights the following skills:

35 MINUTES

- Adding a note

- Closing a note

- Opening a note

- Moving a note

- Resizing a note

- Changing the text in a note

- Changing the font formatting for notes

- Changing note color

- Showing or hiding the date and time on notes

- Deleting a note

- Changing notes views

Adding a Note

GET READY

For this lesson you need the EX14-1.PST and EX14-2.PST files stored in the One Step folder. When you're finished with the exercises in this lesson, you will have created notes such as those shown in the accompanying figure.

CREATING NOTES

Outlook's Notes enables you to create the electronic version of paper sticky notes and keep them right on your computer screen. With Notes you can write down your brilliant ideas, reminders to yourself or for others, questions you want to ask, instructions, directions, and anything you would normally jot down on a paper sticky note. You can leave notes open onscreen as you work, and you can close a note whenever you wish.

For easier viewing, you can move a note (whether it's open or closed) to wherever you want onscreen. You can also shrink or enlarge the note.

After you work with Notes, you'll probably be able to reduce the number of yellow paper sticky notes that you keep on your desk or post all over your computer monitor.

Adding a Note

In this exercise you'll work with the EX14-1.PST file stored in the One Step folder. This file contains several business and personal notes. There are two ways to create a new note: Click the New Note button on the Notes toolbar, or click the New drop-down arrow on any Outlook component toolbar and choose Note.

1 Import the file called EX14-1.PST.

2 Click the New Note button on the Notes toolbar.

A yellow note appears in a window with the date and time in the lower-left corner of the window. Outlook always places a new blank note near the upper-left corner of the Outlook window. This is the default location for a new note.

3 Type **Drink 8 glasses of water today.**

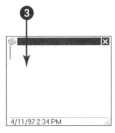

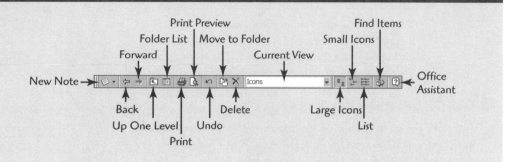

The Notes Toolbar

The Notes toolbar offers tools for adding, deleting, and printing notes, as well as changing the icons onscreen.

The Notes toolbar.

VISUAL BONUS

The Notes Toolbar

The Notes toolbar offers tools for adding, deleting, and printing notes, as well as changing the icons onscreen.

The Notes toolbar.

14

Creating Notes

Closing a Note

After you add a note, the note remains open onscreen. You can leave a note open onscreen as you work and reference it whenever necessary. If you no longer need to reference a note, you can put away that note. Outlook displays the closed note in Notes.

❶ Click the Close button in the upper-right corner of the note window.

Your note appears beneath the first row of notes that you imported, starting a second row of notes. Normally, a new note appears at the far left end of all the notes. When you add a note, it becomes the first note in the list. As you can see, Microsoft provides a default note for you that contains quite a bit of text. This note is long and rectangular and runs into the second row of notes. Remove the default note because you don't need it.

❷ Click the Microsoft note that begins with *Notes are the electronic equivalent of.*

The text in the note is highlighted in a different color, which indicates that the note is selected.

TRY OUT THE

INTERACTIVE TUTORIALS

ON YOUR CD!

Opening a Note

TIP

If you want to select more than one note, click the first note, hold down Ctrl, and then click each additional note you want to select. The text in each of the selected notes is highlighted in a different color.

3 Click the Delete button on the Notes toolbar.

The note disappears. Your notes should now look like the ones in the accompanying figure. You delete another note later in this lesson, and you also learn how to delete more than one note simultaneously.

Opening a Note

You may want to keep one or two of the most important notes open onscreen. It's handy to keep notes open so that you can view them at a glance whenever you need to reference a note or when you're in a hurry. It's a matter of convenience to keep notes open on your screen. In this exercise you open the note you closed in the "Closing a Note" exercise.

1 Double-click the note that begins with *Drink 8.*

Your note opens as shown in the accompanying figure. When you open a note, Outlook always displays the note where it last appeared onscreen. In this case, you created the note near the upper-left corner of the Outlook window; therefore, the note opens in that same location. Now open another note.

2 Double-click the note that begins with *Bring task list.*

The second note opens right on top of the first note you opened. As a result, you cannot see the first note. This happened because Outlook always displays an open note in the same location where it last appeared onscreen. However, you can move a note, and you learn how in the next exercise.

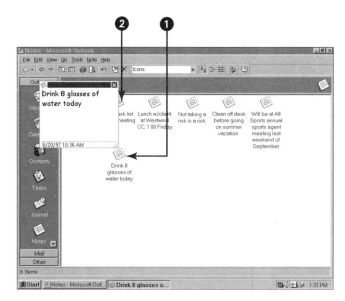

TIP

*If you switch to a different Microsoft program or
another application, Outlook shrinks each open note
to a button and displays each button on the Windows
taskbar. You can open each note again by clicking
each note button on the Windows taskbar. Outlook displays each note
on top of the program window in which you're currently working.*

Moving a Note

As you saw earlier, an open note was placed on top of another open
note. This is one case where you need to move a note. Another
situation might be an open note covering up something that you
want to see on your screen. That's no problem because you can move
the note around the screen. You can also move closed note icons in
Notes to place them in any order you want. In this exercise you move
the open note so that you can see the note underneath it.

1 Point to the title bar (a different colored bar across the top) of
the open note that begins with *Bring task list*.

The mouse pointer shape is an arrow that points up and toward
the left.

2 Drag the note by its title bar down to the left corner of the
Outlook window.

The note appears in its new location. The note's title bar is a
different color, indicating that the note is selected. Now you
can see the first note you created in the upper-left corner of
the Outlook window. This note is not selected because the title
bar is yet another color. Only one open note can be selected at
one time. Now close both notes.

3 Click the Close button on each note to close both notes.

As you can see, the note icons in the Information Viewer are not
lined up in a row. You can change that by moving the individual
notes icons. Move the note in the second row up to the
beginning of the first row.

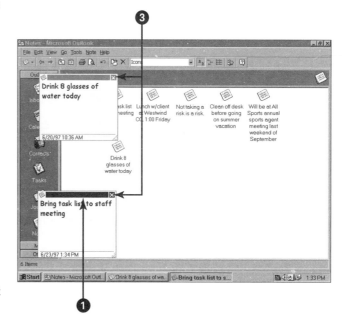

14

Creating Notes

Resizing a Note

④ Drag the note in the second row to the beginning of the first row.

Now the note is the first note icon in the second row. Next, move the *Not taking a risk is a risk* note to the second row.

⑤ Select and drag the *Not taking a risk is a risk* note next to the first note in the second row.

The note now appears as the first note in the second row. Close up the gaps between the notes in the first row by moving the note icons to the left.

⑥ Select and drag each note in the first row so that they are lined up and closer to each other.

You now have two neat rows of notes as shown in the accompanying figure.

TIP   *A quick way to line up the note icons in a row is to select View ➢ Line Up Icons.*

Resizing a Note

Notes come in three sizes: small, medium, and large. By default the note size is set to medium. But you can change the note size whenever you feel like it. For example, when an open note contains a lot of text, you might not be able to see the entire contents with one glimpse. In such a case, you need to enlarge the note to accommodate the lengthy text. You can also shrink an open note so that it doesn't cover up something on the screen you want to see. Enlarging or shrinking a note is just like resizing any window.

NOTE   *By default, the note size is set to the Medium option. To change the default note size, select Tools ➢ Options and click the Tasks/Notes tab. In the Notes defaults section, in the Size list box, choose the size you want. You can select Small, Medium, or Large. Then click OK. All*

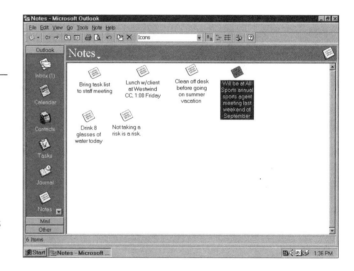

the notes appear in the size you selected. Changing the default note size doesn't affect resizing all notes by dragging.

❶ Double-click the note that begins with *Will be at All Sports* to open it.

The note opens near the left corner of the Outlook window. If a note is near the edge of a window, you won't be able to successfully enlarge the note. You must move the note toward the center of the Information Viewer so that more space surrounds it.

❷ Move the note to the center of the Information Viewer.

❸ Point to the bottom border of the note window until you see a black vertical double-arrow.

The mouse pointer is now a resizing arrow that lets you enlarge or shrink the note window.

❹ Drag the bottom border of the note window down about an inch.

The note becomes taller.

❺ Point to the right border of the note window until you see a black horizontal double-arrow.

❻ Drag the right border of the note window to the right about an inch.

The note becomes wider as shown in the accompanying figure.

❼ Close the note.

TIP

For faster resizing, point to a corner of the note window until you see a black diagonal double-arrow. This arrow lets you resize two sides of the window at once. Now drag the corner of the note in the direction you want to either stretch or shrink it.

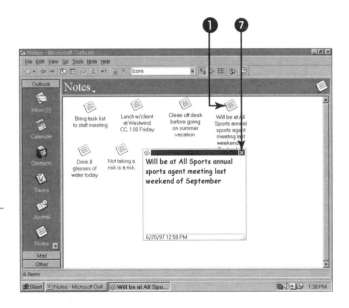

Changing the Text in a Note

FORMATTING NOTES

After you've created a note, you can change its text. You edit text in a note as you would in any word-processing program by using insert, overtype, delete, copy, and move.

Outlook also lets you enhance the text in your note by changing the font formatting. You can pick from a wide variety of fonts, font sizes, and font styles to change the look of your text in a note.

By default, the background color of a note is yellow. However, you have a wide array of other background colors to choose from — blue, green, pink, and white.

The time and date appear at the bottom of a note by default; however, you can hide the time and date for all notes at any time. Then you can redisplay the time and date for all notes whenever necessary.

You can view notes in various ways. By default you see the notes as large icons in Icon Notes view. There are two other icon choices: small icons and list. You can experiment with the icon choices to see what you like best. You'll find that the icon views in Notes and windows in Microsoft Windows are similar. You can switch to several Notes views, including Notes List, Next Seven Days, By Category, and By Color. Outlook also enables you to delete one or more notes whether they're open or closed.

Changing the Text in a Note

The first text you type in a note may not be exactly what you want to convey. Outlook lets you easily make changes to the text. In this exercise you learn how to add and delete text in a note. Go ahead and increase the amount of water to drink to nine glasses.

① Double-click *Drink 8 glasses of water today* to open it.

② Click before the 8.

③ Press the Delete key.

④ Type **9.**

As you can see in the accompanying figure, your note reflects the change.

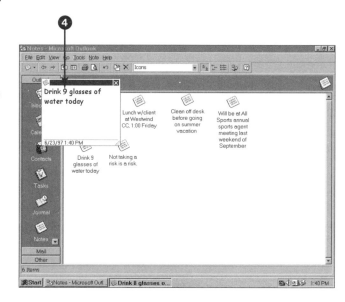

5 Close the note.

Now you've rearranged the notes in a new row beneath the first row of notes, making it easier to find them.

Changing the Font Formatting for Notes

You can also change the font formatting for note text, such as the font, font size, and font style. Font formatting can help you draw attention to an important note by adding bold, italic, or increasing the font size. Outlook lets you change the font formatting only for all notes and not for individual notes. In other words, when you make a font-formatting change for a particular note, this change affects all existing notes, too.

1 Open the Tools menu.

2 Choose the Options command.

3 Click the Tasks/Notes tab.

The Notes options appear in the Notes defaults section at the bottom of the Tasks/Notes tab. Next to the Font button is the default font size and font. You see 10-point Comic Sans MS in the Font box as shown in the accompanying figure.

4 Click the Font button.

The Font dialog box appears. From here you can select a font, font size, font style, special effects such as strikeout or underline, and font color.

5 Choose any options you want; for example, Garamond, Bold, 11-point.

6 Click OK to close the Font dialog box.

7 Click OK again to close the Options dialog box.

8 Open any note.

As you can see in the accompanying figure, the text in the note has changed according to the font formatting you applied.

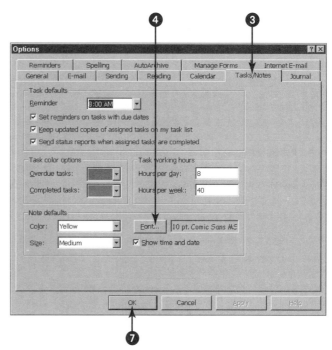

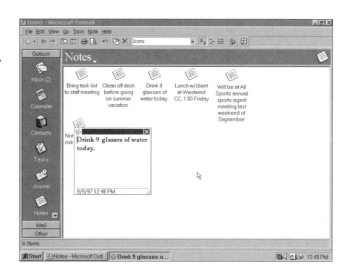

14

Creating Notes

⑨ Open another note.

Font formatting for the text in this note has also changed.

⑩ Close both notes.

Changing Note Color

Outlook gives you other note colors to choose from besides yellow (the default color) — blue, green, pink, and white. Changing the notes to different colors can help you better organize your notes. Perhaps you want your work notes in yellow, personal notes in pink, and famous quotes in blue. In this exercise you change the background color of a note.

① Right-click the *Not taking a risk* note in the second row.

② From the shortcut menu, choose Color.

The Color submenu appears.

③ From the Color submenu, choose Blue.

The background color of the note turns blue.

④ Open the blue note.

As you can see, the note color is blue.

⑤ Close the note.

TIP

If you want to change the default note color for all new notes, select Tools ➤ Options and click the Tasks/Notes tab. In the Notes defaults section, in the Color list box, choose the color you want and then click OK. All the notes appear in the color you selected. If you change the default note color, you will still be able to change the note color for any individual note.

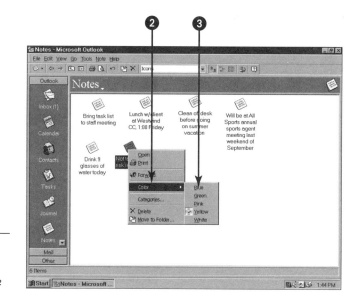

Showing or Hiding the Date and Time on Notes

By default, the date and time appear at the bottom of every note. Outlook displays the date and time when the note was last modified in any way, such as changing the text, font format, color, and so on. This information can be helpful, but if you don't want to display it, you can hide the date and time. Outlook will still keep track of the date and time the note was last changed, but the information will not be displayed on the note. In this exercise you hide the date and time on the notes.

1 Open the Tools menu.

2 Choose the Options command.

3 Click the Tasks/Notes tab (if necessary).

4 Click the Show time and date check box to remove the check mark in the box.

5 Click OK.

6 Double-click any note to open it.

The date and time no longer appear at the bottom of the open note, as shown in the accompanying figure. Now open another note.

7 Double-click any note to open it.

The date and time don't show up on this note, either. Now turn on the Show time and date option to redisplay the date and time on all notes.

8 Open the Tools menu.

9 Choose the Options command.

10 Click the Show time and date check box to insert a check mark in the box.

11 Click OK.

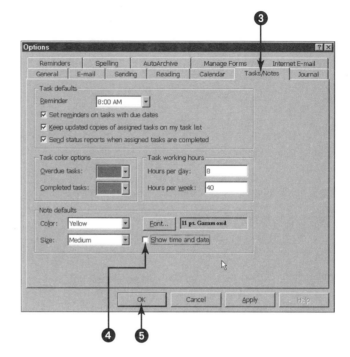

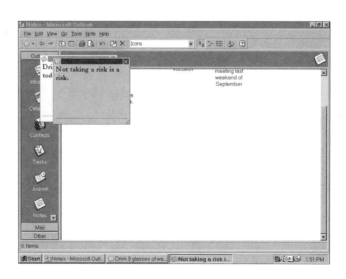

14

Creating Notes

Deleting a Note

⑫ Click each note in the Windows taskbar to open both notes.

The date and time appear at the bottom of the open notes.

⑬ Close both notes.

Deleting a Note

When it's time to get rid of a note or two that you no longer need, you simply delete the note or notes. Follow these steps to delete a note:

❶ Click a note to select it.

❷ Click the Delete button on the Notes toolbar.

The note is gone, but you can bring it back with the Undo feature.

❸ Click the Undo button on the Notes toolbar.

The note reappears in its original location.

Suppose you want to delete more than one note at a time. You can delete a slew of notes or all the notes in the Notes Information Viewer at one time. Try deleting three notes at once.

❹ Click the first note you want to delete in the Notes Information Viewer.

❺ Hold down the Ctrl key.

❻ Click each of the two additional notes you want to delete.

❼ Click the Delete button on the Notes toolbar.

Outlook deletes the three notes you selected. For the purposes of the next exercise, you need all the notes you can get, so undo that deletion.

❽ Click the Undo button on the Notes toolbar.

The notes reappear in their original location.

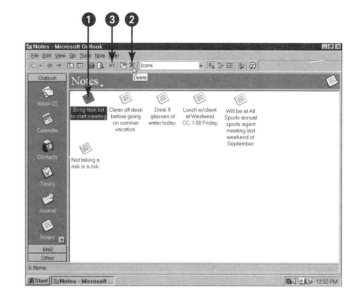

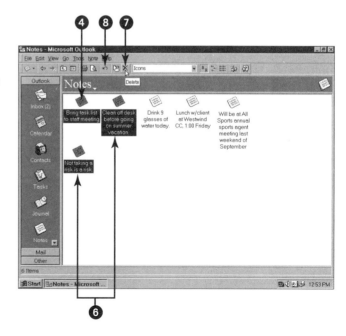

Changing Notes Views

The Large Icons view of Notes is a default option. Now I show you the other two view options: Small Icons and List. Another way to view your notes is to change the Notes views. There are five views:

- **Icons.** Shows notes as icons with their text (default Notes view). You can display large icons (default), small icons, and a list.

- **Notes List.** Shows all notes with details such as item type, subject, created dated and time, and categories.

- **Next Seven Days.** Shows notes only for the next seven days with details such as item type, subject, created date and time, and categories.

- **By Category.** Lists notes grouped by categories. You can assign a note to one or more categories.

- **By Color.** Lists notes grouped by color.

  In this exercise you also change to the Notes List and By Color Notes views.

① Click the Small Icons button on the Notes toolbar.

You see small icons and note text spread across the Information Viewer. You can use the horizontal scroll bar to see all the notes.

② Click the List button on the Notes toolbar.

You see a list of small icons and note text.

③ Click the Large Icons button on the Notes toolbar.

You've returned to the default icons view. Now take a look at a couple other Notes views.

④ From the Current View list on the Notes toolbar, choose Notes List.

Outlook displays a prompt asking if you want to discard the current view settings. In this case you will discard them.

⑤ Click OK.

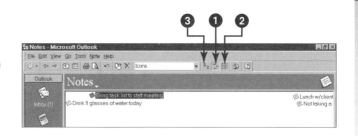

14

Creating Notes

Skills Challenge

Notice the list of notes and their details as shown in the accompanying figure.

6 From the Current View list on the Notes toolbar, choose By Color.

Notice the list of notes grouped by color. Each color group has a plus sign (+) button that enables you to expand the list in a group.

7 Click the plus sign (+) button to expand each color list. The plus sign button turns into a minus sign (−) button when each list is expanded.

As you can see, the blue notes and yellow notes are listed separately.

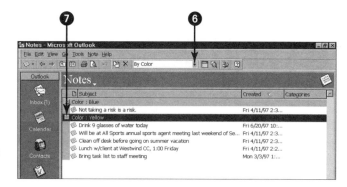

SKILLS CHALLENGE: CREATING NOTES

This final exercise reviews the note skills you've learned in this lesson. Your task is to create, change, and view notes. The EX14-2.PST file contains a few notes.

1 Import EX14-2.PST.

2 Add the following note with directions: **Take interstate North to exit 32B.**

 What are the two ways to create a new note?

3 Close the note.

 How do you close a note?

4 Open the *jog* note and add the words **around track** after the word "jog".

5 Change the font to any font and font size you want for the all the notes.

6 Close the note.

7 Move the last note on the far right down below the first note to make a second row of notes.

3 *How do you move a note in the Information Viewer?*

8 Open any note.

9 Resize the note to make it taller and wider.

10 Change the background color of the note you created to blue.

4 *What command do you select to change the background color of a note?*

11 Hide the date and time for all the notes.

12 Redisplay the date and time for all the notes.

13 Change the icons to small icons.

14 Switch to the Notes List Notes view.

15 Switch to the By Color Notes view.

16 Switch to the Icons Notes view.

TROUBLESHOOTING

You've completed this lesson and learned about Outlook's Notes feature. This table offers solutions to several problems you may have encountered when learning these skills.

Problem	Solution
I need to make some changes to a note I've already added.	Open the note and edit the text using insert, overtype, delete, copy, or move.
I deleted the wrong note.	Click the Undo button on the Notes toolbar to restore the note.

continued

TRY OUT THE
INTERACTIVE TUTORIALS
ON YOUR CD!

14

Creating Notes

Wrap up

Problem	Solution
An open note is covering up an area on the screen that I need to see.	Drag the note by its title bar to a different location on the screen.
After I changed the icons to small icons, I couldn't find some of my notes.	Use the horizontal scroll bar to scroll over to the right to see the rest of the notes.

WRAP UP

In this lesson you learned and practiced how to

- Add a note
- Close a note
- Open a note
- Move a note
- Resize a note
- Change the text in a note
- Change the font formatting for notes
- Change note color
- Show or hide the date and time on notes
- Delete a note
- Change notes views

   If you want more practice with these skills, create some notes for Internet addresses you want to check out. In the last lesson coming up, you are introduced to the new ways you can work with all Outlook components.

Working with Advanced Outlook Components

45 MINUTES

GOALS

This lesson gets you acquainted with advanced Outlook features. You learn about working with components and items beyond the Outlook basics, which were discussed in all the preceding lessons. The advanced features include the following:

- Using natural language for dates
- Managing favorite Web addresses
- Printing all components
- Creating and applying categories across all components
- Creating a new Outlook item from an existing one automatically
- Archiving items
- Creating shared Outlook items
- Creating an Outlook form

Using Natural Language for Dates

GET READY

When you've completed the exercises in this lesson, you will have produced an Outlook form similar to the one shown in the accompanying figure.

MAKING IT EASIER TO WORK WITH OUTLOOK

This lesson shows you how to work with Outlook's AutoDate, how to create shortcuts to Web sites you frequently visit, how to print Outlook items and any view of an Outlook component, and how to create new categories and assign any item you want to any of your custom categories.

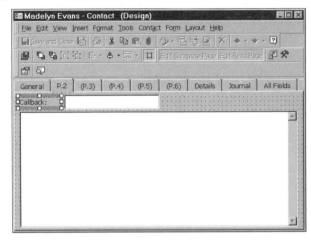

Using Natural Language for Dates

You can use natural language for dates in Calendar and Tasks. In other words, you can type words to describe a date or time for an item. For example, if you type **tomorrow** in a date field, then Outlook shows numbers for the correct month, day, and year. You can spell out or describe a date and time, and you can type abbreviations such as **Jan** for January. The following list contains some examples of natural language for dates and times. This list will give you ideas for trying out some descriptions on your own.

■ **Dates spelled out.** April twenty–first, Sep 7, first of November, this Thu, three days from now, ninety days after, two weeks ago, next week, one month from today.

■ **Times spelled out.** Ten o'clock a.m., four-thirty p.m., noon, midnight.

■ **Descriptions of dates and times.** Now, yesterday, today, tomorrow, next, last, ago, before, beforehand, beginning, previous, start, after, end, ending, following, for, from, that, this, till, through, until.

   In this exercise you use AutoDate to enter a date and time for an appointment.

1 Click Calendar on the Outlook Bar.

2 Click New Appointment on the Calendar toolbar.

3 In the Subject box, type **Tennis luncheon.**

4 In the Location box, type **The Racquet Club.**

5 In the Start time date box, type **this Fri.**

6 Press Tab.

Outlook enters the numbers for the date.

7 In the Start time box, type **noon** and press Enter.

Outlook changes the word *noon* to 12:00 PM.

8 In the End time box, type **two pm.**

9 Click Save and Close.

Managing Favorite Web Addresses

If you have Microsoft Internet Explorer installed, you'll see a list of shortcuts to popular Web pages in the Favorites folder in the Other group on the Outlook Bar. The Favorites folder contains several folders organized by popular topics such as art and literature, career, food, government, travel, weather, and much more. In each of these folders you'll find shortcuts to popular Web pages. When you're online, you can go directly to a Web page listed in the Favorites folder. But if you would like to have a special folder in which to store your favorite Web addresses, you can create a shortcut to the Web History folder. The Web History folder is a subfolder of the Favorites folder.

You can also share your favorite Web addresses with others by inserting a shortcut to a Web page in a mail message in Outlook. Then the recipients can use the shortcuts and browse your favorite Web pages with their Internet browser.

In this exercise you take a look at the shortcuts to Web addresses in the Favorites folder.

1 Click the Other button on the Outlook Bar.

2 Click the Favorites icon in the Outlook Bar.

You see a list of folders for a variety of topics.

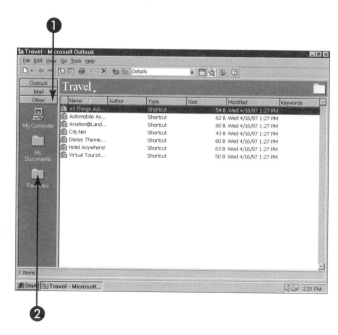

15

Working with Advanced Outlook Components

3 Double-click the Travel folder to open it.

Now you can see a list of shortcuts to Web sites on the Internet related to travel. If you want to go to a particular Web site from here, make sure you have the Microsoft Internet Explorer installed and you're online.

4 Double-click a shortcut in the list to go to that Web page.

5 When you're finished with the Web page, return to Outlook.

6 Click the Outlook button at the top of the Outlook Bar.

Storing Shortcuts to Web Addresses

You can store shortcuts to favorite Web addresses in the History folder in the Windows Explorer. To make the History folder easily accessible in Outlook, you can create a shortcut to the Web History folder. To create the shortcut, make sure you are running Windows 95 with Internet Explorer 3.0. Then follow these steps:

1 Click the Start button on the Windows taskbar.

2 Select Programs.

3 Choose Windows Explorer.

4 Double-click the Win95 folder.

5 Find the History folder and right-click it.

6 Select Create Shortcut on the shortcut menu.

7 In Outlook, click the Other button at the bottom of the Outlook Bar. Then drag the shortcut you just created from the Windows Explorer to the Favorites folder, as shown in the accompanying figure. To use a shortcut in the History folder, follow the steps in the previous exercise.

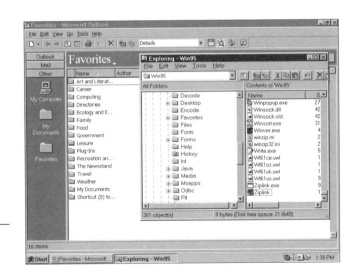

With Microsoft Internet Explorer, you can insert shortcuts to your favorite World Wide Web pages in Outlook mail messages. Then you can share Web addresses to your favorite Web pages with others. The

recipients must have an Internet browser installed to use the shortcuts. To insert a shortcut, first compose a mail message. In the text box in which you type the message, click where you want to insert the shortcut. Select File ➢ Insert, click the Look in Favorites button, and then choose the shortcut to the favorite Web page you want. In the Insert As section, choose Attachment.

Printing All Components

After you enter items in Outlook's components, you can print all items, selected items, and any view of an Outlook component. Each component offers several print styles for printing items. For example, Calendar gives you the Daily, Weekly, Monthly, and Tri-fold print styles; Contacts offers Card, Small Booklet, Medium Booklet, Memo, and Phone Directory print styles; Tasks has the Table print style; and Journal and Notes provides the Memo style.

As you saw in earlier lessons, each Outlook component has several dynamic views. You can print any view except for one based on a timeline or icons. For example, journal entries can be displayed in timeline views with icons, but you can print a view of journal entries with the table-view type.

It's convenient to have a printout of the phone directory near the phone when you're making phone calls to your contacts. You can also give this phone directory to coworkers. In this exercise you print the contacts using the Phone Directory print style.

1 Click Contacts on the Outlook Bar.

2 Click the Print button on the Contacts toolbar.

The Print dialog box opens. From here you can choose a printer, select a print style, specify the print range and number of copies, and decide whether to collate copies.

3 In the Print style section, scroll down to the bottom of the list and choose Phone Directory Style.

There are two options in the Print Range section: All items and Only selected items. Leave the default option, All items, to print all the contacts. If you want, you can select the contacts you want and then choose the Only selected items option.

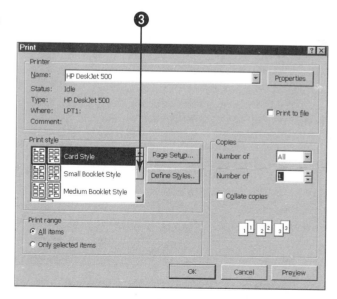

Creating and Applying Categories

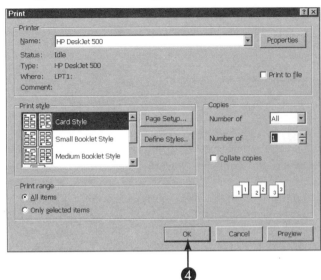

NOTE *The print range options vary in other components. For example, in Calendar you can print a range of dates such as October 1 to December 30. In Tasks you can print all rows in the Task list or selected rows. In Journal and Notes you get two print options: Start each item on a new page and Print attached files with item(s). Also, you must tell Outlook which journal entries you want to print. Before you open the Print dialog box, be sure to select one or more entry-type groups in Journal. Click an entry-type group to select it. To select additional entry-type groups, hold down Ctrl and click each additional entry type you want to print.*

4 Click OK to start printing.

TIP *To preview how your items will look when printed in a particular print style before you actually print the items in a component, click the Preview button in the lower-right corner of the Print dialog box.*

If you would like to see a printout of a particular view of your items in an Outlook component, switch to the view you want to print. To preview the items in a view, click the Print Preview button on the toolbar. If you like what you see, click the Print button on the Print Preview toolbar to print your view. If you prefer a different view, click the Close button on the Print Preview toolbar and choose a different view. To skip the preview, simply click the Print button on the toolbar to print the current view of your items.

Creating and Applying Categories

You've already seen how easy it is to organize your items by category. You assigned items to categories and viewed items grouped by category. Outlook supplies many categories in the Master Category List, but you can make up your own categories. Perhaps your boss wants you to track meetings, contacts, messages, and phone calls for a

Creating and Applying Categories

special project named Spring Sports Blitz. You can add a new category for the project and assign items to it. You can also delete categories you don't use.

You can add categories to the Master Category List when you're in any Outlook component. In this exercise you add a category to track items for a new sports agent project.

1 Pull down the Edit menu.

2 Choose Categories.

TIP

> *If Categories is unavailable (grayed out) on the Edit menu, then select an item and try again.*

3 Click the Master Category List button at the bottom of the Categories dialog box.

The Master Category List dialog box appears. In this dialog box you can add or delete categories.

4 In the New box, type **Spring Sports Blitz.**

5 Click the Add button.

The categories in the Master Category List are listed alphabetically. Your new category has been added to the list.

6 Click OK.

Scroll down to the bottom of the categories list to see your new category with a check box next to it.

7 Click OK again.

At this point you can start assigning items to the new category.

To delete a category in the Master Category List, select the category and click the Delete button.

After you've added and deleted categories in the Master Category List, you may want to revert back to the original list of categories that Outlook supplied. To accomplish this, you can reset

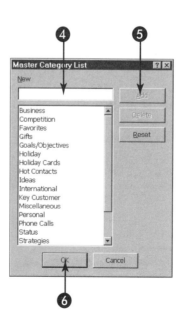

15

Working with Advanced Outlook Components

Creating a New Item

the Master Category List—just click the Reset button in the Master Category List dialog box. Outlook adds any of the original categories you deleted and deletes the categories you added. The items assigned to those deleted categories keep their category assignments. That way you can still find, sort, filter, or group items by those deleted categories.

MANAGING OUTLOOK ITEMS

There are several advanced Outlook features you may find useful and important. With *AutoCreate* you can automatically create a new Outlook item from an existing one. The *Archive* feature lets you store old Outlook items in a file and then retrieve the items whenever you want. You can also share items with others on the network. Another advanced Outlook feature is *Design Outlook Form*, which enables you to create your own form using the fields that appear in Outlook forms.

Creating a New Item from an Existing One

Outlook enables you to take an item of one type and create a new item of a different type from the original item. For example, you may want to quickly create a task from a mail message. The task information from the mail message is automatically added to the fields in the new task. The entire message item appears in text format in the task text box.

You can create only a single new item from the original item. You cannot take multiple items and create different multiple items. The original item is not changed by AutoCreate, except when the original item is moved. For example, if you have a meeting request or task request and create an appointment or task item from it, AutoCreate accepts the request and sends an acceptance reply to the sender. In this exercise you create an appointment from a mail message.

1 Click Inbox on the Outlook Bar.

2 Find a message that contains an appointment.

3 Drag the message to Calendar on the Outlook Bar.

An appointment dialog box opens. The message name appears in the Subject box. The entire message appears in the large text box at the bottom.

4 Make any necessary changes to the appointment information.

5 Click Save and Close.

6 To view the appointment in Calendar, select the appointment's day on the month calendar.

You can use the same procedure for other components besides Calendar to create a new Outlook item from an existing one automatically. Just drag an item to the component's icon on the Outlook Bar.

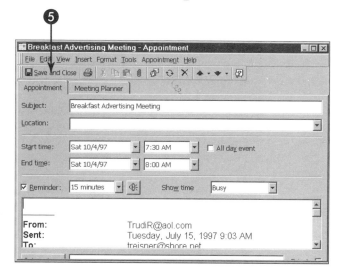

Archiving Items

The more you work with e-mail in Outlook, the more your e-mail can pile up in your mailbox. This is just like your paper mail that can stack up on your desk pretty fast. Periodically, you can file away important paperwork that is rarely used. Paperwork that is not as important, such as magazines and newspapers, can be thrown out based on its issue date. Similarly, Outlook lets you transfer old items to a storage file manually by using the Archive command, or you can have Outlook automatically transfer old items with AutoArchive. The choice is yours.

An item is old when it reaches the age you specify. You can archive all Outlook items. Any attached files, such as Microsoft Word or Excel worksheet documents, must be stored in files in a mail folder before you can archive them. When you archive, the folder structure in the Folder List remains the same, and some of the folders may even be empty.

By default, some of the Outlook folders are installed with AutoArchive turned on. Table 15-1 lists these folders and their default aging periods. The folders that are not archived automatically (by default) are Inbox, Notes, and Contacts.

15

Working with Advanced Outlook Components

Archiving Items

TABLE 15-1 OUTLOOK FOLDERS WITH AUTOARCHIVE TURNED ON

Folder	Aging Period
Calendar	6 months
Tasks	6 months
Journal	6 months
Sent Items	2 months
Deleted Items	2 months

In Lesson 2 you learned about exporting items to a folder in Outlook. Exporting is similar to archiving, with one major difference. Archiving copies the original items to the archive file and then removes them from the current folder. Exporting copies the original items to the export file but doesn't remove them from the current folder. Also, you can only archive to one file type, a personal folder file. However, you can export to many file types, such as .PST, text, and the Timex Data Link Watch.

In this exercise you archive the items in the Contacts folder to a personal folder file.

1 Pull down the File menu.

2 Choose Archive.

The Archive dialog box opens. Notice that the option Archive this folder and all subfolders is already selected. The folder is selected in the folder list.

3 Choose a date in the Archive items older than list box.

4 Click OK.

From now on, any items older than the date you specified will be archived to the archive file named ARCHIVE.PST. You can follow this procedure to archive items in any other Outlook component besides Contacts.

Outlook lets you retrieve archived items in either of two ways:

- Retrieve archived files as a separate file provided that you add an information service to your profile.

Importing Archived Items

- Import archived items into the original file.

If you want to retrieve archived files as a separate file, you first need to add an information service to a user profile. A profile contains predefined settings for an individual Outlook user, which may include any information services your company subscribes to and how to access your Inbox, folders, and address books. Usually, you only need one profile. If you are using Outlook on a company network and have your own profile, follow the steps in Lesson 5, Exercise 2 to add an information service to your profile. Then the archive file will be attached to your mailbox as a separate file that contains all your archived items.

Importing Archived Items

If you want to import archived items into the original Outlook component's file, perform these steps:

1 Pull down the File menu.

2 Choose Import and Export.

The Import and Export Wizard dialog box opens.

3 Choose Import from a personal folder file.

4 Follow the instructions that appear in the Import and Export Wizard dialog boxes.

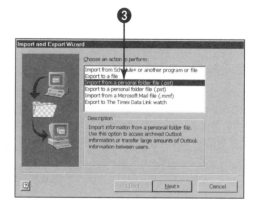

NOTE

Outlook's AutoArchive can delete or move old items from Outlook folders automatically. By default, the AutoArchive option is turned on for several folders, but if you ever need to turn off this option, select Tools ➢ Options and click the AutoArchive tab. Choose the AutoArchive options you want and click OK. You'll also need to set up the AutoArchive properties for the Outlook folders. To do so, right-click a component in the Outlook Bar and choose Properties from the shortcut menu. In the Properties dialog box, click the AutoArchive tab. Specify the aging period and the options for moving and deleting old items.

Creating Shared Outlook Items

Creating Shared Outlook Items

If you want to share your items with others on the network, you can either create a new item in a public folder or add an existing item to a public folder. Sharing Outlook items with others only works when you are connected to the Microsoft Exchange server. Also, you must have permission to create items. Follow these steps to check the type of permissions you have for a public folder:

1 Click the Folder List button on any component toolbar.

2 Click the + (plus sign) next to Public Folders to expand the list of public folders, if necessary.

3 Right-click the public folder for which you want to check the permission status.

4 Choose Properties.

The Properties dialog box appears, and you see a Summary tab. If you have owner permission, you also see a Permissions tab. If these tabs don't appear, then you don't have permission to change the folder properties.

5 Whether you have a Summary tab or a Permissions tab, click the tab to see your permission status.

6 Close the Properties dialog box.

Now you'll see how easy it is to create shared Outlook items.

1 Click the Folder List button on the component toolbar in which you're currently working, if necessary.

2 Click a public folder to open the public folder in which you want to create a shared Outlook item.

3 Pull down the File menu.

4 Choose New.

In the New submenu you see a list of Outlook items, as shown in the accompanying figure. The Outlook items you can share with another person on your network include appointment, meeting, contact, task, task request, journal entry, note, and

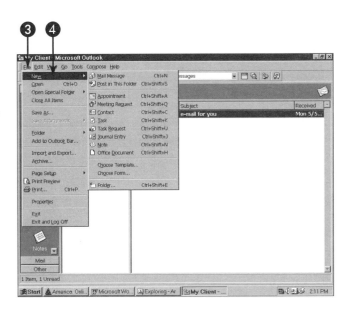

Creating an Outlook Form

Office document. For example, if you have contacts in your public folder that you want to share with others, choose Contact in the New submenu.

5 Choose the item that is the same type as the other items in the folder.

The New dialog box appears.

6 Type a name for the new item.

7 Select any options.

8 Click Save and Close.

If you already have an item you want to add to a public folder, you can add it to a public folder. First click the Folder List button on the toolbar. Under Public Folders, find the public folder to which you want to add the existing item. Then open the folder that contains the item you want to add to the public folder. Click the right mouse button and drag the item to the public folder.

Creating an Outlook Form

When you add new items in Outlook, you enter information into fields in an Outlook built-in form. For example, a New Message form lets you enter a mail message, a New Appointment form is for appointments, a New Contact form is for contacts, and so on. You can change a built-in form that any item is based on to create a new form. You might want to enhance a form to include more details about an item.

In this exercise you create a simple callback form for keeping in touch with contacts and tracking phone calls.

1 Click Contacts on the Outlook Bar.

2 Open Madelyn Evans.

3 Pull down the Tools menu.

4 Choose Design Outlook Form.

As you can see in the accompanying figure, there are several new tabs named P.2, P.3, P.4, P.5, and P.6. These tabs are new pages that you can customize on the form.

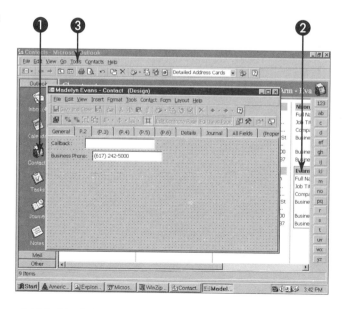

Working with Advanced Outlook Components

15

Creating an Outlook Form

5 Click the P.2 tab.

Notice the grid with dots as shown in the accompanying figure.

You can customize the form using this tab. You can add any fields you want by selecting them from the Field Chooser (see the accompanying figure). The dots on the grid help you line up the fields on the form.

The field names appear alphabetically in the Field Chooser. Now add the Callback field to the form.

6 Click Callback in the Field Chooser.

7 Drag the Callback field to the upper-left corner of the grid.

You see the field name on the form with an empty box next to it. The field name and box are objects you can resize and move on the form. The field name object is currently selected. When an object is selected, you see white squares surrounding the object's border. These squares are called *selection handles.* You can drag the selected object to a new location or drag one of the selection handles to enlarge or shrink the object. Now add a Notes field to the form.

8 Click Business Phone.

9 Drag the Business Phone field to just beneath the Callback field name on the form.

The Business Phone field, including the phone number, appears beneath the Callback field. Now you have a new callback form that you can use to enter callback information such as remarks, comments, and anything else related to a phone call to this contact.

10 Close the Field Chooser.

You can open the Field Chooser at any time by clicking the Field Chooser button on the Form toolbar.

11 Pull down the File menu.

12 Choose Save As.

The Save As dialog box appears.

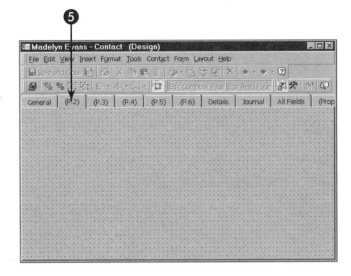

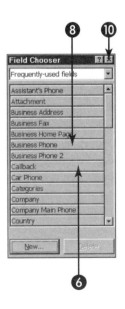

VISUAL BONUS

The Form Toolbar

The Form toolbar provides tools for creating, editing, and publishing a customized Outlook form.

The Form toolbar.

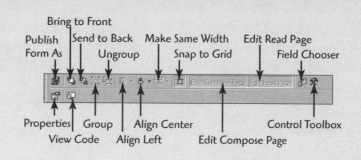

Publish Form As | Bring to Front | Send to Back | Make Same Width | Edit Read Page
Ungroup | Snap to Grid | Field Chooser

Properties | Group | Align Center | Control Toolbox
View Code | Align Left | Edit Compose Page

 Type a name for the form.

 Click Save to close the Save As dialog box.

 Click the Close button to close the design form.

SKILLS CHALLENGE: MANAGING ALL COMPONENTS AND ITEMS

In this last exercise you review all the skills you've learned in this lesson.

1 Create an appointment and use natural language for entering dates.

> **1** *Name the two fields in which you can enter natural language.*

2 Use one of the shortcuts in the Favorites folder to check out a Web page using the Microsoft Internet Explorer.

> **2** *How do you create a shortcut to a Web History folder in Outlook?*

3 Print one of the Outlook components with the print style of your choice.

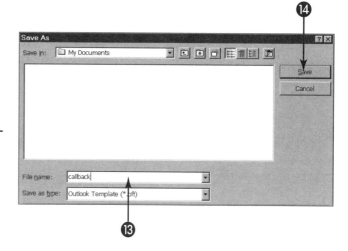

Troubleshooting

④ Create a new category for a project in the Master Category List.

 3 *What command allows you to add a category to the Master Category List?*

⑤ Send a message in Rich Text Format to a contact.

⑥ Create a new Outlook item of one type from a different item type.

⑦ Archive several items to the archive file.

 4 *What is the difference between exporting and archiving?*

⑧ Create an appointment as a shared item in a public folder.

⑨ Create a customized Outlook form for a contact.

TRY OUT THE

INTERACTIVE TUTORIALS

ON YOUR CD!

TROUBLESHOOTING

You've completed this lesson and learned about managing all Outlook components and items. This table offers solutions to several problems you may have encountered when learning these skills.

Problem	Solution
I tried to use a shortcut in the Favorites folder to go to a Web page, but an error message informed me that Internet Explorer couldn't open the site.	Make sure you have Internet Explorer installed and running on your computer and that you're online.
I tried to print Journal items in a timeline view, but Outlook wouldn't print the view.	You cannot print any timeline view in Outlook. Choose the table view and then print the Journal items.
I can't add a category to the Master Category list because Categories is unavailable (grayed out) on the Edit menu.	Select an item and try again.

Problem	Solution
I customized a contact form by adding fields to a page, and I can't save the form using the Save and Close button.	Select File ➤ Save As, type a name for the form, and click OK. Then click the Close button to close the design form.

WRAP UP

You've learned some new skills in this lesson. You learned how to

- Use natural language for dates
- Manage favorite Web addresses
- Print all components
- Create and apply categories across all components
- Send messages in Rich Text Format
- Create a new Outlook item from an existing one automatically
- Archive items
- Create shared Outlook items
- Create an Outlook form

If you want more practice with these skills, create an Outlook form for personal appointments such as visiting the doctor, dentist, or accountant.

In the appendixes that follow, I show you how to install Outlook 97 in Appendix A; give you practice projects to do in Appendix B; give you the answers to the bonus questions in Appendix C; and tell you what's on the CD-ROM in Appendix D. Following the appendixes is a glossary of Outlook 97 terms.

15

Working with Advanced Outlook Components

Installing Microsoft Outlook 97

Installing Microsoft Outlook 97 on your computer is a relatively simple and straightforward procedure. You can use the installation instructions in this appendix to install stand-alone Microsoft Outlook or the Microsoft Office version.

These instructions assume that you are loading Outlook 97 from a CD-ROM, that your CD-ROM drive is labeled (D), and that you have sufficient space to support a typical installation (about 30MB). It is also assumed that you are running Windows 95. Outlook runs only on Windows 95.

Whether you have Microsoft Office 97 or have purchased Outlook 97 separately, here's how you install Outlook on your computer's hard disk:

❶ Turn on your computer and load Windows.

At this point, be sure to quit all other running programs. Also, disable any utility program such as an anti-virus or backup program. If these programs are running, they can cause problems with the Outlook installation.

❷ Insert the Outlook CD in your computer's CD-ROM drive (usually referred to as the D drive).

Installing Outlook

③ Click the Start button on the Windows taskbar.

④ Choose Run from the Start menu.

⑤ Type **d:\setup** (or use the drive letter applicable to your computer).

NOTE *The CD-ROM that Outlook is installed from has an AutoRun program on it. If the AutoRun feature is enabled on your computer, the AutoRun program runs automatically. Usually this feature is the default on Windows 95 installations. If the CD is in the drive when the computer is booted, the AutoRun does not run. However, if the computer is already running, simply insert the CD in the drive, and the AutoRun feature will be enabled and the setup will start on its own (if this feature is enabled on your computer). You will see the Microsoft Outlook 97 dialog box. Click Install Microsoft Outlook. The Welcome dialog box appears. Go directly to Step 6.*

After a moment, the Microsoft Outlook 97 Setup screen appears, as shown in the accompanying figure.

⑥ Choose Continue.

The Name and Organization Information dialog box displays, as shown in the accompanying figure.

⑦ Type your name and, if appropriate, your organization.

⑧ Click OK.

Outlook asks you to confirm the name and organization you entered.

⑨ Click OK.

Outlook asks you to enter your CD KEY, which is the Product ID number. You'll find the CD KEY on a label placed on the back of your CD-ROM case.

⑩ Type the CD KEY number.

⑪ Click OK.

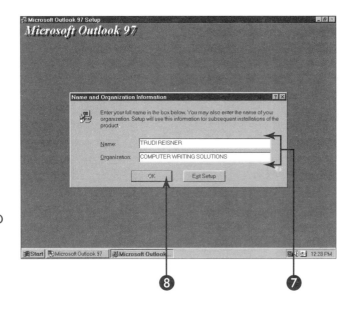

Your Product ID number appears onscreen. Make a note of this number; you will need to provide it if you call Microsoft technical support.

⓬ Click OK to proceed.

The dialog box in the accompanying figure appears.

This dialog box gives you the option of changing the folder in which Microsoft Outlook is installed. Unless you have a previous version of this program that you want to keep, you should accept the default folder name. If you want to have the program installed to a different folder, choose Change Folder and enter a new folder name. Then click OK.

⓭ Click OK to accept the default folder name.

Another dialog box opens, shown in the accompanying figure, offering you a choice of three types of installation (if you are installing Microsoft Office). If you are installing stand-alone Microsoft Outlook, then you will see the first two choices listed here:

- **Typical** installs all of Outlook's features as well as the most commonly used templates. This is the recommended installation for a less-experienced user.

- **Custom** installs only the Outlook features you choose. It gives you an opportunity to pick and choose what you want to install. This is an option if you don't have enough memory for all the programs, or if you don't need one of the components. If you make this choice, you see a Custom dialog box. You can deselect anything you don't want to install.

- **Run from CD-ROM** enables you to run most of Outlook from your CD-ROM drive. However, this option makes running the software slow and much less efficient. This choice appears if you're installing Microsoft Office.

⓮ Click Typical.

The Typical dialog box appears.

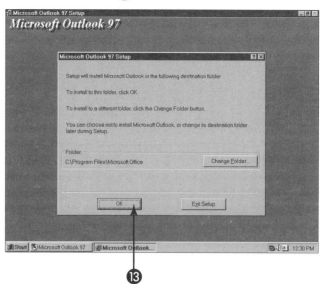

Installing Outlook

Check the Space required and Space available information at the bottom of the dialog box, and make sure you have enough room on your hard drive to install Outlook. The components not selected in the list of Options in this dialog box can always be installed later by running this installation program again. For now, it's best to accept the default Typical installation options.

⑮ Choose Continue.

The screen in the accompanying figure appears, tracking the installation with a percentage complete bar. (If you install Outlook from disks instead of a CD-ROM, you are asked to insert the disks in sequence during this procedure). It may take several minutes for the installation to complete—the installation time varies depending on the speed and configuration of your computer.

Some information on the features of Outlook displays at the top of this screen, which you may want to read to begin to familiarize yourself with the features of Outlook 97. When the installation is complete, you see the screen shown in the accompanying figure. If you have a modem installed and wish to register your software online, you can select Online Registration at this time.

⑯ Choose OK to complete the installation.

If you installed Outlook with the AutoRun program, you will see the Microsoft Outlook 97 dialog box. Click the Close button to close the dialog box.

⑰ Remove the CD or disk from the drive.

Windows has installed the Outlook program files on your computer, creating a program group icon called Microsoft Outlook on the Programs menu in Windows (if that's the program group you chose during setup). The Microsoft Outlook shortcut icon appears on your Windows desktop. You can use this icon as a shortcut for starting Outlook instead of selecting the program from the Windows Programs menu.

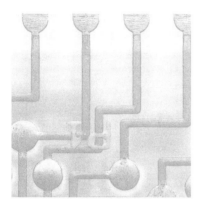

Practice Projects

You did a great job getting through this book and picking up all the basic skills you need to become productive with Outlook 97. However, as with any achievement, you have to stay in practice or you lose all you gained. Now that you've completed *Outlook 97 One Step at a Time,* it's important to set yourself a regular exercise regime so that your Outlook muscles don't get flabby.

The first few days and weeks after learning new skills are the most important. If you can spend 20 minutes each day practicing with the Outlook product over the next week or two, you'll not only reinforce your learning, but you'll also discover other, more advanced Outlook features and devise your own shortcuts for getting things done.

This appendix suggests some projects you might use for follow-up practice. I've tried to include projects that are useful in your daily life, such as creating a holiday database or setting up a meeting.

Project 1: Add contacts to Outlook's Contacts list, such as family members, doctors, insurance agent, and travel agent. Make all your phone calls to these people for the next few weeks using Outlook's phone-dialing feature.

Take a look at Lessons 3 and 4 for details about adding contacts and using AutoDialer.

Practice Projects

Project 2: Add the names of all the people to whom you send holiday greetings to your Contacts list. Assign family and friends to the Holiday category and the Gifts category.

Lesson 3 can help you with assigning items to categories.

Project 3: Send e-mail to all your coworkers giving them some of your favorite Web addresses.

Need assistance with sending e-mail? Go back to Lesson 5. Also, Lesson 15 can help you with Web addresses.

Project 4: Add all the activities for the next few months to Outlook's Calendar. Include your plans for holidays and vacations. Be sure to set a few reminders for yourself of appointments, events, or meetings.

Lesson 8 can help you complete this project.

Project 5: Use Outlook's Meeting Planner in Calendar to plan a meeting. Select attendees from your family or coworkers and deal with any scheduling conflicts. Send an e-mail to attendees if you have access to an e-mail system on a network in your office.

Don't forget, Lesson 10 can help you with Meeting Planner.

Project 6: Input all the errands you need to run for the upcoming week into your Outlook Tasks list. Assign some of the tasks to family members. Print a list of task items to take along with you to the office or as you run errands.

Outlook's Tasks feature is covered in Lesson 11.

Project 7: Use Journal to record all your business and personal projects in the upcoming month.

The skills you learned in Lesson 13 come in handy for this project.

Project 8: Using Notes, create several notes to remind yourself of special concerns about attending a conference, such as your airline ticket, hotel confirmation, and directions to a four-star restaurant. Print the notes to take along with you.

Remember, Lesson 14 can refresh your memory about the steps involved in creating notes.

These are some suggestions. Feel free to put on your thinking cap and come up with others. The important thing is to keep at it and take advantage of all your hard work with *Outlook 97 One Step at a Time.*

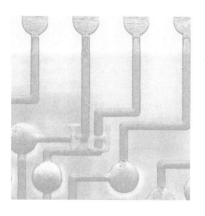

Answers to Skills Challenge Questions

LESSON 1

 1 *Can you identify the Window Control buttons on the Outlook window?*

The Minimize button has a minus sign, the Maximize button contains a window, and the Close button has an X. These buttons are located in the upper-right corner of the Outlook window.

 2 *What does an ellipsis next to a menu command indicate?*

An ellipsis next to a menu command indicates that a dialog box appears when you select the command.

 3 *If you're unsure of what a toolbar button does, how do you find the button's name?*

Leave the mouse pointer on the button to display the button's name, which is called a *screen tip.*

Answers to Skills Challenge Questions

 4 *What are the two shortcuts for exiting Outlook?*

You can either double-click the Outlook Control menu icon or click the Close button to exit Outlook quickly.

LESSON 2

 1 *Name two ways to open the Journal folder.*

You can click the Journal button on the Outlook Bar, or you can click the Folder List button on a component's toolbar and choose the Journal folder in the Folder List.

 2 *Before you name a subfolder, what is the folder called that you select in the Folder List?*

You select the parent folder for which you are creating a subfolder.

 3 *What does a minus sign (–) next to a folder in the Folder List mean?*

The minus sign (–) indicates that the folder has subfolders and can be collapsed.

 4 *What does a plus sign (+) next to a folder in the Folder List mean?*

The plus sign (+) indicates that the folder has subfolders and can be expanded.

LESSON 3

 1 *How do you move backward from box to box in the Contact window?*

Press Shift+Tab.

Answers to Skills Challenge Questions

 If you want to add a few contacts consecutively, what button on the Contact toolbar helps you do it?

Click the Save and New button on the Contact toolbar.

 What's the shortcut for opening a contact's file?

Double-click the contact in the list.

 Can you describe what a contact looks like when it's selected?

A selected contact is enclosed in a dotted-line border, and the contact's name is highlighted in a different color.

LESSON 4

 What are the four tabs that appear in the Letter Wizard dialog box?

Letter Format, Recipient Info, Other Elements, and Sender Info.

 How do you redial the last number you called?

Click the AutoDialer drop-down arrow on the Contacts toolbar, choose Redial, and choose the first phone number in the Redial list.

 What is a more technical name for a Web page address?

URL, which stands for Uniform Resource Locator.

 Can you name the five print styles for printing a Contacts List?

Card Style, Small Booklet Style, Medium Booklet Style, Memo Style, and Phone Directory Style.

Answers to Skills Challenge Questions

LESSON 5

 1 *Which tool on the Inbox toolbar creates a new message?*

The New Mail Message button.

 2 *How do you send a message?*

Click the Send button on the Message toolbar.

 3 *How do you attach a file to a message?*

Click the Insert File button on the Message toolbar.

LESSON 6

 1 *How do you read a message?*

Click the message to select it, and then double-click the message to open it.

 2 *Which tool on the Reply toolbar lets you reply to all names in the To and Cc boxes?*

The Reply to all tool.

 3 *Which tool on the Reply toolbar lets you forward a message?*

The Forward tool.

 4 *Which command enables you to sort mail message items?*

The View ➢ Sort command.

Answers to Skills Challenge Questions

LESSON 7

 1 *Where can you view the tracking results?*

Click the Tracking tab in the original message.

 2 *Which command lets you recall a message?*

Tools ➤ Recall This Message.

 3 *What are the two types of message flags?*

Flagged is red and completed is gray.

 4 *Which command enables you to add a custom signature?*

Tools ➤ AutoSignature.

LESSON 8

 1 *Identify the three ways to add an appointment.*

❶ Click the New drop-down arrow on any Outlook toolbar and choose Appointment.

❷ Click the New Appointment button on the Calendar toolbar.

❸ In Calendar, type the appointment information into a time slot in the schedule.

 2 *What is the difference between an appointment and an event?*

An *appointment* is an activity scheduled in a block of time and marked as busy so that its time slots are unavailable. An *event* is an activity that lasts 24 hours or longer and is marked as free so that its time slots are available.

Answers to Skills Challenge Questions

 3 *What are the three major categories of options you can set for a recurring appointment in the Appointment Recurrence dialog box?*

Appointment time, recurrence pattern, and range of occurrence.

 4 *What are your choices when the Reminder dialog box appears?*

You can dismiss, postpone, or open the appointment.

LESSON 9

 1 *How do you change months?*

Click the left or right arrow on the Month Calendar, or use the vertical scroll bar to scroll through the Month Calendar.

 2 *Can you identify the two types of multiple days that you can view in Calendar?*

Continuous and discontinuous days.

 3 *How do you change the order in which time zones appear in Calendar?*

Click the Swap Time Zones button in the Time Zones dialog box.

 4 *How do you import holidays to Calendar?*

Select Tools ➢ Options and click the Calendar tab. Click the Add Holidays button, choose the countries you want, and click OK.

LESSON 10

 1 *What are the four major steps involved when planning a meeting?*

Answers to Skills Challenge Questions ◀

 Enter the attendees.

2 Choose a meeting start and end time.

3 Specify a meeting location.

4 Send a memo to attendees.

 2 *How do you remove an attendee?*

Select the attendee in the Attendees list and press the Delete key.

3 *Can you describe the colors and pattern that indicate the block of time for a person's schedule?*

Tentative is light blue, *busy* is dark blue, and *Out of Office* is purple. If an attendee's block of time is free, it will be clear or have no color. If the schedule is unknown, then the block of time will have diagonal lines.

4 *In Calendar, what does a meeting icon look like on the schedule?*

Two people's heads.

LESSON 11

1 *What are the three ways to add a task?*

1 Click the New Task button on the Task toolbar.

2 Click the New button on any Outlook component's toolbar.

3 Type the task item directly into the Task list.

2 *What is a regenerating task?*

A task that repeats based on the completion date.

Answers to Skills Challenge Questions

 3 *What are the two ways to assign the Completed status to a task?*

1 Open the task and choose the Completed option from the Status drop-down list.

2 Click the Completed check box in Simple List view.

 4 *What are the two ways to assign a due date to a task?*

1 Open the task, choose the Due option in the Due date section, and then choose a date.

2 In Simple List view, choose a date in the Due Date column.

LESSON 12

 1 *How do you change task views?*

Open the Current View list on the Task toolbar and choose a view.

 2 *How do you show completed tasks for selected days on the TaskPad in Calendar?*

First select the days on the calendar. Then select View ➢ TaskPad View and choose a view from the TaskPad View submenu.

 3 *Where do you see a recipient's acceptance of a task assigned to him?*

A recipient's task acceptance message appears in your Inbox.

Answers to Skills Challenge Questions

LESSON 13

 1 *Which command do you use to set up recording journal entries automatically?*

The Tools ➢ Options command.

 2 *How can you tell Outlook to start manually recording the item immediately?*

Type **now** in the start date and time boxes.

 3 *What are the two ways to record an item manually?*

1 Click the New Journal button on the Journal toolbar.

2 Open the item and select Tools ➢ Record in Journal.

 4 *Which Journal views list all the entries recorded in Journal?*

By type and Entry list.

LESSON 14

 1 *What are the two ways to create a new note?*

1 Click the New Note button on the Notes toolbar.

2 Click the New drop-down arrow on any Outlook component toolbar and choose Note.

 2 *How do you close a note?*

Click the Close button in the upper-right corner of the note window.

How do you move a note in the Information Viewer?

Drag the note to the new location.

 What command do you select to change the background color of a note?

The Colors command on the shortcut menu.

LESSON 15

 Name the two fields in which you can enter natural language.

Date and Time.

 How do you create a shortcut to a Web History folder in Outlook?

In the Windows Explorer, select the Win95 directory and find the History folder. Right-click the History folder and choose Create Shortcut. Drag the History folder to the Favorites folder in the Other group on the Outlook Bar.

 What command allows you to add a category to the Master Category List?

The Edit Categories command.

 What is the difference between exporting and archiving?

Exporting copies the original items to the export file but doesn't remove them from the current folder. Archiving copies the original items to the archive file and then removes them from the current folder.

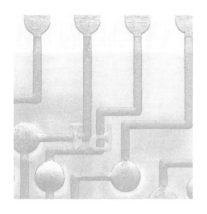

What's on the CD-ROM

The CD-ROM in the back of the book includes the exclusive *One Step at a Time On-Demand* software. This interactive software coaches you through the exercises in the book's lessons while you work on a computer at your own pace.

USING THE ONE STEP AT A TIME ON-DEMAND INTERACTIVE SOFTWARE

One Step at a Time On-Demand interactive software includes the exercises in the book so that you can search for information about how to perform a function or complete a task. You can run the software alone or in combination with the book. The software consists of three modes: Demo, Teacher, and Concurrent. In addition, the Concept option provides an overview of each exercise.

- **Demo** mode provides a movie-style demonstration of the same steps that are presented in the book's exercises, and works with the sample exercise files that are included on the CD-ROM in the One Step folder.

Installing the software

- **Teacher** mode simulates the software environment and permits you to interactively follow the exercises in the book's lessons.

- **Concurrent** mode enables you to use the *One Step at a Time-On Demand* features while you work within the actual Outlook 97 environment. This unique interactive mode provides audio instructions and directs you to take the correct actions as you work through the exercises. (Concurrent mode may not be available to all exercises.)

■ Installing the software

The *One Step at a Time On-Demand Interactive* software can be installed on Windows 95 and Windows NT 4.0. To install the interactive software on your computer, follow these steps:

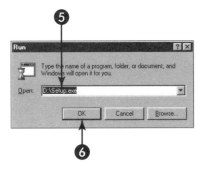

① Place the *Outlook 97 One Step at a Time* CD-ROM in your CD-ROM drive.

② Launch Windows (if you haven't already).

③ Click the Start menu.

④ Select Run. The Run dialog box appears.

⑤ Type **D:\Setup.exe** (where D is your CD-ROM drive) in the Run dialog box.

⑥ Click OK to run the setup procedure. The On-Demand Installation dialog box appears.

⑦ Click Continue. The On-Demand Installation Options dialog box appears.

⑧ Click the Full/Network radio button (if this option is not already selected).

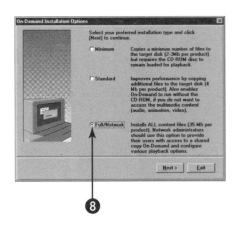

NOTE *Full/Network installation requires approximately 150MB of hard disk space. If you don't have enough hard disk space, click the Standard radio button to choose Standard* installation. If you choose standard installation, you should always insert the CD-ROM when you start the software to hear sound.

9 Click Next. The Determine Installation Drive and Directory dialog box appears.

10 Choose the default drive and directory that appears, or click Change to choose a different drive and directory.

11 Click Next. The Product Selection dialog box appears, which enables you to verify the software you want to install.

12 Click Finish to complete the installation. The On-Demand Installation dialog box displays the progress of the installation. After the installation, the Multiuser Pack Registration dialog box appears.

13 Enter information in the Multiuser Pack Registration dialog box.

14 Click OK. The On-Demand Installation dialog box appears.

15 Click OK to confirm the installation has been successfully completed.

■ **Running Demo, Teacher, or Concurrent mode**

NOTE *If you run the One Step at a Time On-Demand software in Windows 98, we recommend you don't work in Teacher or Concurrent modes unless you turn off the* Active Desktop feature. However, Teacher mode and Concurrent mode may not work properly at all in Windows 98. At the time of the writing of this book, the final release of Windows 98 wasn't available and we couldn't test all the topics in Teacher mode and Concurrent mode.

Once you've installed the software, you can view the text of the book and follow interactively the steps in each exercise. To run Demo mode, Teacher mode, or Concurrent mode follow these steps:

1 Click the Start menu on the Windows desktop.

2 Select Programs ➤ IDG Books ➤ Outlook 97 One Step at a Time. A small On-Demand toolbar appears in the upper-right corner of your screen.

3 Launch Outlook 97.

4 The On-Demand Reminder dialog box appears, telling you that the On-Demand software is active. If you don't want to display the dialog box, deselect the Show Reminder check box. Then, click OK.

D

What's on the CD-ROM

5 Click the icon of the professor. The Interactive Training — Lesson Selection dialog box appears.

6 Select the Contents tab, if it isn't selected already. The contents appear, divided into six parts.

Please select the Module option, and follow the software using that option (rather than All Topics).

7 Click the plus icon next to the part you want to explore. Lessons appear. The list of lessons corresponds to the lessons in the book.

8 Click the plus icon next to the lesson you want to explore. Topics appear.

If you wish to work in Concurrent mode, start with the first topic of the lesson, because the software will direct you to open a specific file which you will use to complete the steps in that lesson.

9 Double-click a topic of your choice. A menu appears.

10 Select Concept, Demo, Concurrent (if available), or Teacher.

11 Follow the onscreen prompts to use the interactive software and work through the steps.

NOTE

In Demo mode, you only need to perform actions that appear in red. Otherwise, the software automatically demonstrates the actions for you. All you need to do is read the information that appears onscreen. (Holding down the Shift key pauses the program; releasing the Shift key activates the program.) In Teacher mode, you need to follow the directions and perform the actions that appear onscreen.

GETTING THE MOST OUT OF USING THE ONE STEP AT A TIME SOFTWARE

We strongly recommend that you read the topics in the book while using the software (especially while working in Concurrent mode). In those instances where the onscreen instructions don't match the book's instructions exactly, or when the software appears to stop before completing a task, the book will provide the instructions necessary for you to continue.

STOPPING THE PROGRAM

To stop running the program at any time, press Esc to return to the Interactive Training – Lesson Selection dialog box. (To restart the software, double-click a topic of your choice and select a mode.)

EXITING THE PROGRAM

Press Esc when the Interactive Training – Lesson Selection dialog box appears to exit the program. The On-Demand toolbar appears in the upper-right corner of your screen. Click the icon that displays the lightning bolt image. A menu appears. Choose Exit. The On-Demand – Exit dialog box appears. Click Yes to exit On-Demand.

INSTALLING THE EXERCISE FILES

To access the exercise files for the lessons in this book, you'll need to set up a folder for the exercise files on your hard drive (also covered in Lesson 1). Follow these steps:

1 Double-click the My Computer icon on your desktop.

2 In the My Computer window, double-click the hard drive (C).

3 Open the File menu.

4 Choose the New command.

5 Choose Folder from the submenu. A new folder appears at the end of the list with the name New Folder.

6 Type **One Step** to name the folder.

7 Press Enter.

8 Place the *Outlook 97 One Step at a Time* CD-ROM in the CD-ROM drive.

9 In the My Computer window, double-click the CD-ROM icon, usually labeled D:, to open the drive in which you placed the CD-ROM.

10 In the CD-ROM (D:) window, copy the folder named Exercise by selecting it and pressing Ctrl-C. Then, close the CD-ROM window and all other open windows.

11 Double-click My Computer.

12 Double-click the hard drive (C:).

13 Double-click the One Step folder.

14 Paste the Exercise folder into the One Step folder by pressing Ctrl-V. All of the exercise files are now located within the Exercise folder, inside the One Step folder.

D

What's on the CD-ROM

Using the Exercise Files

USING THE EXERCISE FILES

You need to make sure that you have removed the Read Only attribute from the file(s) you copied to your hard drive before you start using those files. Otherwise, when you attempt to save your work, your screen will display an error message. To remove the attribute, open the Exercise folder (inside the One Step folder) on your hard drive. Select the files by opening the Edit menu and choosing the Select All command. Open the File menu and choose Properties. The Properties dialog box appears. Click the Read Only attribute to remove the check from the checkbox.

RUNNING THE DEMO PROGRAM

You may install additional modules of On-Demand Interactive Learning and find out more about PTS Learning Systems, the company behind the software, by using a file on the CD-ROM included with this book. Follow these steps:

1 Start your browser.

2 Select File from the menu.

3 Select Open.

4 Type **D:\info\welcome.htm**, where D is your CD-ROM drive.

5 Click OK to view the contents.

A

appointment An arrangement you set up for a meeting, activity, or event.

archive file A file Outlook creates to archive your Outlook items, moving the items into the archive file and deleting them from the original folder.

archiving A backup procedure in which Outlook backs up or moves your Outlook items to an archive file and deletes them from the original folder.

ascending order A sort procedure in which Outlook items are arranged from first to last, such as A to Z; or smallest to largest, such as 1 to 10.

attachment A file, such as any Microsoft document, that you can attach to an e-mail message and transfer to the recipient. You can also attach a file to an Outlook item such as a task item or journal entry.

attendee A person you invite to a meeting by sending him/her a meeting request and who agrees to attend the meeting.

AutoArchive An automatic backup feature that archives Outlook items.

AutoCreate An automatic item-creation feature that enables you to create a new Outlook item by dragging an item and then dropping it onto the icon for another kind of item. For instance, you can create a new task by dragging an appointment on to the Tasks icon on the Outlook Bar.

AutoDate An automatic date-entry feature that enters the correct date when you type descriptive words such as "today" or "next Monday."

AutoPreview An automatic preview e-mail message feature that shows the first three lines of an e-mail message in a table view.

AutoSignature An automatic signature feature that inserts a chunk of text, such as your name and phone number, at the end of a new e-mail message, a reply, or forward that you send.

B

browser A software program that enables you to view Web pages on the Internet, such as Microsoft Internet Explorer, Netscape Navigator, or Mosaic.

C

Calendar An Outlook miniprogram that enables you to schedule appointments, events, and meetings.

Card view A way of looking at contact information in Contacts that shows each contact item in a business-card form arranged in columns and rows.

categorize To organize files and items by one or more categories so that you can easily find them, especially when you find, sort, filter, or group.

Glossary

category A word or phrase that helps you keep track of items in Outlook, such as holiday, gift, or phone call.

Cc An e-mail feature that enables you to send a carbon copy of an e-mail message to an additional recipient.

check box A small, square box that appears next to an option in a dialog box you choose to toggle an option on or off. Click the check box to turn on the option, and a check mark appears in the box. Click the check box to remove the check mark and turn off the option.

collapse a group In a table view with items grouped by one or more fields, you click the small minus sign next to a group heading to hide the list of items in the group.

column A vertical segment of items in a table view, also known as a field (*see field*).

column heading The name across the top of a column in a table view that describes the column's content, also known as the field name (*see field name*).

command A word or phrase that executes a specific operation. Each menu,

shortcut menu, or toolbar consists of commands.

Contacts An Outlook miniprogram that stores names, addresses, phone numbers, e-mail, and Web page addresses, and other contact information. Enables you to maintain a simple database in the same way you would keep business cards for your business and personal contacts.

copy Duplicate a selection of information in one location and place a copy of the selection somewhere else.

criteria To identify information in any one of the fields, such as the last name Anderson or the category Holiday so that you can locate an Outlook item. Criteria you specify to filter a view hides or shows the Outlook items containing the criteria.

Ctrl A special key on your keyboard that you press with other keys or mouse clicks to execute commands. In Outlook, for example, holding down Ctrl while clicking items in a list selects multiple items that are not next to each other in the list.

D

default A standard setting that the program uses unless you specify a different setting.

Deleted Items A special Outlook folder that holds items you delete in other Outlook folders. To permanently delete items from Outlook, you need to delete them from the Deleted Items folder.

descending order A sort procedure in which Outlook items are arranged from last to first, such as Z to A; or largest to smallest, such as 10 to 1.

dialog box A type of window that opens when you select certain commands or actions, giving you information about the current settings and requiring one or more responses from you before executing the command or action. For example, if you choose File ➢ Save As, you see the Save As dialog box.

document An organized set of text and/or graphic elements identified by a single name. The electronic form of a document stored on disk is also called a file.

double-click To press and release the left mouse button two times in rapid succession.

drag To hold down the left mouse button while moving the mouse and pointer to a different location on the screen, and then release the mouse button.

drag-and-drop A method for moving or copying information over short distances using the mouse. To use drag-and-drop, point to the object, hold down the left mouse button while you move the mouse to drag the object to where you want it, and then release the mouse button to drop the object in the new location.

E

e-mail Stands for electronic mail. An electronic communications system that lets you send and receive mail messages, exchanging mail with other Outlook users and many other e-mail systems such as the Internet, America Online, and CompuServe. E-mail uses a modem and telephone lines instead of paper, envelopes, and stamps.

Glossary

e-mail message An electronic mail message that contains a letter or file sent by one person to another.

event A Calendar item that you can schedule, which lasts for a minimum of 24 hours.

expand a group In a table view with items grouped by one or more fields, you click the small plus sign next to a group heading to show a list of the items in the group.

export To convert and save Outlook information in a file that has a different file type (*see import*).

F

field A single piece of information in an Outlook item, such as First Name, Last Name, Company, or Phone Number. A field can be a column in a table view or a labeled box in a card in a card view.

field name The name given to a field, also known as a column heading (*see column heading*) that helps you identify the field's contents.

file A collection of information stored on disk with a unique name, such as a Word document, an Excel

worksheet, or an Access database.

filter A feature that enables you to specify criteria to display certain items and hide the others.

flag A symbol that represents the type of follow-up necessary for an e-mail message. Outlook displays flag symbols in the Flag Status column in Table view.

folder An onscreen representation of a file folder into which you can place files, items, and other folders to organize your work stored on the hard disk. A folder was called a directory in the DOS world.

Folder banner A horizontal bar that appears beneath the Outlook toolbars, which shows the Outlook folder name that you are currently viewing.

font A collection of letters, punctuation marks, numbers, and special characters in a given typeface, weight, and size, such as Arial Bold 10-point.

font formatting Changing text attributes to enhance the appearance of text, such as adding bold or italic, applying

color, and increasing or decreasing font size.

format The layout of elements such as characters, lines, and paragraphs and how they appear onscreen and on a printed page.

forward To send a message you've received to one or more additional recipients.

G

grouping A way to organize Outlook items by any field so you can easily locate an item in a folder.

I

icon A small onscreen symbol that represents a program, file, or folder you click to perform an action or operation.

import To convert and load a file that you created in one program into a different program (*see export*).

Inbox An Outlook folder that stores the e-mail messages you receive from others.

Internet The global network of networks that enables some or all of the following: exchange of e-mail messages, files, Usenet newsgroups, and

World Wide Web pages. Also known as the Net.

Internet service provider (ISP) A company that provides access to the Internet by dialing into their computer across a phone line, and then connecting to the Internet via a server. ISP is also known as a local service provider and mail delivery service.

item An individual set of information in an Outlook mini-program, such as an e-mail message, appointment, contact, task, or journal entry.

J

Journal An Outlook miniprogram that enables you to record your activities in Outlook and any Windows program as you perform them.

journal entry The details about an activity that you perform, which is recorded in Journal.

K

key One or more fields used for criteria by which you sort items in a list in Outlook.

Glossary

L

list box A box that contains a list of items for you to choose from. Sometimes a down-pointing arrow appears to the right of the list box; clicking it makes the list drop down to reveal additional options.

local service provider *See Internet Service Provider.*

M

mail delivery service *See Internet Service Provider.*

maximize To enlarge a window so that it fills the entire available window space. Click the Maximize button in the upper-right corner of a window to maximize the window.

meeting A type of appointment you can schedule in Calendar, whereby you invite other people to attend a meeting.

meeting request An Outlook meeting invitation you send as an e-mail message to invite meeting attendees.

menu When you click on a menu name such as File, Edit, or View on the menu bar, it causes a list of commands or menu to drop down.

message An e-mail message or the text you type into the large message box at the bottom of an item dialog box.

Microsoft Exchange Server A Microsoft network server. Some Outlook features work only on a company network using the Exchange Server.

Microsoft Network (MSN) Microsoft's online service that provides an electronic mail service, online information such as the news, sports, and weather, technical questions with answers, downloadable programs, and access to the Internet. Similar to America Online and CompuServe.

minimize To reduce the size of a window so that it is minimized to a button on the Windows Taskbar. Click the Minimize button in the upper-right corner of a window to minimize the window.

move To transfer a selection of information in one location and place it somewhere else.

My Computer An icon on your Windows desktop and in the Outlook bar that opens a window in which you can browse through the contents of your computer or get information about the disk drives, control panel, and printers you have on your computer.

N

Notes An Outlook miniprogram that enables you to create little notes for ideas, reminders, instructions, or directions that look like yellow sticky notes.

O

Office Assistant A quick way to search for help on a particular topic and find shortcuts in Outlook. Replaces the Answer Wizard in Office 95.

Outbox An Outlook folder that holds the e-mail messages that are ready to be sent. When you dial up and connect to your mail delivery service, Outlook mails the messages in the Outbox.

Outlook Bar The vertical toolbar on the left side of the Outlook window, which contains icons for Outlook miniprograms and folders.

Outlook Bar Group A group of icons that appears in the Outlook Bar. You click the Outlook, Mail, or Other button to display a particular group of icons.

P

print style A set of special formatting attributes such as font formatting, headers, footers, and miscellaneous attributes that controls the layout and printout of an entire page.

program A set of instructions written in a computer language that is delivered in a complete and ready-to-run form, such as a word processor, spreadsheet, or database program. Also known as software or application program.

R

recall To retrieve or *unsend* a message in the recipient's Inbox or mail server that your recipient hasn't opened or read yet.

recipient The one who receives a message.

recurring task A task that automatically reappears in your Task list at specified time intervals, for example, once a month or once a year, even if you don't complete the previous occurrence of the task.

regenerating task A task that regenerates automatically and appears in your Task list again when you complete the previous occurrence of the task.

reminder A message that appears onscreen and/or a sound that plays to remind you of an upcoming appointment you had scheduled in Calendar.

reply To respond to a sender's message.

Rich Text Format An e-mail message that contains formatted text such as bold, italic, underline, and color.

S

select an item To click on the item. In a table view and card view, a selected item has a bar across it in a color. In an icon view, a selected item's text appears highlighted in a color. The color that appears is dependent upon the default Windows colors that are set.

select text To click the left mouse button and drag the mouse pointer across the text you want to select. Selected text appears highlighted.

sender A person who sends a message.

Sent Items An Outlook folder that displays the e-mail messages, task requests, and meeting requests that have been sent to recipients.

shortcut menu A menu of commands that pops up when you click the right mouse button on an object. This context-sensitive menu includes just those commands you need to use for the object you clicked.

sorting A feature that arranges the items alphabetically and numerically in ascending or descending order, making it easy to locate the items you want.

T

Table view A type of view that displays items in columns and rows.

Task list A list of tasks that need to be done or have been completed. A Task list appears in Outlook's Tasks.

task request To assign a task to another person and send an e-mail message asking the recipient to perform the task.

TaskPad A smaller version of the Task list that appears in

Tasks, but it appears in Calendar and contains the same tasks.

Tasks An Outlook miniprogram for creating a list of tasks that need to be done.

Timeline view A type of view that displays the mail message, task, and journal entry items on a timeline based on when the item occurred.

toolbar A bar that runs across the top of the Outlook window, containing buttons you can click as shortcuts for executing frequently used menu commands.

U

URL Stands for Uniform Resource Locator. A URL is a Web site address (location). Most URLs consist of the service, host name, and directory path. An example of a URL is `http://www.idgbooks.com`.

V

view The way that Outlook items are displayed onscreen.

W

Web *See World Wide Web.*

World Wide Web A graphical part of the Internet that organizes millions of documents, thousands of sites, and dozens of indexes on the Internet. The Web is a fluid and often surprising collection of information and activity. Also called *WWW*.

WWW *See World Wide Web.*

X

X Close box A button with an X on it in the upper-right corner of every Windows 95 window. Click the X Close box to close the program, file, or item in the window, or a dialog box.

Glossary

C–D

C

Calendar component, 15, 134-135
  allowing outside access, 165
  assigning Calendar items to categories, 161
  AutoDate (natural language) feature, 136, 250-251
  continuous day views, 152
  current day, displaying, 153
  daily schedule, 153
  discontinuous day views, 152, 156
  displaying two time zones, 158-159, 167
  holidays, displaying, 161
  monthly schedule, 155, 156, 157-158
  More Appointments icon, 143
  Print Range options, 254
  TaskPad, 204-205
  time availability categories, 135, 137
  viewing meetings, 176
  views, 45-46, 160-164
  weekly schedule, 154, 167
  See also appointments; events; Calendar toolbar
Calendar tab, Options dialog box, 158-159, 161, 175
Calendar toolbar, 138
  Current View drop-down arrow, 46, 49, 161-162
  Delete button, 148, 167
  Find Items button, 167
  Go to Today button, 153
  New Appointment button, 136, 137, 140, 141
  New drop-down arrow, 205
  Office Assistant button, 30-31
  Week button, 154, 167
  See also Calendar component
Calendar ➢ New Appointment command, 136
Calendar ➢ New Meeting Request command, 176-177
Callback field, adding to custom form, 262
calling contacts with AutoDialer, 75-76, 84
categories, 54-55
  assigning, 60, 161
  Master Category list, 60, 254-256, 264
  time availability categories, in Calendar, 135, 170, 172
  See also By Category view
Categories button, Appointment window, 161
Categories dialog box, 60
category lists, expanding and collapsing, 162
changing
  appointment and meeting time, 144-145, 150, 172, 178
  contact's information, 58-59, 69
  due dates assigned to flagged messages, 124
  journal entries, 223, 226
  meeting locations, 179
  notes, 240-242, 247
  order of folders, 40
Choose Template dialog box, 127
Clear All button, Sort dialog box, 207
clearing message flags, 124
clipboard task icons, 185, 188
Close button, 31
closed envelope symbol, 104

closing
  Folder List, 40
  notes, 235-236
  Outlook 97, 31
collapsing folders, 40
colors, 96, 242
commands. *See* shortcut menus; toolbar buttons; *individual command names*
communications activities, recording manually, 224-225
companies involved with tasks, recording, 212
company directory lists, 64
completed tasks, 190
conflicts in schedules
  conflicting appointments, 136, 140, 150
  when scheduling meetings, 170, 172, 178
Connect To dialog box, 95
connecting to online services, 94-95
Connection tab, Mail Account Properties dialog box, 94
contact files, saving, 78
Contact window, 55, 58, 62, 69, 79
contacts
  adding, 55-56, 56-58
  assigning tasks to, 191-193, 199, 201
  assigning to categories, 54, 60
  birthday reminders, 69
  calling with AutoDialer, 75-76, 84
  changing contact's information, 58-59, 69
  deleting, 43, 60-61, 70
  e-mail options, 95, 98
  File As feature, 78-79
  filtering messages from, 47
  Internet addresses, 76-77
  inviting to meetings, 176-177
  locating, 64-65, 65, 70
  printing address book, 80-82, 84
  recording contact-related items in Journal, 212, 221
  restoring deleted contacts, 61
  scheduling appointments with, 142-144
  selecting, 60, 61, 70, 191
  sending letters to, 72-75
  sending messages to, 95, 96, 98, 101
  Web pages, exploring, 76-77, 84
  See also Address Cards; Contacts component; contacts list
Contacts component, 15, 54
  displaying Contacts folder, 24
  views, 46, 63-64, 66-67
  See also Address Cards; contacts
contacts list, 75, 80-82, 84, 254
  See also contacts
Contacts toolbar, 62
  AutoDialer button, 75
  Current View drop-down arrow, 66
  Explore Web Page button, 77
  New Contact button, 55
  Print button, 80
  Print Preview button, 80, 84
  Save and Close button, 56, 57
Contacts ➢ New Letter to Contact command, 73
context-sensitive help, 29

continuous day views, 152
Control Panel, creating user profile, 18
copying
  messages with Remote Mail, 122
  Outlook items, 256-257
  vote responses to another item, 128-129
Ctrl+G (Go to Date command), 156, 158
Ctrl+N (New Appointment command), 136
Ctrl+P (Print command), 80
Ctrl+Shift+A (New Appointment command), 136, 149
Ctrl+Shift+Q (New Meeting Request command), 176-177
Current View drop-down arrow
  Calendar toolbar, 46, 49, 161-162
  Contacts toolbar, 66
  Inbox toolbar, 110
  Journal toolbar, 230
  Notes toolbar, 245
  Task toolbar, 189, 200-201
custom forms, 261-263, 265
custom signatures, 124, 125-126
customizing reminder sound, 147

D

daily schedule, Calendar component, 153
dates
  AutoDate (natural language) feature, 250-251
  correcting in journal entries, 227, 232
  due dates, 123-124, 191
  end dates for tasks, 184
  Go to Date command, 156, 158
  showing in notes, 243-244
day schedule, Calendar component, 153
Day/Week/Month, Calendar view, 46, 160
Delegate Access feature, 210
Delegates tab, Options dialog box, 210
Delete button, 123, 148, 167, 228
delete function, 58
Delete key, 49, 56
Deleted Items button, Outlook Bar, 24
Deleted Items folder
  deleting messages, 106-108
  displaying, 24
  emptying, 39
  log files, 44-45
  See also restoring deleted items
deleting
  appointments, 147-148
  attendees for meetings, 171
  categories, 255
  contacts, 60-61, 70
  folders, 39, 49
  holidays, 167
  journal entries, 227-228, 232
  messages, 106-108, 122
  notes, 244
  Outlook items, 39

continued

continued

Now it's easy to remember what you just learned and more...

With *On-Demand*, you'll never rely on the help function again – or your money back.

Introducing *On-Demand Interactive Learning*™ — the remarkable software that actually makes corrections to your documents for you. Unlike the standard help function that merely provides "canned" responses to your requests for help or makes you write down a list of complicated instructions, *On-Demand* lets you learn while you work.

Concurrent Mode — makes the *changes for you* right in your document.

Teacher Mode — *guides you* step-by-step to make changes safely outside your document.

Demo Mode — *shows you* how the changes are made safely outside your document.

Let *On-Demand* take care of the software commands for you. Just follow the on-screen pointer and fill in the information, and you'll learn in the fastest and easiest way possible — without ever leaving your document.

In fact, *On-Demand* makes your work so easy, it's *guaranteed* to help you finish complicated documents neatly and on time. With over eleven years in software education and a development staff that's logged more than 5,000 hours of classroom teaching time, it's no wonder that Fortune 500 corporations around the world use *On-Demand* to make learning for their employees quicker and more effective.

"On-Demand Interactive Learning for Word 97. The best training title of this group..." —*PC World*

The Concurrent Mode Difference

Concurrent Mode guides you through learning new functions without having to stop for directions. Right before your eyes, a moving pointer clicks on the right buttons and icons for you and then lets you fill in the information.

"On-Demand lets me get my work done and learn without slowing me down." —*Rosemarie Hasson, Quad Micro*

TITLES AVAILABLE FOR: Windows® 3.1, 95, NT, Microsoft® Word, Microsoft Excel, Microsoft PowerPoint, Microsoft Access, Microsoft Internet Explorer, Lotus® SmartSuite, Lotus Notes, and more! Call for additional titles.

---

30 DAY GUARANTEE:
Try *On-Demand* at the introductory price of $32⁹⁵ (U.S. dollars) for one title or pay $29⁹⁵ (U.S. dollars) each for two titles. That's a savings of almost 10%. Use *On-Demand* for 30 days. If you don't learn more in a shorter period of time, simply return the software to PTS Learning Systems with your receipt for a full refund (this guarantee is good only for purchases made directly from PTS).

On**Demand**
Interactive Learning

Call PTS at 800-387-8878 ext. 3053 or 610-337-8878 ext. 3053 outside the U.S.

© 1997 PTS Learning Systems

IDG103197

IDG BOOKS WORLDWIDE, INC.
END-USER LICENSE AGREEMENT

my2cents.idgbooks.com

Register This Book — And Win!

Visit **http://my2cents.idgbooks.com** to register this book and we'll automatically enter you in our monthly prize giveaway. It's also your opportunity to give us feedback: let us know what you thought of this book and how you would like to see other topics covered.

Not on the Web yet? It's easy to get started with *Discover the Internet*, at local retailers everywhere (see our retailer list at IDG Books Online).

Discover IDG Books Online!

The IDG Books Online Web site is your online resource for tackling technology — at home and at the office.

Ten Productive and Career-Enhancing Things You Can Do at www.idgbooks.com

1. Nab source code for your own programming projects.

2. Download software.

3. Read Web exclusives: special articles and book excerpts by IDG Books Worldwide authors.

4. Take advantage of resources to help you advance your career as a Novell or Microsoft professional.

5. Buy IDG Books Worldwide titles or find a convenient bookstore that carries them.

6. Register your book and win a prize.

7. Chat live online with authors.

8. Sign up for regular e-mail updates about our latest books.

9. Suggest a book you'd like to read or write.

10. Give us your 2¢ about our books and about our Web site.

CD-ROM Installation Instructions

The CD-ROM includes the interactive *One Step at a Time On-Demand* software. This software coaches you through the exercises in the book while you work on a computer at your own pace.

INSTALLING THE ONE STEP AT A TIME ON-DEMAND INTERACTIVE SOFTWARE

The *One Step at a Time On-Demand* interactive software can be installed on Windows 95 and Windows NT 4.0. To install the interactive software on your computer, follow these steps:

1. Launch Windows (if you haven't already).

2. Place the *Outlook 97 One Step at a Time* CD-ROM in your CD-ROM drive.

3. Click the Start menu.

4. Select Run. The Run dialog box appears.

CD-ROM Installation Instructions

⑤ Type **D:\Setup.exe** (where D is your CD-ROM drive) in the Run dialog box.

⑥ Click OK to run the setup procedure. The On-Demand Installation dialog box appears.

⑦ Click Continue. The On-Demand Installation Options dialog box appears.

⑧ Click the Full/Network radio button (if this option is not already selected).

NOTE *Full/Network installation requires approximately 150MB of hard disk space. If you don't have enough hard disk space, click the Standard radio button to choose Standard installation. If you choose standard installation, you should always insert the CD-ROM when you start the software to hear sound.*

⑨ Click Next. The Determine Installation Drive and Directory dialog box appears.

⑩ Choose the default drive and directory that appears, or click Change to choose a different drive and directory.

⑪ Click Next. The Product Selection dialog box appears, which enables you to verify the software you want to install.

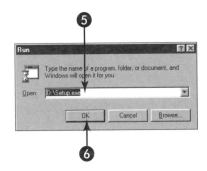

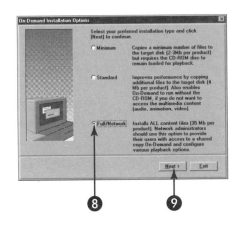

⑫ Click Finish to complete the installation. The On-Demand Installation dialog box displays the progress of the installation. After the installation, the Multiuser Pack Registration dialog box appears.

⑬ Enter information in the Multiuser Pack Registration dialog box.

⑭ Click OK. The On-Demand Installation dialog box appears.

⑮ Click OK to confirm the installation has been successfully completed.

Please see Appendix D, "What's on the CD-ROM," for information about running the *One Step at a Time On-Demand* interactive software.

INSTALLING THE EXERCISE FILES

To access the exercise files for the lessons in this book, you'll need to set up a folder for the exercise files on your hard drive (also covered in Lesson 1). Follow these steps:

❶ Double-click the My Computer icon on your desktop.

❷ In the My Computer window, double-click the hard drive (C).

❸ Open the File menu.

❹ Choose the New command.

❺ Choose Folder from the submenu. A new folder appears at the end of the list with the name New Folder.

❻ Type **One Step** to name the folder.

❼ Press Enter.

❽ Place the *Outlook 97 One Step at a Time* CD-ROM in the CD-ROM drive.

❾ In the My Computer window, double-click the CD-ROM icon, usually labeled D:, to open the drive in which you placed the CD-ROM.

❿ In the CD-ROM (D:) window, copy the folder named Exercise by selecting it and pressing Ctrl-C. Then, close the CD-ROM window and all other open windows.

⑪ Double-click My Computer.

⑫ Double-click the hard drive (C:).

⑬ Double-click the One Step folder.

⑭ Paste the Exercise folder into the One Step folder by pressing Ctrl-V. All of the exercise files are now located within the Exercise folder, inside the One Step folder.

Using the Exercise Files

USING THE EXERCISE FILES

You need to make sure that you have removed the Read Only attribute from the file(s) you copied to your hard drive before you start using those files. Otherwise, when you attempt to save your work, your screen will display an error message. To remove the attribute, open the Exercise folder (inside the One Step folder) on your hard drive. Select the files by opening the Edit menu and choosing the Select All command. Open the File menu and choose Properties. The Properties dialog box appears. Click the Read Only attribute to remove the check from the checkbox.